# The
# Surrealist
# Revolution
# in
# France

# THE
# REVOLUTION

## HERBERT S. GERSHMAN

# SURREALIST

# IN FRANCE

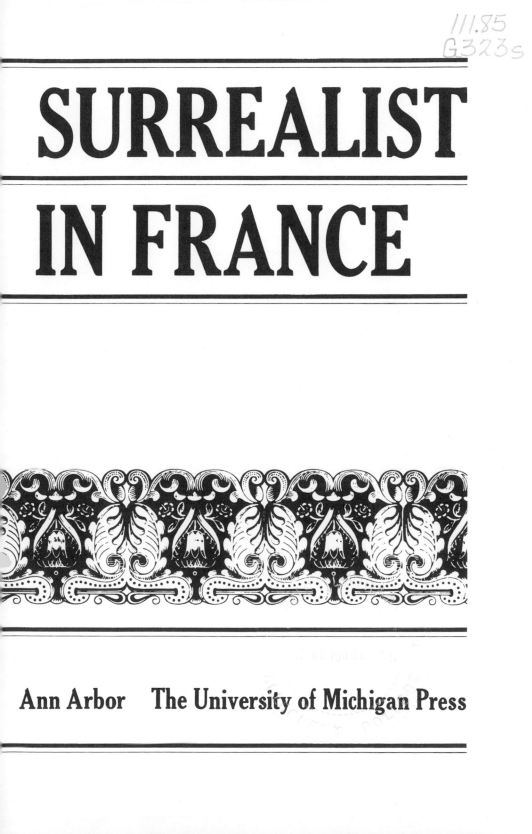

Ann Arbor    The University of Michigan Press

*Grateful acknowledgement is made to the following authors, publishers, and agents for kind permission to quote copyrighted material:*

Louis Aragon for his poems "Persiennes" and "Suicide," and for excerpts from *La Grande gaîté.*

Editions Gallimard for an excerpt from *Le Paysan de Paris* by Louis Aragon, © Editions Gallimard.

Mme André Breton for excerpts from *Les Champs magnétiques* by André Breton and Philippe Soupault.

Editions Gallimard for excerpts from *Poèmes* by André Breton, © Editions Gallimard, and for excerpts from *Le Surréalisme et la peinture* by André Breton, © Editions Gallimard.

Editions Gallimard for excerpts from *Domaine public* by Robert Desnos, © Editions Gallimard.

Faber & Faber Ltd. and Harcourt, Brace & World, Inc. for excerpts from *Four Quartets* and *Collected Poems 1909-1962* by T. S. Eliot.

Mme Cecile Dreyfus-Valette for the poem "Critique de la poésie" from *Poèmes pour tous* by Paul Eluard, published by Les Editeurs Français Réunis-Paris.

Editions Gallimard for excerpts from *Choix de poèmes* by Paul Eluard, © Editions Gallimard.

New Directions Publishing Corporation for excerpts from *Sunday after the War* by Henry Miller. Copyright 1944 by Henry Miller.

Jonathan Cape Ltd. and The Macmillan Company for excerpts from *The History of Surrealism* by Maurice Nadeau, translated by Richard Howard. Copyright © The Macmillan Company, 1965.

Le Terrain Vague for excerpts from *La Brebis galante* by Benjamin Péret.

Lettres Modernes for an excerpt from *Vingt poèmes, Péret's Score,* by J. H. Matthews.

Editions Gallimard for excerpts from *Paroles* by Jacques Prévert, © Editions Gallimard.

Editions Jean-Jacques Pauvert for excerpts from *Dada à Paris* by Michel Sanouillet.

Editions du Rocher for excerpts from *L'Amour noir,* edited by Albert-Marie Schmidt.

Philippe Soupault for excerpts from *Les Champs magnétiques* by André Breton and Philippe Soupault and for his review of the film *Charlot voyage.*

New Directions Publishing Corporation for title of poem "And Death Shall Have No Dominion" from *The Collected Poems* of Dylan Thomas. Copyright 1943 by New Directions Publishing Corporation.

Christophe Tzara for excerpts from *Morceaux choisis* by Tristan Tzara.

Southern Illinois University for "Toward Defining the Surrealist Aesthetic" by Herbert S. Gershman from *Papers on Language and Literature,* © 1966 by the Board of Trustees, Southern Illinois University.

*to my wife*
SALLY

# Acknowledgments

Summer research grants (1957, 1960, 1963, 1966) from the University of Missouri Research Council enabled me to carry on the necessary reading and writing for this study. My very sincere thanks to that conscientious group. My thanks also go to the American Philosophical Society for a travel grant to France (Summer 1960), which permitted me to work in the Fonds Doucet. Part of the material found in this study originally appeared in *Italica* (June 1962), *Myth and Reality*, a collection of essays by several hands published by the University of Nebraska Press, Bernice Slote, ed. (1963), *Yale French Studies* (Spring 1964), *The French Review* (Jan. 1965, Dec. 1964), and *Papers in Language and Literature* (Winter 1966). My appreciation to their respective editors for permission to adapt this material.

# Contents

# Introduction

A proper history is a death mask. A living movement rarely has time to contemplate its yesterdays, for today and tomorrow are here with their impatient tasks. Still, there are circumstances which justify a momentary pause. One who has witnessed a specific event may stop to give an account of it. One who has observed unusual adventures under vanishing conditions may pause to describe them. And perhaps he also may be given a hearing who, without having ventured out of familiar paths, without having achieved any signal surrealist triumph, has listened and read, and believes he has discovered in one literary movement a reflexion of some universal phenomenon.

Surrealism was unusual but not unique. This is the core of the matter. If I consider it worth recording, it is because I consider its history, in its broader outlines, to be typical of many histories—a concrete illustration, in short. It is one strand of the cable binding past to future. Before surrealism, the outside world ill knew the inside; but since it has been among us, as a movement, the two realms have learned to walk hand in hand seeking a common destiny. The essence of surrealism was born millennia past, yet is still with us, our contemporary in the twentieth century, alive to our latest objections. It was much more vital before it began to explore its past so seriously, ferreting out lost ancestors—for a long past vividly remembered clings when you would run. Like a sad clown surrealism advances, grimacing, gesticulating, tumbling—amusing and frightening at the same time, for its features are not familiar. It has a unity that would warm a mystic's soul, or Baudelaire's. Its ears see and its mouth hears. Dreams are its reality, but like the characters in a Balzac novel it is never quite the victim of its own illusions. The illusions are for the others, those whose intelligence is firmly established upon the bedrock of tangible reality and certainty. Rebels? Yes, and Outsiders too, to borrow a term from Colin Wilson. Without doubt the surrealists produced the humus without which a Sartre or Camus could not have existed in quite the same form. The surrealists' views on man and the world about him, given body in the antinomies of dream and reality, chance and determinism, total liberty and political commitment, have since become commonplaces. The uniqueness of man's role, the equation of life with art (it requires quite as much talent to *live* a poem as to write one), the stress upon responsibility as a substantial reality impossible to assign (except to the surrealist group) or to refuse (except by ascribing it to one's Unconscious)—all this is surrealism, and at the same time a prelude to the New Novel and to the Theater of the Absurd with its faultless idiocy and carefully contrived automata. If everything is meaningless except as we grant it meaning, so say the surrealists, let us be serious about this comedy of gestures and words, deeds and misdeeds, which together make up the spectrum of our lives. The absurdity of it all can be overcome. But in which direction shall we move?

# I: Toward a Definition of The Surrealist Aesthetic

"The lunatic, the lover, and the poet
Are of imagination all compact.
One sees more devils than vast hell can hold;
That is the madman. The lover, all as frantic,
Sees Helen's beauty in a brow of Egypt.
The poet's eye, in a fine frenzy rolling,
Doth glance from heaven to earth, from earth to heaven;
And as imagination bodies forth
The forms of things unknown, the poet's pen
Turns them to shapes and gives to airy nothing
A local habitation and a name.
Such tricks hath strong imagination. . . . "
—Shakespeare, *A Midsummer Night's Dream*, V. 1, 1.7-18.

"Only on the analogical plane have I ever experienced
any intellectual pleasure. For me the only real *evidence*
is a result of the spontaneous, extra-lucid and defiant
relationship suddenly sensed between two things which
common sense would never bring together."
—Breton, "Signe ascendant" (1948), in *La Clé des champs*
(Paris: Editions du Sagittaire, 1953), p. 112.

The surrealist aesthetic can be reduced to one theme: the attempt to actualize *le merveilleux*, the wonderland of revelation and dream, and by so doing to permit chance to run rampant in a wasteland of bleak reality. Not *le mystère*, the willful introduction of obscurity into art and life, which to Breton was a confession of weakness, but the lucidity that is a product of conviction and which will bind men together in a faith against which reason must falter and ultimately succumb.[1] This private heaven could be attained in several ways, and the surrealists tried them all at different times. Taken together these several attempts help explain the evolution of the movement from the starveling, internecine revolt against Dada in the early twenties to its present Cheshire cat sleekness.

A penchant for the absolute is not peculiar to surrealism. Much of Baudelaire, for example, reflects this same longing for an effortless beatitude—what T.S. Eliot called (with reference to Baudelaire) his "leave-taking poetry" or "waiting-room poetry."[2] And whether this new land to which he is going, where "all is ordered and beautiful,/Luxurious, calm and voluptuous," is a heaven or a hell, we must of necessity "Dive to the depths of the abyss . . . in our never-ending search for *something new*."[3] No sooner is the poet baffled by the maze of reality, no sooner does he succumb to the complexity, the irrationality (the absurdity) of existence, the so-called tragic sense of life, than there wells up the temptation to seek refuge in the trash cans of familiar myths, in the manner of Beckett. Where Baudelaire naively sought revelation "through forests of symbols,"[4] Rimbaud proposed a path through the forest, a technique—deliberate sensory confusion—which would permit the inspired poet to storm the gates of his Dionysian heaven.[5] Mallarmé, despairing of locating a paradise beyond the blue, set out to create one, a purely formal, verbal one. Proust worked out his salvation in the past, in the realm of pure being where nothing changes, except as our memory (involuntary or other) so wills it. Valéry spied his amorphous will-o'-the-wisp heaven at each turn of a thought: could he but fix its shape, describe its relationship to man, then salvation, were it nothing more than dissolution in his own thought, would be his.[6]

Surrealism is essentially a multi-faceted method for eliciting revelations, and as such it is indeed the prehensile tail of romanticism that Breton once termed it.[7] There is, first in both time and importance, the much discussed and often mocked technique of automatic writing.[8] The effort of choice, of decision, here gives way to the facility of free association—Protean chance bound by the silken threads of caprice, drowned in the inky well of unconscious objectivity. Where Valéry sought to observe his *Moi*, to enclose his thought in a coat of alexandrine mail, the surrealists became willing receptacles for the oracle, mimes of dark frenzy, to paraphrase Valéry.[9] If the liberated (or tortured, if one prefers) syntax of the surrealists has no parallel in the 1920's, it has many parallels in the poetry of Mallarmé and his disciples. The element of mystery inherent in the surrealist world, where dreams fulfill wishes and words mean more than they seem to (charged as they

are with emotional and erotic overtones), has only a distant analogy in the romantic wonder at the grandeur of the universe, but
does recall the tales of Villiers and Lautréamont's enigmatic *Chants
de Maldoror* (1869). It is therefore no great surprise that the surrealists, as passive toys of an other-world message, welcomed the
aid of mediums. Given a choice between the limitations of reason
and the calm conviction of spiritism, they opted for a mystic flight,
one which would take them to the frontier where Being and Nothingness clasp uneasy hands and nonconformity touches on insan-
ity.[10] We have come a long way from the nihilism of Dada and its
exuberant spoof of a prim, smug, and *prudhommesque* society, one
which could neither fight a just war nor win a decent peace. Now
that the old table of values had been smashed, thanks to Dada, new
ones had to be found—or rather revealed, so as to give them their
proper sacred character.

Yet as Breton himself admitted, neither automatic writing nor
recourse to mediums was regularly effective or a sure way of in-
ducing any persuasive series of oracles.[11] What was required was
a more intimate revelation, one that would passionately and eter-
nally commit the small chosen clan of surrealists. Such was the role
to be played by love, by the myth of the child-woman (*la femme-
enfant*) and mad love (*l'amour fou*).[12] To the surrealists love was
an advanced form of automatism, the bolt from the blue canonized,
normalized to a way of life, a vivid objectification of chance. It
would free man from humdrum reality, lead to new discoveries, to
the intimate possession of new worlds; it ignores logic, encourages
dreams, and rescues the ideal from its season in hell, brings it to
earth in an embraceable body and soul. In a word it fixes a goal
for the *poésie des départs,* puts an end to that period of waiting
which is our life.[13] But surrealism was destined to remain millen-
nial promise and the surrealists themselves seekers more than finders. In their search, however, lay their literary salvation.

This new mythology, recalling the neo-Platonists more than
the romantics, had as its specific goal the conjuring up of an earthly
paradise.[14] Between 1925 and 1935, the leaders of the group, spo-
radically occupied with politics, had found little time for the elaboration of earlier theoretical positions. The earthly paradise, during
the decade in question, was thought to be attainable by essentially
political means.[15] But with Breton's article "Revelation versus Mystery" (1936) and the more explicit *Mad Love* (1937) a new turning becomes manifest.[16] Themes little in evidence since "Here

Come the Mediums" (1922) and "Introduction to a Lecture on Reality and Its Limits" (1924) are suddenly picked up and developed.[17] Specifically love—not simply love as the high point of life, the physical fusion of dream and reality, but love as a myth, one of the "exalting and incredible myths which will send one and all to lay siege to the unknown."[18] The importance of love in literature is too obvious to need illustration; its rejuvenating qualities and socially revolutionary effects are equally evident, if less often referred to specifically. This *amour fou,* as Breton called it, invariably shatters the daily routine that society has so laboriously set up for the individual and implies that happiness, the exaltation that gives a measure of value to life, can be found beyond the traditional frame of family, work, and community effort.[19] When the Beloved (*l'idole*), Dreams (*le rêve*), and Poetry (*la poésie*) are deemed as necessary to life as the air one breathes, then the divinization of love is a *fait accompli.*

This mythology of love is new in two important respects. It differs from the neo-Platonic conception in fixing the idealization on earth: the party loved is of flesh and blood; there is no beyond. On the other hand it differs from the Stendhalian *amour-passion* in being something more than crystallized passion. The person loved has the attributes of the Bride of Saint John of the Cross; she is the *idole,* as Mme Sabatier was to Baudelaire, as Bouton de Chamilly was to the *religieuse portugaise,* Maria Alcaforado. "All myths," as Péret said, "reflect man's ambivalence both with regard to the world and with regard to himself . . . . The vital element in a myth is the striving after happiness which one finds there . . . . They express, in short, the feeling that there is a duality in nature, and in man, duality and paradox which he is not likely to resolve in his lifetime."[20] When faced with an example of *amour sublime* (or *fou*), society's initial reaction is normally condemnation, for the two persons involved are capable of any action, however antisocial, in the pursuance of their goal. Religion must of necessity condemn it, for it tends to "replace God by man" and make available to man a happiness in which religion has had no part.[21]

Having experienced little but deception in their attempts "to change our way of life" and "to transform the world" by militant political means,[22] the surrealists hit upon another approach: rather than accept a political myth not of their own making, they determined to refurbish one with deep roots in poetry and in the world of dreams, the twin realms of language and desire. That this myth of *l'amour fou* has often been confused by the public with eroticism is unfortunate. Not that the surrealists were averse to eroticism or indeed to any exotic attempt to arouse or reveal desire—one of their many international exhibitions was devoted to that very theme. But the common elements are their unconscious origin and their anti-social posture: *le merveilleux* and the almost religious moral elevation of the one are completely absent from the other. Neither, of course, should be confused with pornography, which is eroticism travestied, the very antithesis of sublime love.[23]

This conscious myth-making on the part of the surrealists (of which *l'amour sublime* is but one example), this raising of the *femme-enfant* to a position comparable to that held by Mary in the Church, is not without its dangers. The surrealists have long been manifest-happy, and were it not for the quality of related literary productions—the poems of Eluard and Desnos, the stories of Péret and Aragon, the longer works of Breton, Crevel, and others—these incurable pattern-makers would have left no enduring mark on the intellectual slate. For a while it was not clear that the movement had escaped the creeping monadism that seemed to be overcoming it, that it had not indeed taken refuge in a cloud of bogus mysticism, with talk of magic, intoxicating exuberance, and hallucinatory throbbing of misplaced heartstrings. But in the context of the aims of the group, and these have evolved within guidelines that were clear from the very beginning, the myth of *l'amour sublime* is seen as a literary weapon designed to defend the individual at his most intimate from a society become oppressively addicted to routine and, at the same time, to offer to society an illusion capable of both revivifying and liberating it.[24]

➤ A love of this intensity implies a distinctive attraction, according to Breton, a "disruptive beauty" that is "erotic-veiled, explosive-fixed, magic-circumstantial."[25] As this is the only beauty recognized as such by the surrealists, it may be of some interest to examine one of its more striking illustrations, the Baudelaire sonnet "Le Possédé," which has the additional merit of highlighting some of the more traditional aspects of this phenomenon.[26] From its baroque opening line to its exalted (or depraved) conclusion, a passion is unfurled before which all—salvation included—must give way. A passion of this violence, demanding only its own liberty and submitting only to the discipline of a fixed poetic form,[27] could not fail to be applauded by the surrealists for its revolutionary potential. A person so in love of necessity calls into question the virtues associated with normalcy and the *juste milieu*. Every Romeo is a threat to society the way no one else can be, which is why Breton could say that "Baudelaire is surrealist in his morality."[28] While Baudelaire did not live as surrealistically as did, say, Rimbaud,[29] his absolute devotion to what Breton would later term *l'amour fou*, his total commitment to love as an all consuming passion, clearly revealed in "Le Possédé," make of this poem a key to the surrealist definition of love.

Le soleil s'est couvert d'un crêpe. Comme lui,
O lune de ma vie! emmitoufle-toi d'ombre;
Dors ou fume à ton gré; sois muette, sois sombre,
Et plonge tout entière au gouffre de l'Ennui;

Je t'aime ainsi! Pourtant, si tu veux aujourd'hui,
Comme un astre éclipsé qui sort de la pénombre,
Te pavaner aux lieux que la Folie encombre,
C'est bien! Charmant poignard, jailli de ton étui!

Allume ta prunelle à la flamme des lustres!
Allume le désir dans les regards des rustres!
Tout de toi m'est plaisir morbide ou pétulant;

Sois ce que tu voudras, nuit noire, rouge aurore;
Il n'est pas une fibre en tout mon corps tremblant
Qui ne crie: *O mon cher Belzébuth, je t'adore!* [30]

There is much in this poem that needs no comment: the literary commonplaces of love and jealousy, the woman's desire to be seen in public (the "lieux que la Folie encombre"), and such. Certain elements, however, are peculiar to Baudelaire. From the initial somber image, which recalls Nerval's *"soleil noir* de la *Mélancolie,"*[31] to the frenzied cry in the last line, the poet possessed takes us on a rapid trip through the land of passion, whose curious geography recalls both wasteland and paradise. The dislocated rhythm of lines 1 and 14, one being a mirror image of the other, the exaltation implied by the frequent ejaculations—"O lune de ma vie! . . . Je t'aime ainsi! . . . C'est bien! . . . jailli de ton étui!," lines 9 and 10, and the ultimate sigh of "je t'adore!"—all deny the formal evidence of a *classic* sonnet.[32] Rather does the reader have the impression of a challenge accepted and won: how to keep the skeleton of the classic form—quatrains, tercets, alexandrines, and rhyme scheme—and yet write a truly original piece. And original it is, with the rhythmic parallelism of lines 1 and 14, the exacerbated emotion implied by the exclamation marks, the absence of a clear caesura in line 11, suggesting the poet's lassitude after the excesses of lines 9 and 10, and above all the fantastic series of metaphors: a crêpe-covered sun (alluding simultaneously to the time of the poem, evening, or at least to an overcast sky, to his ill-defined mourning, and also to his beloved hidden by the lengthening shadows), moon of my life where one might expect the more banal *soleil de ma vie*,[33] a plea that his love dress in shadow as others might garb themselves in expensive furs . . . for darkness and mystery are essential to love. Or, as Baudelaire suggested, they are necessary before the final plunge can be made into the abyss of Ennui. This Ennui, incidentally, in the context of the poem, clearly has the added force of love-induced agony or anguish, of repressed rage and total, if here impotent, involvement associated in more recent times with *l'amour fou*.[34]

Nor do the above exhaust the baroque elements in the sonnet. There is the asymmetry of line 1, where in the space of nine syllables Baudelaire sets the stage for the tortured outpouring of the next four lines. After a pause following "Je t'aime ainsi," we have a rapidly rising crescendo which reaches a plateau with "C'est bien"— in midverse once again—and the convulsive climax indicated by three brief imperatives of unequal length. The emotional peak, contrary to traditional sonnet form, is reached in the second line of the first tercet. From "Tout de toi" (l.11) to the final italicized cry in line 14, there is a significant fall in intensity. Neither the verse form nor the stanza division, in short, corresponds to the intimate reality of the sonnet. The real "breaks" do not come where the eye expects them: the first rhythmic stanza ends with "Je t'aime ainsi" (l.5), the second with "C'est bien" (l.8), the third with "rustres" (l.10), followed by the decrescendo "Tout de toi m'est plaisir morbide ou pétulant," and the ultimate resolution in the final (visual) tercet. As for baroque resemblances in the imagery, one need go no further than the excellent anthology of Albert-Marie Schmidt:[35]

> Astre dont la noirceur semble former la gloire
> Et qui fait ton éclat de ton obscurité. . .
> > Urbain Chevreau (p. 87)

> Si c'est un Soleil par les yeux
> C'est une ombre par le visage
> > Urbain Chevreau (p. 88)

Ce chef d'oeuvre que tu vois peint
Pourrait enfin nous faire croire
Par l'éclat qui sort de son teint
Que la lumière serait noire.

Urbain Chevreau (p. 89)

Astre noir et brillant ombre éclatante et belle (l.1)
Comme l'astre des mois quand la nuit l'appelle (l.5)
Beau portrait de tourments noire prison de flamme (l.9)
Ciel brun Soleil à l'ombre obscur et clair séjour (l.11)

Anon. (p. 92)

Qui vit jamais sortir tant d'éclairs d'un nuage

Claude de Malleville (p.95)

What Baudelaire added to the saturnine images he may have borrowed is the element of *possession,* a torment that damned convention, and that is precisely what appealed to the surrealists. Their
attraction to the poem does not of course imply that it is a surrealist work, or even presurrealist, except in the most ambiguous
sense of that term. Baudelaire, in a word, is not Jarry . . . or Raymond Roussel. Only the poet's acceptance of his passion, all per-
vading and transcending brute physical possession, fits easily into
a surrealist mold. Baudelaire (at least in this poem) was as un-
affected by, if not indifferent to, the vagaries of his beloved as ever
was mortal at the feet of the divine. Possessed he was indeed, and
by love.

The sonnet in question not only develops some of the most
common themes in lyric poetry, love and death (or at least the
death of the soul implied by *possession*), liberty and servitude, *la
femme fatale* and *la belle endormie,* but does so in a typically
surrealist fashion, that is by confusing the opposites (*érotique-
voilée, explosante-fixe, magique-circonstancielle*). The poet is destroyed by his love just as certainly as he is recreated by it; he has
freely chosen his servitude and could not now retract if he wished;
the fatal woman is also his beloved in idle reverie. What is *convulsive* (or surrealist) in the poem is the intolerable tension between
opposites which cannot logically coexist; the erotic (which implies
something seen or sensed) and the hidden, the volatile and the un-
changeable, magic and the world of cause and effect. "The new
beauty," as Breton regularly pointed out, "beauty 'considered exclusively as a means toward a passionate end'. . . can be assimi-

lated only to the almost painful shock of seeing something revealed."[36] This could serve as a commentary on "Le Possédé."

To the surrealists their method was their miracle, and as prophets glorying in the political gloom of the twenties and thirties,
for whom all tenses paled save the future,[37] they attracted an audience by proclaiming verities immune to logic, though not for that
reason necessarily false: that free association was intrinsically superior to traditional, presumably commonplace association, and
that the collage of intellectual debris, randomly ordered, was superior to a work produced by recourse to any traditional discipline.
The conviction so common to the true believer, and which bobs un-
easily in the wake of occult phenomena, lit their path. And so was
born the original ash-can school of unconscious wits, one which
became strikingly effective in incorporating into literature a domain
previously (and illogically) excluded. Love was their latest and
greatest mystery, a treasure trove of limitless surprises. Amenable
neither to logic nor to common sense, resisting reality more efficaciously than even a medium's pronouncements, it led directly to
heaven, violently on occasion, and with complete indifference to
social norms. It is the one-man revolution, for the partner is of no
great importance, any more than he (or she) is in the writings of
the neo-Platonists. In a nutshell, it converts dream to reality without ever changing either.[38]

If automatic writing, spiritism, and l'amour fou are the major
surrealist weapons for releasing revelation from the wall of mystery
surrounding us, they are not the only ones. Almost from the very beginning the surrealists devoted what must have seemed to onlookers
as an inordinate amount of time to games. "Play," as Huizinga wrote
in Homo Ludens, "is a function of the living, but is not susceptible of
exact definition either logically, biologically or aesthetically."[39] It is
a voluntary activity, which removes it from the realm of the unconscious, but at the same time it serves to shut out reality as formal
truths always shut out the world.[40]

> Play is distinct from 'ordinary' life both as to locality and dura-
> tion. . . . It contains its own course and meaning . . . .
> Just as there is no formal difference between play and ritual, so
> the 'consecrated spot' cannot be formally distinguished from
> the play-ground. The arena, the card-table, the magic circle,
> the temple, the stage, the screen, the tennis court, the court of
> justice, etc., are all in form and function play-grounds, i.e. for-

bidden spots, isolated, hedged round, hallowed, within which special rules obtain. All are temporary worlds within the ordinary world, dedicated to the performance of an act apart. . . . Play demands order absolute and supreme. (*Homo Ludens*, pp. 9-10)

Huizinga then goes on to define the special position that play occupies in life: it requires that its rules, arbitrary though they are, be accepted without question; it promotes the formation of social groupings in its nonserious undertakings and, at the same time, serves to divorce each playful group from others surrounding it (*Homo Ludens*, pp. 11, 13). Breton and his group could have served as models for that portrait.

To the surrealists games were a method by means of which they might detach themselves from the world, a gesture meaningless in the context of "ordinary" life, but pointing toward a social distinction and suggesting a distinctive metaphysical outlook. For many of the same reasons that the typical romantic wore his hair long (as did Breton) and the dandy, ever conscious of his role in the world, set himself apart by his foppish attention to his clothes, so the surrealists did not hesitate to distinguish themselves by their numerous and often exotic games.[41] These were a gesture of defiance directed at the world of reality, a thumbing of the nose at adult (utilitarian) logic, a retreat to a paradise where the liberty so loudly proclaimed in other spheres could not possibly obtain, for, to quote Huizinga again, the least deviation from the rules of the game "robs it of its character and makes it worthless" (*Homo Ludens*, p. 10). The beauty of a game lies in its being so clearly, so irrevocably ordered. No trespassing of the rules is permitted at the risk of denying the game, of breaking the magic circle, of opening the hothouse doors to the cold wind of the world beyond. The game, in short, is a formal construction which shuts out one reality while creating another, more nearly ideal one. Baudelaire might have been describing a game as much as an artificial paradise when he wrote:

> Là, tout n'est qu'ordre et beauté,
> Luxe, calme et volupté.
> ("L'Invitation au voyage," *Les Fleurs du mal*)

The triumvirate of automatic writing, spiritism, and love stormed the gates of Wonderland directly. Play was more oblique. It created an artificial paradise closed to outsiders and, for the time of the game, within the rules of the game, gave free reign to chance, which no throw of the dice could ever abolish. Or perhaps it would be more accurate to say that automatic writing and its two avatars wooed *le merveilleux*, while play created it anew at each moment. Play, the art form of the rebel, is the rigid mask of the aesthete. It is liberty itself (always, however, within the confines of the game), for the real world is in no way involved. It relaxes the tense by displacing the tension. It frees the fool from the sentence of history, makes man a God and bloats his stomach with hope. It was, in a word, a divine artifice to which the surrealists were not insensitive.

The concept of total liberty, along with the practice of automatic writing and games, was of vital importance to the group: at any moment these pure spirits might have to demonstrate, either by word or deed, their detachment from things mundane. The *concept* of liberty, however, rather than its practice, was primary. If I think I am free then I am, and the irons which bind my body are unable to bind my thoughts, my soul. In a world in which everything is possible, even revelation, anything is possible, including freedom in slavery. The surrealists not only saw pie in the sky but insisted that they partook of it. "Only liberty still thrills me," wrote Breton in his first *Manifesto,* the liberty to shut his eyes and, by so doing, annihilate the world, for, he implied, his imagination knew no limits.[42] This is the freedom to make of one's life a work of art as did, say, the dandy in the nineteenth century, if only superficially, or the Sun-King in the seventeenth. Liberty, here, rejoins play and becomes pure form, a new version of the creative imagination.[43] Bit by bit we see the elaboration not of a hoax, as is on occasion put forward, but of a myth, whether it be that of the pythoness in Breton's *Nadja* or of the *femme-enfant* in much of Eluard's poetry. Its goal is ever the same: to reorient reality. Will you play at being mad? There is *L'Immaculée conception* and its passages simulating the writings of those suffering from a variety of mental illnesses. Will you play at being God? The surrealists' refusal to recognize the world is matched only by Kafka's hunger artist caught in a web of his own creation, convinced that the game will indefinitely shut out reality.[44] "Inspire me," says Breton, invoking a mythical Orient, "so that I may become he who has no shadow."[45] So might have spoken the hunger artist had he a goal other than the crowd's admiration or a less finicky palate. phenomenon, then it must include that part of him which dreams If man's freedom is to be something more than a simple physical and is capable of flights of fancy which, for being wild, are nonetheless human. "The mind of the man who dreams," wrote Breton, "is at peace with its environment."[46] The dream is as real as the other reality, and indeed has the additional advantage of permitting us to strut uninterrupted through the night. The terrors of the night become *ours* as those of our waking hours rarely can. One must be quite sensitive, or perhaps sensitized, to perceive the *incredible* which surrounds us—the very pattern of our existence—where others see only a mundane reality. For the surrealist there is no *fantastic*, there is only reality, and the stranger it seems the more revealing and valuable it becomes: "Revelation is always beautiful, every revelation is beautiful, indeed nothing but revelation is beautiful."[47] It almost seems on occasion that the entire surrealist movement, its numerous theoretical positions and even more numerous collections of poetry, stories, and essays, has as its principal purpose the conquering of the romantic *ennui* by a *beau rêve* or a *beau geste*: the never-ending embrace with the divine Lady of one's dreams, or the threat of wildly firing a revolver into a crowd.[48] These formal dandies, delicate murderers, and exalted lovers lived naked on a stage performing rites designed to capture a harmony that could only have existed before the Fall. Their essence lay in their mask, in their play, and was the product of a glance.

Liberty, to the surrealists, has a pronounced negative aspect— or perhaps it would be more accurate to say that it recalls the principles and goals of Riesman's inner-directed man.[49] If it seeks martyrdom and oracular revelation, at the same time it denies the world and man's flesh and blood existence. How else can one explain the scorn for the innocent (though worldly) crowd, the scattered scandalous gestures which separate the surrealist elect from the *vulgus*, the numerous political interventions, but always as an independent force, except for their brief flirtation with the Communist Party?[50] The surrealists were the elect, in their own eyes, if only by dint of frequent communion with the unconscious oracle; all others were to a greater or lesser extent compromised, crassly so, with the world. A gesture, however, regardless of its nobility, its disinterestedness, regardless even of its consequences, is futile in isolation, without a coherent doctrine to lend it meaning. In the battle for a better world it is what fireworks are to an artillery attack, illumination without substance.

In the crisis of sensibility which begins with romanticism, surrealism was but another attempt to resolve the logically irreconcilable, to fill by fiat the void of Being. Its most impressive conquest, according to Robbe-Grillet, was its ability to highlight, to bring to the attention of a blasé public, the wonders of daily life: "The most ordinary phenomena are therefore, in all probability, the most revelatory, the most striking."[51] If indeed their most impressive conquest is

> To see a world in a grain of sand,
> And a heaven in a wild flower,
> To hold infinity in the palm of your hand,
> And eternity in an hour,

then we have not come far from Blake's *Auguries of Innocence*. But to Breton, "What is eye-opening about the fantastic is that there is no fantastic, there is only reality."[52] The Englishman and the Frenchman here join hands.

Surrealism was born of a desire to wrest from the Unknown, knowledge born of revelation, *le merveilleux*. This was its origin and its aesthetic. Adding together the two axioms that nothing but *le merveilleux* is beautiful and that to be beautiful something must be *convulsive*, it seems clear that the intimate sense of the movement from its very beginnings has had extraliterary implications. When literature lost its ancient meaning, saw its function as servant to God and crown disappear, its continued existence was called into question.[53] For some, no class, no group or ideal merited their allegiance: hence the bacchanale that was Dada. The surrealists, however, recognized early the pointless and ultimately dreary circularity of spoofing the ridiculous, of parodying the pompous, of mocking society, themselves included. Had they been able, they would have pulled the trigger of Kirilov's gun, or Vaché's, tossed bombs as did Malraux's Chen and Desnos' anarchist friends. Instead their revolt was dissipated in two distinct directions: (1) toward the creation of new myths out of whole, if imaginary cloth, using Freudian techniques as a sort of springboard—and here they were well served by the cacophonous trio of automatic writing, mediumistic pronouncements, and the sensual anarchy, the *dérèglement de tous les sens* produced by a passionate commitment to love; (2) given the new social myths, they moved toward a radical Marxist interpretation of society, less for the purpose of elevating the proletariat, with which they had no extensive contact, than for bringing down, for casting into hell, their bourgeois brothers who were still untouched by surrealist grace.

Concomitant with the creation of new myths, or the refurbishing of old ones, came an ever-increasing reliance on games. These too could serve to elicit *le merveilleux* and so fill bleak reality with a pack of suggestive revelations. Man is a god in his games; they are his creation. Once in the game, however, his hands are tied, unless he is willing to be a spoil-sport and so destroy this thing of pure form. But the surrealists were not spoil-sports; games were to them a way of life:

> How many evenings did we spend lovingly creating a race of *cadavres exquis!* . . . All cares were banished, all thought of our poverty, our boredom, all thought of the outside world. We played with images and there were no losers. Everyone wanted his neighbor to win, and to continue winning ever more until he had everything. No longer was revelation an outcast. Its features disfigured by passion seemed far more beautiful to us as a group than when we are alone, for when we are alone we are struck dumb by our vision.[54]

So wrote Eluard. The surrealists were actors on a mirrored stage, and were their roles sufficiently well played then the play itself would become life and life the shadow cast by the play. Each gesture counted, each word. Those who felt obliged to acknowledge the reality of the outside world, if only for the purpose of seeking employment without which they could not live, were soon excluded. Into the Ubu-like *trappe* went all those expelled, be it for literary, political, or financial reasons: Soupault, Desnos, Vitrac, Artaud, Aragon, Tzara, Eluard. No hunger artist, committed to his fast, can ever admit that existence may well precede essence in importance. Committed to a certain technique of revelation, the sole granting access to paradise, the true believer rarely can look kindly upon those who, once having seen the light, turn their backs upon it to follow other stars.

The belief in liberty, total and uncommitted liberty, subsumed everything the surrealists did or attempted. It was implicit in Dada, which saw the world as a scandal and itself as an irreverent gadfly or parodist. This liberty can never be assigned. It is the Church's free will and Gide's *disponibilité* combined and suggests that in life every act is gratuitous and every encounter meaningful. The world thus

becomes a web of *hasards objectifs* in much the same way that for
an earlier generation it was a forest of symbols.[55] This sacred liberty,
this "desire for *complete* freedom," whose shifting swamps are strewn
with specters and soluble fish, prophecies of doom and at least a
half-dozen suicides successful or attempted, is more a function than a
thing and, alone, would be incapable of storming a heaven, even a
surrealist heaven.[56]   For refusing to accept this limitation the surrealist adventure could not but end in a baroque failure, except
paradoxically in the realms of art and literature, where its wonderland techniques blew up the desires innate in all of us into a shim-
mering balloon large enough to be easily recognized and gaudy
enough to appeal. When the cardboard sphinx of traditional values
was scornfully rejected, nothing was left to serve as a measuring
rod, except perhaps a shadowy impressionism, which the Voltaires
of all time have distrusted and the Rousseaus embraced. Surrealism
brought the Unconscious into the world of letters, where it will likely
remain long after the debate over the merits of the movement has
subsided to an academic drone, or to paraphrase Philip Rieff, long
after mortician professors conclude their attempt to let the blood out
of its ideas.[57]

# II: Surrealism and Art

"Many persons who first hear of surrealism wonder what
criteria are used to determine whether a work of art
is surrealistic. Need we repeat that the criteria are
*other than aesthetic*? We can say in brief that surrealist
art is bounded on one side by *realism* and on the other
by *abstractionism*."
 —Breton, "Comète surréaliste" (1947), in *La Clé des champs*
   (Paris: Ed. du Sagittaire, 1953), p. 100.

"In the subway and on public benches we sometimes
see little old ladies wearing an unlikely pink hat over
their white hair and their wrinkles—a hat that dates
back to their twentieth birthday, and which they have
cherished ever since.
  "It is one of those silly, yet touching apparitions
that I saw at the Maeght Gallery, avenue de Messine."
 —Marie-Louise Barron, "Surréalisme 1947.
En retard d'une guerre comme l'état-major,"
*Les Lettres françaises,* July 18, 1947, p. 2.

Because it is a state of mind reflected in a body of doctrine, surrealism can exist without literature, without art, without revolution, indeed without society. But as a matter of course it feeds on all of
them, and the shoots it gives forth in different terrains all bear witness to the same underlying principles. Because he proclaims that
life *is* art and that life-as-a-work-of-art is its own justification, the
consistent surrealist must of necessity oppose society's demands for
conformity, which implies the acceptance of a discipline imposed
from without and denies the uniqueness of the work of art that each
individual, whether consciously or otherwise, is in the process of
acting out. It follows, therefore, that novelty is always inspired (i.e.,
"good"), for it suggests an active *non serviam* to the yoke of habit.
Reason, having been corrupted by society and its educational sys-

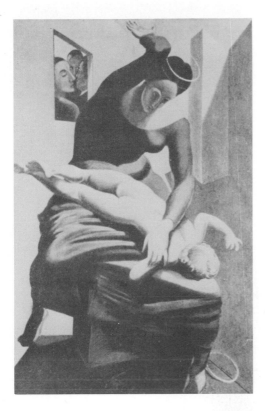

*The Virgin Spanking the Infant Jesus Before Three Onlookers* (1928) By Max Ernst
Permission SPADEM 1968 by French Reproduction Rights Inc.

*The Fearless Sleeper* (c. 1930) By René Magritte
Permission ADAGP 1968 by French Reproduction Rights Inc.

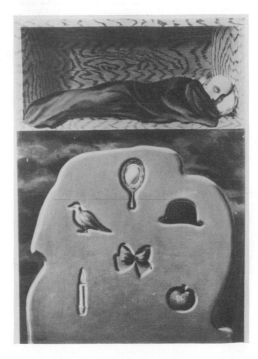

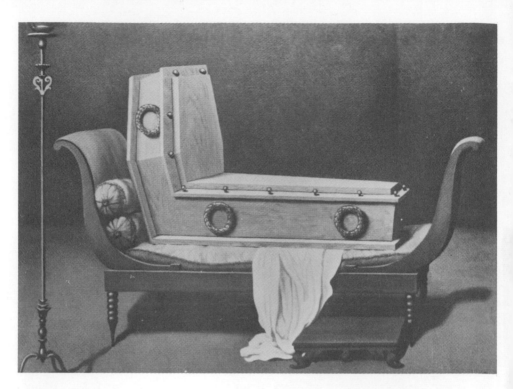

*A View of David's Painting of*
*Mme Récamier* (1951) By René
Magritte
Permission ADAGP 1968 by
French Reproduction Rights Inc.

*The Hour of Traces* (1930)
By Alberto Giacometti
Permission ADAGP 1968 by French
Reproduction Rights Inc.

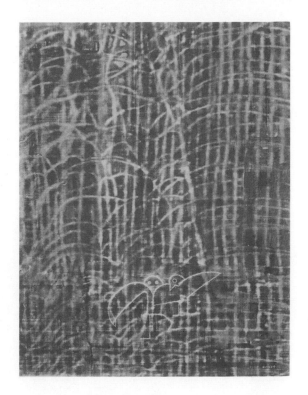

*The Mysteries of Love*
(1955) by Max Ernst

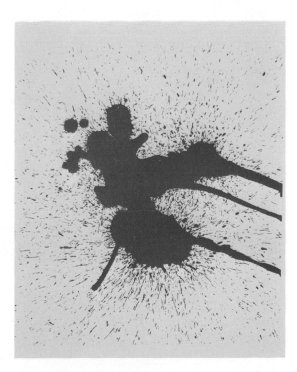

*The Holy Virgin* (1920)
By Francis Picabia

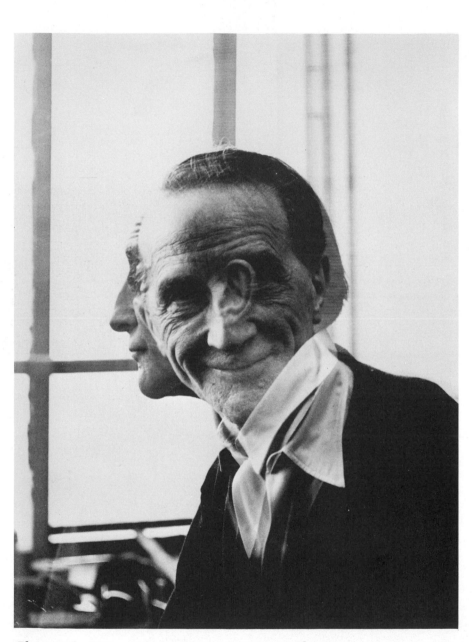

Photograph of Marcel Duchamp (1953) By Victor Obsatz
Permission of the photographer

*Ladders like Wheels of Fire Cross the Blue Sky* (1953) By Joan Miro

Permission ADAGP 1968 by French Reproduction Rights Inc.

*Melancholy and Mystery of a Street* (1914) By Giorgio de Chirico

Collection: Mr. and Mrs. Stanley R. Resor

*Illumined Pleasures* (1929) By Salvador Dali

Sidney and Harriet Janis Collection Gift to The Museum of Modern Art, New York

*Through Birds, Through Fire, but
Not Through Glass* (1943)
By Yves Tanguy
Collection: Mr. and Mrs. Donald Winston

*Nude Descending a Staircase,*
No. II (1912) By Marcel Duchamp
Louise and Walter Arensberg Collection,
Philadelphia Museum of Art
Permission ADAGP 1968 by French
Reproduction Rights Inc.

*Hands* (1941) By Paul Delvaux
Collection: Richard S. Zeisler

*Two Children Threatened by a*
*Nightingale* (1924) By Max Ernst

*Soft Construction with Boiled Beans;*
*Premonition of Civil War* (1936)
By Salvador Dali

Louise and Walter Arensberg Collection,
Philadelphia Museum of Art

*L.H.O.O.Q.* (1919) By Marcel Duchamp
Permission ADAGP 1968 by French Reproduction Rights Inc.

tem, must be held in check. It is suspect as other human attributes and tendencies are not, for example, those of the Id and the Unconscious, the Destructive, the Constructive (but outside of the normal framework of compromise with bourgeois reality), the Nihilistic, the Mystic (without God), the Anarchistic, or the Peace-at-any Caustic. Hence the surrealists' pronounced opposition to France's entering World War II, though they had no use for Hitler. Rational thought lends itself too easily to the creation of ambiguous defense mechanisms. As society's great wall of China, reason regularly becomes the Ego's protection against the maraudings of the Id and desires long dammed up. As these desires, or at least their fulfillment, presumably spell pleasure and happiness, man's goal should be to outflank the enemy in his midst, to oblige the surrender of his intelligence to a greater, all-encompassing vitalism. Only in this way can be reconciled the opposing views of those who, like Baudelaire and G.B. Shaw, hold that reason is a searchlight man turns on the future and those others, like J.J. Rousseau and Henry Miller, who maintain that all thought is antilife, that the essence of life is to be found only in the heart or the gonads, the former being preferred in the period before 1900, the latter after that date. Specialists become unnecessary, for if art be life then the very fact of living includes an artistic component: all words are literary and all constructions artistic. If this broad generalization is accepted we arrive at the ultimate democratization of art and literature. Even anti-art is art and formless literature, literature. This attitude, Dadaist in the extreme, but utilized by the surrealists, helps explain the inadequacy of so much of the critical comment on surrealism. The critic traditionally proceeds by analysis, one intelligence peering through a peephole at another. But here questions of composition, color harmony, draftsmanship, and insight are only peripheral to the more fundamental one of *revelation*, revelation not of a divine order but rather of a dimly human one. Talent becomes talent-to-express, and genius the opening of the flood gates of desire—it being assumed that one man's flood gates look very much like another's.[1] Hence the garish tricolor of Love, Liberty, and Poetry—the suggestive androgyne, unfettered desire, and the confusion of opposites, all of which, the surrealists felt, would make of man a god on earth.

One of the curious phenomena of the late nineteenth and the early twentieth centuries is the emergence of writer after writer either directly engaged in the creation of plastic works of art or writing in defense of the newest techniques. This tradition, which goes back to

Baudelaire, was picked up by Pierre Reverdy, Pierre Albert-Birot, F.T. Marinetti, Guillaume Apollinaire, and made an integral part of the philosophy of those who, like the surrealists, see all endeavor as unitary. The arts are conceived to exist not in and of themselves but as a function of desire, of pleasure, of the need for a change—which change must be social as well as aesthetic. The typical *realist* attitude toward literature and art, that of a Balzac or a Courbet, for example, is considered untenable. Art is more than holding up a mirror to nature, more than passivity, a fictitious consolation against the horrors of reality. Years before existentialism was known in France the surrealists had evolved an existential line of criticism: not only society but the author (or artist) too must be transformed by his work. To illustrate or illuminate was no longer sufficient. An active *engagement* leading toward a radical transformation of society and its individual parts must be the goal of all who worked in ink, paint, or clay. To this end the lamp of reason, reflecting traditional techniques and serving as society's searchlight, would have to be modernized so as to accept the *real* insights, the *pure* revelations of the Id. What to Freud had been a therapeutically useful hypothesis derived from experience became for the surrealists a portrait of Man suggesting a philosophy of life. Obscurity was equated with excellence, as it implied that the author-artist had succeeded in approaching the well-guarded treasure trove of Reality. Analysis as such was secondary, the revelation alone being more than sufficient. But is it? Surrealist art shocks. It does so by definition. The work of Dali, Magritte, Giacometti, and a host of others attests to this. But while the initial break with traditional reality—seen in the melting watches, the capricious reflection of erratic desires, or the metallic distortions of linear men—may initially overwhelm or exhilarate, or even stir the receptive onlooker to action, only exceptionally can it convince. Novelty alone is inadequate against the merciless buffeting of time. It is like the shadow cast by a phantom, too volatile to be fixed, too ephemeral to endure. Witness the recent exhibition devoted to the *object* held in Paris (at the Galerie Breteau, Dec. 1965), in which replicas of Duchamp's *porte-bouteilles* (1914) and other equally "revolutionary" items were shown with not a murmur from the spectators, or the repetitive XIth International Exhibition of Surrealism held at the art gallery L'Oeil (3, rue Séguier, Paris).[2]

The surrealists would agree with Leonardo da Vinci's whimsical answer to the question of how to find a subject: stare intently at the cracks of a blank wall until one appears. Technique, composition, media, colors—all that will depend on the artist's talent. The subject itself, however, comes from within, call it a product of the Id, a gift of the nether Gods, or an exteriorization of repressed desires in communion with Chance. An approach of this type to painting, or indeed to any work of art, makes it practically impossible for the observer to distinguish between a valid surrealist production and a fraudulent imitation. Only the artist—and even then!—can bear witness to the honesty of his work, that is, unless one is willing to accept the decision of some master judge, say Breton, whose Code of the Id would permit him to decide doubtful cases. But there is also an objective code of sorts, although Breton never cared to spell it out. Its major headings stress the *eroticism* of Dali and his brilliant "trompe-l'oeil technique for reproducing dream sequences"[3] (with subheadings for the wonderland of Chirico and Delvaux), the *meaningless horror* of Brauner and Bellmer, the *hermeticism* of Ernst with his parody of a parody to the nth degree (a stylization of a stylization, or a pictorial story about a story about still another stylized story), the ambivalent *anticlericalism* of Picabia, "one of the two or three great pioneers of what is called, for want of a better term, *the modern spirit*,"[4] the *jemenfoutisme* of several dozen others, the multiplaned *sentimentality* and *allusiveness* of Picasso, *the forms from another world* of Arp and Tanguy—everything in short that might be dream-like or unnatural by nineteenth-century criteria. If the scene depicted is too normal—that is, too logical or easily recognizable—its origin is immediately suspect. For what is wanted is pure reality untouched by interfering Censor or meddling Ego. Behind this surrealist call for liberation lay a Kantian misunderstanding: that a given individual was typical of all. To this was added the Freudian assumption that everything is significant, from which it is but one step to see in the most extravagant pictorial representations a reflection of the deepest layers of the Unconscious, a sort of bedrock human norm.

Art criticism, at least in its present verbal form, is fundamentally unsatisfactory to the surrealists. The only really convincing criticism of a painting, as they see it, would be another painting, or a series of paintings, just as the best criticism of a piece of music would be another piece of music. This is especially true of non-representational painting and a-traditional music; the hooks of logical discourse can find few edges among the fanciful shapes and colors, the unreal flora and fauna. Consider the example of clear titles affixed to the semantically ambiguous paintings of Miró and Picabia. Instead of a commentary of one on the other we are left with two parallel inspirations, one pictorial, the other verbal, both perhaps having the same point of departure, but speaking two different languages: form and color vs lexicon and grammar. The painting is seen instantaneously, its composition and contours strike the viewer all at once, as a unit; the prose passage is sensed in time, colorless and formless to the eye. While music, too, has a temporal existence similar to that of prose, its substance, its picture of reality (or "surreality"), is so radically different from either of the other two arts as to warrant separate treatment. Even less than with painting or sculpture can the unstructured "meaning" of a piece of music be fixed in the lumbering syntax of a natural language—which, incidentally, may explain the surrealists' indifference to music.

In spite of the above reservations the association between writers and painters, from Dada to the present, has been intimate and mutually rewarding. The mystery in Chirico, the directed whimsy of Picabia, both point to a layer of reality rejected or unrecognized by the Establishment. If one had to pick a date, a *terminus ab quo,* when this technique of revolutionary painting was first consciously utilized in a surrealist context, as contrasted with a purely artistic one, the most convincing would be March 1920. By the simple technique of adding a pair of moustaches to a copy of the Mona Lisa and presenting the "completed" work as his own, Duchamp extended to the realm of painting the same conceit which had previously found expression in his *Fountain,* the urinal signed "R. Mutt," submitted to the New York Independents Exhibition of 1917.[5] As long as the artist was a craftsman striving to reproduce reality, or certain of its details, his work could be judged according to the canons of his craft. But once he moved in the direction of pictorial puns, or tied his talent to a star and claimed to speak with the voice of the muse, or to have goals similar to those of the scientist seeking new ways to express the world, offering a new language for a new age, then the old touchstones of criticism became less certain. By what criteria could the work of art be evaluated? By its approximation to immediately sensed reality or to that subjective truth made manifest in the choice of color, sand, and stone? And if it is the artist's choice that elevates the work to the rank of art, then why not choose, say, a urinal? For those sensitive to art and willing to face the questions posed by the newer forms, the dogmas of the past were of little aid. With each passing year the canvases grew more outlandish, the forms more suggestive and jarring, for the artists felt that only by keeping the question of criteria alive might an answer be found. If Ernst is art, then surely Dali is. And why not Tanguy, or Matta, or the action, Pop, and Op people? Or a donkey waving a paint-swabbed tail, or a worm daubed in the color of one's choice, or even his? What *is* art?

The surrealist reply is implicit in Breton's first Manifesto—specifically in the phrase "it is not a question of painting, *but rather of tracing*"—and was developed with only slight modification in subsequent writings.[6] It is a two-part answer which can be put as follows: (1) art for art's sake is meaningless; it must *serve*, must reveal what is at present hidden, or it becomes a futile pastime;[7] (2) the work of art must be revolutionary; it must *shock*, or at least surprise, and preferably amuse. The specific subject matter is of no importance, any more so than the materials used. The painting (or whatever) should be a mirror on the unknown, or at least a key which will open the door to revelation. If it does this, it is good art, it is surrealistic; if it doesn't, it is worthless. To an extent this recalls certain symbolist poems, the hermetic works of Mallarmé and the unstructured *Illuminations* of Rimbaud, which, having no overt, immediately accessible meaning, offer the occasion for a leap into the unknown, indeed encourage it, and so half open the door to reverie—and revelation. Until Duchamp's time art was high seriousness, the litmus paper of a great civilization. Humor, whether in the form of a Rabelaisian outburst or in the wry smile at the antics of Molière's misanthrope, might have its place in the republic of letters and colors—but only on the periphery. For humor sees something wrong; and while a great civilization may tolerate humor, it can scarcely be expected to encourage it. Duchamp's mustachioed Mona Lisa, along with Picabia's ink-blot Virgin and any number of comparable farces, is a direct attack on a humorless tradition—an attack all the more telling in that it was directed by insiders, artists with acknowledged talent and everything to gain by fitting in.[8] The effect of surprise or shock, in art as elsewhere, is to disorient, to oblige the viewer to reexamine his baggage of beliefs and convictions, and hopefully to prepare him for that descent into the unknown, into himself, which one tradition from Socrates' time on has held to be the basis of all true knowledge.

Is art considered immortal? Then the surrealists will work in shoddy materials. Is it noble? Then their paintings will not shy away from baseness. Are care and craftsmanship desirable? Then chance and caprice will take their place. At no time, it might be pointed out, were their intentions masked; but they were sufficiently revolutionary to elicit little more than outraged disbelief—like the poetry of Lautréamont or the murals of Monet in an earlier period. The latter, however, and this is of some importance, were, as far as we can determine, trying to convey a message. In a true surrealist work there is no message, only an invitation, an invitation to examine the wretchedness of a society gone sour and to acknowledge the only true values in a fraudulent world: liberty, love, and the poetry which expresses them and makes both possible. In the eternal battle between moralists and revolutionaries, the first striving to change human nature, the second the society in which men live, the surrealists walked jerkily on both sides at the same time. To their Parisian peers they were *farceurs* perpetrating an overly long joke, summer revolutionaries with neither arms nor following, sometime writers damning literature—in a word, prissy virgins in a brothel. Yet would Sartre have declined his Nobel Prize if the groundwork had not been laid by Breton's long-standing refusal to be considered for any literary award (e.g., the 1950 award of the Prix de la Ville de Paris), by Julien Gracq's rejection of the Goncourt Prize for his novel *Le Rivage des Syrtes* (1951), by Ernst's expulsion from the movement, after over thirty years of intimate collaboration, for his acceptance of first prize at the Venice Biennale in 1954, not to mention the earlier expulsions of Soupault, Artaud, and Vitrac for their presumed interest in traditional literature? When a revolutionary is crowned by the enemy, so goes the thought, the revolution has failed, and neither Breton nor Sartre would accept the implications of a bourgeois coronation.

In much the same way that Chirico's studies of invisible horrors lurking behind the turn of a pillar do more to draw attention to the mystery of existence than, say, Renan's confident *Avenir de la science,* Duchamp's ready-mades do more to question the relevancy of individual craftsmanship (often masked by the term "art") than the articles of Apollinaire who, while still recognizing the storm on the horizon, did little more than indicate its general origin.[9] Love and marriage become tools or quasi-mathematical relationships in Picabia's "Novia" and Duchamp's several versions of "La Mariée mise à nu par ses célibataires, même"; the unknown takes on body with Dorothea Tanning and Max Ernst, while the irrelevant and the fanciful tag play in Miró.[10] Puns and eroticism, play and love—surrealist art is a Garden of Eden, a modern Garden of Delights by a collective Hieronymus Bosch, lacking only in transcendental implications. Dali's contribution to this artistic current, by far the best known if not always the most substantial, reflects a number of superficial surrealist paradoxes. There is the highly realistic fashion with which he portrayed the phantasmagoria of the irrational, his *méthode paranoiaque-critique,* broached as early as 1930, and whose one real merit is its fanciful title. (By concentrating on a painting with sufficient intensity, Dali assured the reader that he would eventually "see" the "real" subject.) The following year he lent his growing prestige to the discovery and creation of surrealistic objects, that is, objects having no practical value but only a symbolic function, like many of the so-called "executive pacifiers" that have been on the market these past few years. On the whole, he is less important as a theoretician—none of his techniques is fundamentally new—than as a latter-day Dadaist. His flamboyance and ridiculous poses caught the public's imagination as the bickerings of Breton & Co. never could.[11]

The history of surrealistic art has already been told in its broad outlines by a number of competent artists and historians. In going over the same terrain our goal is less to summarize than to reexamine the development of this art form (if we may use this shorthand term) in the all-embracing context of surrealism. In addition to the numerous painters, sculptors, and photographers who have appeared in surrealist-sponsored reviews, and who can therefore be considered as fleetingly representative, Breton himself has singled out a number for special mention. These include, among others, Picabia, Arp, Ernst, Chirico, Miró, Braque, Picasso, Man Ray, André Masson, Tanguy, Dali, Victor Brauner, Arshile Gorky, the Algerian Baya, and the Brazilian Maria.[12] He has at different times collaborated with artists as dissimilar as Marcel Duchamp and Joan Miró.[13] Primitives of all times and from all continents have long been favorites, along with the fantastic works of Bosch, Grünewald, Gustave Moreau, and similarly oriented painters.[14] What these, along with Bellmer, Svanberg, the early Matta, and Wifredo Lam, have in common is an obsession with the world as it *isn't,* but as it could be, perhaps as it should be. Theirs is a world of magic scenes, of enchanted forests, of unlikely pictorial metaphors: "Neither conscious nor unconscious," as Breton quotes approvingly, but mechanically produced, as Ernst's collages and frottages, and inspired by obsessional impulses.[15] Both the act of creation as well as the end result are presumed to open a door on the unknown. The magic wand here enables both artist and spectator to vault through the looking glass into the never-never land where desires take on flesh—and Alice plays Beatrice—in a Paradise of one's own creation. But the ultimate goal is more than sheer fantasy, more than caprice unleashed, for the unconditional liberty the surrealists seek must be for the betterment of man. [16] While Breton avoids giving that betterment a specific content, his political posture from 1925 to his death leaves little doubt as to the form it would take.

The idea of painting or poetry in the service of some cause, *engagé* would have been the term several years ago, is not especially new. In the course of time artists have served gods and kings and given imaginative contours to mysteries and to prospective brides. To defend the proletarian revolution is a logical extension, particularly if one assumes that the proletariat will eventually replace the now dominant classes and install its own mysteries, its own justice. What made this surrealist commitment even simpler was that it in no way obliged them to fraternize with those whom they were defending; this, together with their own class origins (bourgeois almost without exception), made them suspect, understandably so, to their Communist brothers. It is not only that the doctrine of socialist realism in art bears little resemblance to the magic realism of the surrealists, but even where they rub shoulders—such as in their idealization of reality—the one looks upward, all brightness and light, the other peers inward at the dark recesses of the soul (or the Id, for the squeamish). Both are idealizations, but one of the possibilities of reason and science, the other of desire and magic; one purports to speak the language of high seriousness, of purposeful activity, the other points to the land of Oz, but an Oz where the triumvirate of whimsy, irrational violence, and eroticism reigns supreme. But even this is a simplification. Dali, for example, describes the artistic sensitivity of the surrealists in the early days of their friendship. While they were delighted with his subject matter in general, they were also visibly disturbed by certain scatological themes:

> Blood was acceptable. Even a little excrement. But not excrement alone. I could portray sexual organs, but not anally oriented optical illusions. The arsehole was frowned upon! Lesbians were welcomed, but not homosexuals. Sadism, umbrellas, and sewing machines could all be found in dream imagery, but all references to religion or mysticism, except sacrilegious ones,

were taboo. If you innocently dreamed of a Madonna by Raphael, without manifestly blasphemous intentions, you were forbidden to mention it.[17]

The Unconscious, in short, is fine as long as it toes the line of a preconceived surrealist morality and aesthetic.

When one examines the exemplars of surrealist art, one cannot help but be struck by their Dadaist affinities. Duchamp and Picabia made their mark long before surrealism was conceived. Their suggestive objects, be they ready-mades, mechanical constructions, or doctored paintings, owe little to any specifically surrealist concepts, except those found also in Dada. Much the same can be said for Man Ray, who was introduced to the Paris art world by Duchamp,[18] and for Arp and Max Ernst who, each in his own way, had previously exposed the soft underbelly of fantasy which concrete reality masks but cannot eliminate. There are, of course, others, Tanguy and Dali among them, who came to the movement after Dada had been metamorphosed into surrealism and who therefore, we may suppose, best illustrate surrealism's peculiar contribution. But leaving aside for the moment the undoubted qualities of these late arrivals, and that a latecomer can always develop a technique or theme of a predecessor, there is in their work nothing that is substantially new, nothing that had not previously been tried in the so-called Dada period. This is not to say that Tanguy imitated Arp, Masson, Picasso, Dali or anyone else, but rather that what Breton found particularly praiseworthy is exactly what the Dadaists had years before applauded in earlier works. With this one difference: whereas the farce and the *canular* were integral parts of Dada, surrealist humor is much more of a reluctant afterthought. One welcomed the ridiculous, the other feared it; the playful violence of Dada, amorphous and uncommitted, took on a more strained air when Breton tried to lead the movement to the Communist Party and to specific social reforms. Only someone like Breton, thoroughly impatient with the imperfect world of reality and convinced of his own merits (quite real, especially as a publicist), could possibly have conceived so radical a goal.

In at least one way surrealist art recalls that of prehistoric times. The picture for paleolithic man probably had the value of a *double*: it was designed to capture the animal figured, or in some way conjure with it. The modern surrealist has a similar goal in that he wishes to fix the invisible, to describe the relations binding objective and subjective in all their crudity and hidden complexity. This is not magic in the narrow sense of the term—a system of operations or beliefs which grant to certain human acts the power to control natural phenomena—for art clearly lacks this operational character.[19] But it is magic in the broader (surrealist) sense, for which every *known* includes an unknown aspect and every unknown is potentially *magic,* that is, capable of revealing a whole new universe to the adept. Revelation, Wonderland—and material human progress. It is this apparent confusion of opposites—Breton would say antinomies—that gives surrealism its very special appeal and is at the same time so frustrating. More than anything else it is this recourse to magic, the revelation which can surge forth at any time from the most common objects, which colors the humanism of this movement. For revelation, in this context, must of necessity be human, since the divine, to the surrealists, is by definition nonexistent. Revelation thus becomes the third term in the dialectic starting with objective and subjective, the synthesis of poetry and politics, of desire and material resistance, of innocence and violence, of the real and the unreal.

If painting is indeed the "lamentable expedient" that Breton once called it,[20] it surely is no more so than any other means to an end. At its most effective surrealist art recalls a series of brilliant improvisations, in many ways like the best of modern jazz. What it lacks in formal coherence, in neo-academic finish, it more than makes up for by its atmosphere. Its unity is gratuitous, its sense provocative; it is, as the catalogue to Max Ernst's first Paris exhibition notes, "beyond painting."[21] Where Malraux speaks of an imaginary museum, referring to the influence of photography, the surrealists can with equal justification speak of the museum of the imaginary, which is nonetheless real for being intangible. The very organization which the artist of an earlier generation imposed on his material implies a convention and a simplification antithetical to the modern "superrealist." Reality, to the latter, to be effective must be presented *as it is,* that is, as it is sensed by the artist, in all its immediacy and arbitrariness. It is brute reality or it is nothing. This return to the source of inspiration, with none of the conventional prettiness encouraged by a taboo-conscious culture, is perhaps the major innovation of twentieth century art. A view of this type helps explain the sudden interest in so-called primitive art at the turn of the century. Not only do the African statuettes and masks admired by Picasso reflect a new way of seeing, a fusion of outside reality with an inner vision of what it *should* be, but their inadvertent disregard for Western prohibitions could not help but shock, and by so doing help liberate both artist and public from attitudes long held to be universal and, hence, natural or "good."

It has become a commonplace nowadays to point out that the *weltanschauung* of the surrealists and their immediate precursors in the art world is erotically charged—and powerfully so. If this is most blatantly evident in the hallucinatory paintings of Dali, it is rarely absent anywhere, except perhaps in the nonrepresentational canvases of people like Tanguy, and then only if one refuses the aid of Freudian symbolism. With some the eroticism hides behind terror, with others it is veiled in an equivocal game; in Chagall it has the magic of tenderness, in *le douanier* Rousseau it is luxuriant, in Dali frankly libidinous—everywhere, it would seem, it is a homeopathic cure for two endemic human afflictions, the absence of love and the fear of death. Magic, the stylized attempt to find remedies for those attributes of the human condition, is never far from surrealist think- ing. Though too sophisticated to indulge in meaningless gibberish, the surrealists welcomed the several myths proposed by Freud as offering a working description of man's inner clockwork far more convincing than those of more timid moralists. The recurrence of the fantastic in folk myth, painting, and literature, the appeal of love themes in all media and in all periods for which records exist, the universality of verbal incantations, all suggest that there is a firm biological or social anchor for surrealism, that it is a significant at- tempt to renew acquaintance with a part of man long ignored by a narrowly rational civilization.[22] The surrealist painter would be the first to recognize the irreality of his work, but he likely would react to it as he would to an exorcism. He is both its master and its slave: though he has created it, he too is caught by the spell.

If all art is a lamentable expedient, to quote Breton once again, limited in principle by color, technique, and the rest, the ideal sur- realist work would be one in which those principles played no role, where the will and talent of the artist were rendered inoperative:

> To open your window at will
> on the most beautiful landscapes of this and other worlds

Spread by means of a large brush some black gouache, more or less diluted here and there, on a sheet of white glossy paper. Cover with a similar sheet and apply moderate pressure with the back of the hand. Slowly lift the top sheet, as you would in making a decalcomania, replace and lift again until almost dry.

What you will have may be nothing more than Da Vinci's old paranoiac wall, but it will be that wall *brought to its ultimate degree of perfection.* All that remains is to give the picture obtained a title which accurately reflects what you see in it, taking some care to express yourself in the most personal and surrealistic fashion possible.[23]

Some years after having made the suggestion just cited, Breton offered an alternate approach to bedrock surrealist art, the "happening." In 1939 he pointed out that all art, to the extent it lent itself to commercialization, was a disservice to surrealist activity. The time had come, he proposed, to do away with the relatively durable, measurable work of art, "l'oeuvre d'art-ruban," and to replace it with its more ephemeral complement, the happening, "l'oeuvre d'art-événement,"[24] a moment of intense meaninglessness which would reflect and concentrate the absurdity of the world about us, and thus serve to make us more aware of our precarious human condition. Impossible to place in a museum, but nonetheless visually exciting, the happening would have all the virtues of a work of art (spontaneity, ability to surprise, to elicit *le merveilleux,* and so on) with none of its disadvantages (reflection of a conscious talent, possibility of commercialization, etc.).

Music, which might at first glance appear to lend itself most readily to surrealist adaptation, was to Breton "la plus profondément confusionnelle" of all artistic expressions.[25] What music lacks—or lacked, for the situation has changed with the advent of concrete music and its several offshoots—is a point of origin in the unconscious. As Breton has stated many times, and perhaps nowhere so clearly as in "Genèse et perspective artistiques du surréalisme" (1941), the two major contributions of surrealism are "automatism, inherited from mediums,"[26] popularly understood to be automatic writing, but quite as capable of being utilized in painting, sculpture, and elsewhere as well, and "the fixation called trompe-l'oeil,"[27] dream imagery, the overt portrait of a covert paradise. Both techniques bypass the conscious censor and presumably permit us to discover our *real* desires, and to the surrealists their desires were their dogma. Music, however, as Breton saw it, quiets the rebellion that stirs within us. At its best it might offer the semblance of paradise, but only for the time of the music. Whereas the results of an hour of writing automatically or making random blots and scrapings on a canvas might reveal a vein of gold hidden beneath the surface of some rational discipline, music—like poetry for Sartre—can reveal nothing, being primarily ornament and opiate.[28] In spite of its plausibility one may legitimately wonder if Breton's attitude toward music was not influenced by certain events in the ill-fated Congrès de Paris (early 1922), specifically Eric Satie's siding with Tzara rather than with Breton, for the very arguments the latter uses against music were earlier used by Pierre Naville in denouncing the inappropriateness of painting as a surrealist art.[29] Theoretically, of course, musical notes can be jotted down quite as randomly as colors can be applied to a canvas. The surrealist objection, therefore, would appear to have more subtle roots, or more personal ones.

Although Breton regularly stresses the primary importance of revelation elicited by the techniques of free association and dream analysis, he is careful never to reject reason completely. On one occasion he even questions the importance of Miró to surrealism because he is too unsophisticated, too unintellectual.[30] Given the fundamental goal of understanding and controlling the world, ourselves included, reason is obviously a handy tool, if not the only one. It is here that Breton parts company with the great majority of his contemporaries for whom reason and science *alone* are capable of affording reliable answers to the problems which beset modern man. If the surrealists have long been considered anti-intellectual, it is more for their reliance upon techniques unsubstantiated by present-day science than for their total rejection of reason.

One of the more striking innovations of surrealist art was the deliberate mixing of categories: a canvas, for example, combining elements of painting, sculpture, and poetry. As early as 1924 Breton had set the tone by proposing the construction of objects seen in dreams, objects which would bear witness to the latent desires of the dreamer and serve as either a magic talisman or a treasure from another world. Some eight years later, when the Charles Ratton Gallery held its surrealist exhibition of *objets mathématiques, objets naturels, objets sauvages, objets trouvés, objets irrationnels, objets ready made, objets interprétés, objets incorporés,* and *objets mobiles* (Calder), there was little doubt that a successful breach had been made in the wall separating several distinct art forms.[31] These dream objects, as with surrealist poetry, happenings, and the like, were "a means more than an end."[32] That this aspect of surrealist art is not lacking an intellectual component is perhaps nowhere more in evidence than in Breton's *poèmes-objets.* There is, for example, his baroque construction of December 1941, "Portrait de l'acteur A.B.

dans son rôle mémorable l'an de grâce 1713," in which he has meticulously brought together a hodgepodge of allusions to 1713 (suggested by the initials "A.B."), and which he then proceeds to explain.[33] All of this leaves little doubt that the prime purpose of surrealist art is other than aesthetic, at least if that term be understood as the recreation of yesterday's beauty. On the individual level it permits exorcism of personal obsessions, on the collective level it purports to reveal a hidden wonderland.

On the other side of the coin called Reality, implied Breton, lies Magic, and in his hands surrealism became an organized, collective search for the unknown in our midst, an attempt to make the two sides of the coin one, to see the other side of the moon, so to speak, intuitively. Some twenty years after Tristan Tzara had proposed drafting a poem from words drawn randomly from a hat, Breton used the same theoretical framework in praising a contemporary painter: "After having distributed his colors at random on a piece of wood [he] scrapes the results obtained with a razor blade in an arbitrary fashion, taking care only to emphasize the lights and shadows. At that point an invisible hand guides the blade so as to actualize the hallucinatory figures which previously existed only potentially in the amalgam."[34] The surrealist artist, in short, *creates* reality, or perhaps *reveals* it, where others are content to reflect surface phenomena. "Nature," as Breton once remarked, "is a cryptogram on which the artist places his *grid,* hoping thereby to discover the very rhythm of life."[35] More than an artisan, the artist in this view becomes the Adventurer, the Explorer. He is Alice seeking a way back through the looking glass.

It has recently become stylish to see in the motion picture the ideal means of surrealist expression—"the means," said Breton, "we at one time thought best adapted for bringing 'the true life' into existence."[36] The reason is quite clear: to the surrealists the film is not only a picture-poem, as was, say, Max Ernst's *La Femme 100 têtes,* but a moving-picture-poem resembling the dream state.[37] "The analogies suggested by the images" are crucial because they permit us to bypass the conformist Censor and drink at the source of all surrealist knowledge.[38] Before surrealism and before Dada, Breton and Vaché had made a practice of wandering at random from movie house to movie house seeking surcease from pain, or perhaps "kicks," from this newest of drugs. Without regard for programs, actors, beginning, or end, they strolled the streets of Nantes in search of a pictorial escape from mundane reality.[39] Thanks

to its "uprooting power," the cinema was ideally suited for getting
out of this world, as Baudelaire might have said, and for recharging
run-down batteries, as Breton did say.[40] For Breton, the great merit
of the film over literature or the theater is the speed with which it
affects the spectator: it places him almost instantly in that never-
never land between dream and reality, actualizes as no book ever
can desire and the picture of love, and can do all this even in a film
of little merit.[41]

The universe of the surrealist film maker is in principle identical
to that of his ink-oriented colleague, except that one works in words
and the other handles sets. If the value of the word lies in its evoca-
tive power, so does that of the film sequence. Meaning, logic, story
line, and aesthetic considerations are as irrelevant in this medium
as they are elsewhere in the movement. The touchstones of excellence are as ever shock and novelty, with a consolation prize to all
who had good intentions. One can assume, therefore, that the best
surrealist films would be those that bring together disparate items
(or people), photograph them in unlikely (but stylized) situations,
explain nothing (but do so in oracular terms), add a bit of wry
humor (or horror), and break two or three of the more obvious taboos (incest, sadism, gross anticlericalism, and so on). Such a film,
by surrealist definition, would reveal the latent in man and his universe, and by so doing permit him to know himself and his normally
repressed desires better.[42] The viewer must be affected by the screen
as he would be by a contagious germ, or at least by an exalting example. If we are to be made aware of the mystery that surrounds us,
of the revelation just beyond our grasp, the conjuring film must contain it, or be structured so as to elicit it.[43]

If surrealist theory remained fundamentally unchanged in moving from literature to the seventh art, the surrealists themselves were
avid film critics whose views were not always in harmony. Eluard
bears witness: "During the period when several friends and I were
regular moviegoers, there arose a very curious situation. We were
normally in agreement on just about everything. But never with regard to the movies. There were never so many interminable discussions, unshakable positions, as those concerning films we had
just seen."[44] As Sadoul put it: "We called one another every name
in the book because we had, or had not, liked a given Western or
some American actress. . . . However intransigent it might be in other
fields . . . surrealism had no guidelines in dealing with movies."[45]
With the exception of *Le Chien andalou* (1929) and *L'Age d'or*

(1930), the group found few films it could applaud wholeheartedly. And the former, while surrealist in tone, was completed some time before Buñuel or Dali met the group.[46]

The importance of surrealism in this genre, as elsewhere, lay in its liberating power. In a medium where every trained technician knows how to make a "good" film, surrealism had an explosive force. A close-up of an eye being slit by a straight razor, clergy in situations showing their humanity rather than their divinity, grotesque violence or madness, uncompromising love—all tended to metamorphose into a pictorial poem what to others was the ideal form of the picture-novel.[47] But if the automatic film poem is to survive beyond the private showing for friends-of-the-director, it must be a short, for to subject an audience to several hours of inspired images would be, to use Man Ray's term, barbaric.[48]

In his fanciful study of surrealism in the movies, Ado Kyrou, using a shifting series of measuring rods, succeeds in finding surrealism everywhere.[49] Although many of his examples are unconvincing, the movement's influence is apparent—if only indirectly and to differing degrees—in any number of films. Nonetheless, to the extent that surrealism is "inseparable from a certain automatism," as Pieyre de Mandiargues puts it so nicely, its obvious means of expression are in poetry (writing) and painting, not in a domain requiring technical knowledge of a fairly high order, which would be only too likely to filter out the inspiration of either author or director.[50] While automatism and dream analysis are the high roads to surrealist self-knowledge, they are not necessarily the most efficient techniques for opening to *others* the gates of horn. The film does just that: it *simulates* a world where dream and reality are one. Are there then two types of surrealist production, one automatic, aiming at REPRODUCING *le merveilleux,* the other highly controlled and endeavoring to ELICIT it? The paradox is sufficiently real for the early surrealists and Breton himself to have confused the issues. Eluard, for example, once wrote that "the poet is he who inspires more than the one who is inspired."[51] If we are correct it would have been more accurate to say that there are two types of poets, the inspired and those who inspire—and sometimes they change roles, or even overlap. The cinema, through its resemblance to a conscious dream, "can give the illusion of being surrealist in its very essence," as Michel Beaujour points out; but the *spectacle* of a revelation is only one of the goals the surrealists set for themselves, and indeed one they virtually abandoned in the thirties as being far less important, it would seem, than *evoking* some revelation in the spectator or reader.[52]

With the advent of sound, especially speech, the filmed image found a worthy rival competing for the spectators' attention. And quite as important, though on another level, the increased cost of making a film placed it beyond the reach of the surrealists.[53] The only full-length "talkies" that could be made would have to be commercially successful, as the new equipment was expensive and there simply were not enough surrealist cinema technicians around to make up a voluntary crew. A brief film review by René Crevel and Paul Eluard is evidence of the authors' annoyance at an art form turned commercial: "Between creatures purified by silence, speech places a sordid link," say the two surrealists. "One film is just like the next, and not very good at that, especially when it tries to conceal the essential, or worse to glorify it by means of noisy, moving pictures."[54] The movie, as the surrealists view it, is a dream larger than life, which because of public demand has been turned from its legitimate goal and made subservient to the laws of verisimilitude and decency. At best, then, it is more catharsis than preparation for revolt.[55] Its spectacle will purge the audience without in any way elevating it. The film thus becomes a simulation of a dream in much the same way that *L'Immaculée conception* simulates, without sharing them, certain mental illnesses.[56] If there is any revelation forthcoming when witnessing a non-surrealist film, it will be because the spectator takes what he sees before him to be an unstructured reality and structures it to please himself. What results is a sort of *critique synthétique,* of which a concrete example is Soupault's commentary[57] on a Chaplin film:

> Rolling and boredom fill our days. We have walked long enough on the bridge: the sea has been colorless ever since we left port. Not even the dice we toss or the cards we play can make us forget that city which we will shortly see: our life is at stake.
>
> It's the rain which greets us in those deserted streets. Birds and hope are far off. In all cities the restaurants are warm. We no longer even think; we look rather at the faces of the diners, at the door, or at the light. Are we aware that we will have to leave and pay? Isn't the present moment sufficient? It would be best to laugh away these concerns.
>
> And we laugh sadly like a fool.

If this tells us little about the film—who does what, when, and where—it tells us a great deal about the spectator's reaction to *The Immigrant.* We have what amounts to a prose parallel to the film, a complementary vision more than an analytic one. As one critic indicated, "it is not surprising that the surrealists considered the movies to be a superior type of drug; like a drug, it changes both man and the picture he has of his surroundings: 'My friends,' said Aragon, 'opium, the shameful vices, and the alcoholic symphony are all out of style: we have invented the movies.' And echoing him, Jacques Rigaut replies: 'We know what reproaches the youth of ten years from now will toss our way because of our attraction to the movies. They will say this was the last refuge of sentimentality. Women and trips, what pretexts! But drugs need no justification.' "[58]

It is not difficult to see why the surrealists, especially the surrealists, should be attracted to the cinema. Neither logic nor conventions govern its sequences. Speed up the camera and men dash about at dizzying speeds, slow it down and they are caught in some thick, transparent syrup. Mountains can move and phantoms speak. The dead rise. Heroines are breathtakingly beautiful, dangers chilling, embraces passionate—and it is all played for you alone, in a darkened dream-inducing atmosphere, perhaps with a lonely Pearl White next to you, also wondering if dream and reality can ever coincide. The true surrealist film, one that combined an automatic technique with a revelatory result, and ideally was produced by a member of the clan, was "regularly a failure," to borrow Breton's phrase from another context.[59] But if the surrealists set their sights too high, they did not fail completely. How could they? The very medium encourages a trance-like atmosphere of total receptivity, and even in the worst of the films there was always "the appealing gesture of a woman on the screen when *at long last* everything is lost."[60] The cinema offered the surrealists an animated mirror image of the inner theater of the mind, the projection on a screen of simplified passion and horror, comedy and death, without any commitment on the part of the viewer. It was *his* film being shown in the darkened theater, but he was no more responsible for it than he was for his dreams, or his poetry. This was *real* life, unencumbered with the details of *daily* life. And when this two-dimensional, bloodless projection was over, as with a dream, the spectator could rise and leave, leaving to others the tiresome task of rewinding the reels and preparing for the next *séance.*

# III: The Early Literature of Surrealism

The writings of surrealism, rejecting the techniques of hypothesis and controlled observation normally associated with an empirical science, and lacking the trappings of a religion, fall most easily into the categories of literature and art. The verbal automatism which is characteristic of much surrealist work and more surrealist theory, though relying heavily for its theoretical underpinnings on Freud's description of the Unconscious, can only be called a pseudo-science—while the later stress on occultism and related attention-getters represents little more than a restatement in esoteric terms of the value of automatism and of the benefits to be derived from this mental magic. The *surréel* itself, always immanent, is a result of the fortuitous encounter between the infinite within man and the infinite without. Breton's definition,[1] much quoted but little understood, pinpoints the goals of the movement as no comparable definition of romanticism, realism, or symbolism ever did:

> *Surrealism* (dictionary meaning). Pure psychic automatism by means of which we propose to express either verbally, in writing, or in some other fashion what really goes on in the mind. Dictation by the mind, unhampered by conscious control and having no aesthetic or moral goals.

> *Encyc. Philosophy*. Surrealism is based on the belief in the higher reality of certain types of association previously neglected, in the omnipotence of dreams, and in the free unmotivated play of the mind. It tends to undermine all other psychic mechanisms and to take their place in the resolution of the principal problems of life.

In spite of the problems one critic saw in this definition, both statement and intent, especially in the context of the Manifesto, are remarkably clear.[2] Surrealism's goal, to paraphrase Breton, is to let the Unconscious express itself, free as far as possible of the normalizing restraints of the Censor. The question of technique, *how* to bypass the Censor, whether by drugs, dreams, mediums, imitation of the writings of psychotics, inspiration, love, group collaboration in some verbal or pictorial game (such as that of the *cadavre exquis*), is not touched on at all in this definition, indeed is only alluded to fleetingly and jocularly (almost Dadaistically) elsewhere in the Manifesto. The second part of the definition, the one destined for some hypothetical encyclopedia, is less concerned with automatism and literature than with the philosophical basis of the preceding "dictionary" entry. Where Breton refers to "higher reality," the simplest restatement would be "greater meaningfulness or profundity," the sense it regularly has in the movement. Objective reality is here assumed to be one side of the coin whose other face is the Unconscious, with its storeroom full of repressed bits and snippets of obscure situations, thoughts and desires too sensitive for the conscious mind and too important to be summarily forgotten. Hence surrealism's reliance upon dreams and relaxed, undirected reverie, which presumably will lull the Censor into carelessness, and so permit one to observe what lies beneath the surface: a lay psychoanalysis, in short, which Breton saw as undermining our conventional, taboo-ridden society.[3] This attitude implies, of course, a complete rejection of that form of realism having its basis in positivism, St. Thomas, and Anatole France. To Breton, theirs was an ungenerous refusal to grant reality to anything but the average, the overt, and the mediocre. The exceptional, in either the intellectual or moral spheres, was suspect—an attitude no surrealist (or humanist) could accept. Even the doctrine of materialism, unacceptable though it was, had more merit, as it at least recognized the unity of man and of all of his acts and granted him the possibility of locating an earthly paradise, a possibility rejected by competing spiritualists.[4] "Surrealism, as I see it," said Breton, "highlights to such an extent our complete *nonconformism* that there can be no question of having it testify in favor of the world-as-it-is. Its sole purpose, on the contrary, is to turn our attention away from the so-called real world. . . . True life lies elsewhere."[5] For Breton, true life lay in searching for the unknown, much as it had for Baudelaire and Rimbaud, in inventing a new form of love, of finding virgin truths in hallucination, profundity just beyond reality.[6] The principal concern was the search; the treasure itself, which lay just beyond the surrealist drill-bit, was assumed to be a gift of the gods. "There can be no question of merit in having written a surrealist work," Breton remarked years before he was asked to put that phrase to the test in the comedy of errors that was *l'affaire Aragon.*[7]

Surrealist literature regularly appears as a pilgrimage down to the underworld of desire unlimited. As in some modern buildings in which the architects have sought to underscore the integrity of the materials and the honesty of the techniques, we see the props, the struts, the pillars, almost the very tools that were used in the con-struction—and the debris—so it often is with the surrealist work. Is it because the writer is uncertain in which of the "automatic" mes-sages the revelation is to be found? Yet all the communications pre-sumably derive from the "same surrealist oracle which shook Cumae, Dodona, and Delphi."[8] What was theory and therapy to Freud became active search to the surrealists. Much as the scientist does for the purpose of illustrating some theory, the surrealists, rarely the slaves of the data dredged up from the Unconscious, would *organize* their findings: "Even in the best of our automatically produced texts, a conscious element is present—although I like to think that we will eventually find a means of eliminating it. Nonetheless, there is a small amount of direction, found generally in the *organization of the poem.*"[9] If Breton here says "poem," it is because the only true lit-erature for him is poetry, whether rhymed or not, and regardless of whether even the ghost of a meter is present. The equation Litera-ture = Poetry = Provocative Image(s) has as its converse the other category of "literature," the one described by Verlaine, a commercial product designed to please rather than to reveal.[10] This double sense can be confusing to the unwary, as, for example, when Breton cautions us that "literature is one of the most unfortunate roads to success."[11] It is unlikely that he here has surrealist literature in mind, for success was at no time one of its overt goals. What Breton rejects out of hand is uninspired, superficial writing: "In literature [second meaning], only the spark of revelation can brighten novels and similar works whose very anecdotal nature place them in a lower category."[12]

While the traditional prose tale is essentially concerned with describing what everyone sees or does, or has heard of, or would take some pleasure in doing or witnessing, the surrealist poem, pro-posing as it does a window on the unknown, cannot avoid presenting a picture quite at variance with the formal gardens of homespun reality. In seeking to expand the domain of the real, the surrealist work looks beyond the plausible and tends to explode the concept of a closed universe. There is inevitably an element of grandeur in the surrealist aspiration and a unity of style and content which, while at worst obscure and at best opaque, signals a revolutionary turbulence of no mean proportions. In a discussion some years ago Pierre Reverdy remarked, "I have always thought that the style [of a poem] is merely the most visible part of the content—what the skin is to what lies beneath." To which Breton replied, "Absolutely," and then added: "The poet's role is less to move the reader than to *exalt* what he writes about."[13] To the early surrealists, if we may judge from *La Révolution surréaliste,* there were three principal genres: dreams (*rêves*), surrealist texts (*textes surréalistes*), and literary commentary in the broadest sense (*chroniques*). The first, a potpourri of scenes presumably dreamed, give every indication of careful reconstruction; the second, tales quite as brief as the dreams (1-2 pp.), differ in no significant way from the first, except that they were apparently not dreamed; the third in any other context would be termed essays, literary criticism, or *reportages.* That none of these examples truly succeeds in conveying that touch of random improvisation peculiar to automatic writing was recognized by Breton, years later, when he suggested that stenographic notation might permit the practicing surrealist to jot down his dream or text *in the form it came to him*—but *that* was never attempted.[14] When Breton took over the direction of *La Révolution surréaliste,* the tripartite division was modified to reflect his own literary orientation and that of his closest associates, though this was never mentioned in the magazine! From the July 1925 issue of *La Révolution surréaliste* (no. 4) on, we find a section devoted to poetry, sometimes in first place (as in no. 4), sometimes placed after the surrealist texts (nos. 5, 6, 8), sometimes after the dreams but before the surrealist texts (no. 7), sometimes after both (no. 11), or on occasion there are poems but no overt section devoted to surrealist texts (no. 9-10), while in the final number (no. 12), all earlier divisions go by the board: the final table of contents includes everything from poetry to a poll, from a manifesto (Breton's *Second manifeste du surréalisme*) to a scenario (Buñuel-Dali, *Un Chien andalou*), political notes, and a short story. Automatic writing is little in evidence, much less so, for example, than carefully contrived, baroque imagery. The period from 1924 to 1930 reflects a conscious desire on the part of the surrealists to test the pronouncements of Breton's first Manifesto. Literature's function was to open wide the gates of the Unconscious, permitting the flood waters of chance and desire to inundate reality. When nothing but a trickle came forth, the more formal systems of Marxism and magic, already present, were pressed into more active service.

How automatic was automatic writing? To what extent, even in their earliest productions, did the authors collaborate on any given text? In *Les Champs magnétiques* we see a perfectly normal prose, far less troubling than that of Mallarmé or even Proust. The syntax is that of standard French, with no slang, no esoteric technical terms, no neologisms. Is this the shorthand of the Unconscious? If the *content* is a jungle of disparate revelations, with all the incoherence of unrelated themes, the *frame* is that of a highly disciplined prose, this in spite of Breton's affirmation: "Let no one be mistaken, I know the meaning of all the words I use, and it is without conscious effort that I obey the rules of syntax (syntax is not, as some fools may think, a discipline)."[15] *Les Champs magnétiques* was a product of the joint efforts of Breton and Philippe Soupault, "the fruit of the first systematic application of automatic writing,"[16] but that did not prevent Soupault from publishing one section under his own name (with no reference to Breton), nor Breton from incorporating among his poems two other prose passages (with no reference to Soupault).[17] All of this tends to cast some doubt on the extent to which the two authors felt that the texts published separately were *joint* efforts. Was the poet really nothing more than a mouthpiece for the unconscious oracle, one who "does not consider himself the author of his book," for "he has done nothing more than transcribe without commentary, a document received"?[18] The theory and the practice of surrealism clearly do not always dovetail. The content of *Les Champs magnétiques* does little to substantiate the view that surrealism was radically different from what had preceded. To someone who has read Rimbaud's *Saison en Enfer* or his *Illuminations,* passages such as the following have a disturbingly familiar ring:[19]

> Les pupitres naviguent trois-mâts sur le zéro de conduite avec l'étonnante poussière des vasistas qu'on trouvera moyen de fermer. Je fais ce que je peux pour que mes parents aient du monde le soir. J'admire beaucoup la canne de ce monsieur; ce sont les premières nouvelles que j'ai reçues d'Ethiopie. Son neveu s'offrait à m'envoyer des tortues de là-bas: c'est, je crois bien, la plus belle promesse qu'on m'ait faite, et j'attends aussi toujours ces fleurs de Nice, gravure d'un calendrier. Voici que les prières se replient. . . .

La couleur des saluts fabuleux obscurcit jusqu'au moindre râle: calme des soupirs relatifs. Le cirque des bonds malgré l'odeur de lait et de sang caillé est plein de secondes mélancoliques. Il y a cependant un peu plus loin un trou sans profondeur connue qui attire tous nos regards, c'est un orgue de joies répétées. Simplicités des lunes anciennes, vous êtes de savants mystères pour nos yeux injectés de lieux communs.

On occasion there are reminiscences of Lautréamont:[20]

Un agent de police du VI[e] arrondissement rencontra un homme qui sortait d'un café et qui courait. Un carnet tomba de sa poche mais l'homme avait disparu. A la lumière d'un haut réverbère, il lut ces quelques lignes écrites au crayon:

*La rougeur des crépuscules ne peut effrayer que les mortels. J'ai préféré la cruauté.*

*Les manufactures anatomiques et les habitations à bon marché détruiront les villes les plus hautes.*

*A travers les vitres des hublots, j'ai vu toujours les mêmes visages: c'étaient des vagues échappées.*

*La fièvre tourne doucement dans ma poitrine; on dirait le bruit plus lointain des villes vers onze heures du soir.*

Indeed, the very format of the Breton-Soupault work points to Lautréamont. Instead of the latter's five *Chants de Maldoror*, we have seven *Champs (Chants?) magnétiques* by the two pre-surrealists: "La Glace sans tain" (pp. 9-17), "Saisons" (pp. 21-27), "Eclipses" (pp. 31-40), "En 80 jours" (pp. 43-52), "Barrières" (pp. 55-69), "Ne bougeons plus" (pp. 73-83), "Gants blancs" (pp. 87-91), followed by a section of poems, "Le Pagure dit" (pp. 95-111).[21] The principal point of resemblance, however, between Breton-Soupault and Rimbaud-Lautréamont is their rejection of what the French would call *la littérature de consommation*, a literature written to be sold. Hence the absence of any carefully contrived story, clever characterizations, or pretty rhythmic lines. But where Rimbaud-Lautréamont give the illusion of pagan priests officiating at some magic ritual, Breton and Soupault, far less certain of their witching powers, offer the less provoking picture of poets seeking a subject and delving for it in some forged image: the spellbinding quality of one becomes overly rhetorical in the other. Where Rimbaud could write, "I became a fabulous opera: I recognized that everyone is doomed to happiness . . . ," Breton-Soupault follow, "The color of fabulous salvations masked even the slightest death-rattle." Where Lautréamont marveled that "There exists an insect that men nourish at their own expense," Breton and Soupault add, "There is in deepest Africa a lake peopled by male insects who know how to die only at day's end."[22] Where Lautréamont and Rimbaud direct their attention to the horror that often lies at fingernail depth beneath a daily routine, Breton and Soupault appear to be at some distance from "this river swollen with our despair."[23] The disciplined frenzy of the earlier duo has been metamorphosed into a discipline in search of a frenzy: imagery born of substance has become talent seeking images—and the spell is broken.

We see this even more clearly in Aragon's early parody on Rimbaud (*Anicet*) and in Breton's *Poisson soluble*.[24] The thirty-two chapters (poems?) of the latter work survey a latter-day *pays du Tendre*. In this land of magic innocence we have a paradise of delights from which violence has been banished, the images tamed, and the hours spent pursuing vaguely female forms in a wonderland Alice would have nodded to familiarly. How automatic is section 31, for example, in which we find a carefully arranged dialogue among four people—stage directions and all; or section 12, which relates an interview between a reporter and a mad scientist; or the remainder, with their revamping of Rimbaldian themes.[25]

Le parc, à cette heure, étendait ses mains blondes au-dessus de la fontaine magique. (*Poisson soluble*, sec. 1, p. 67) L'aube d'or et la soirée frissonnante trouvent notre brick en large en face de cette villa et de ses dépendances, qui forment un promontoire aussi étendu que l'Epire et le Péloponnèse. . . ("Promontoire," *Illuminations*, p. 299)

Sur le bord des nuages se tient une femme, sur le bord des îles une femme se tient comme sur les hauts murs décorés de vigne étincelante le raisin mûrit, à belles grappes dorées et noires. (*Poisson*, sec. 1, p. 69) Sur la pente des talus les anges tournent leur robes de laine dans les herbages d'acier et d'emeraude. Des prés de flammes bondissent jusqu'au sommet du mamelon. ("Mystique," *Illumin.*, p. 283).

Elle disparut en effet et j'étais déjà enchanté d'en être quitte avec elle à si bon compte quand je m'aperçus que le Génie de la place, d'ordinaire fort éveillé, semblait pris de vertige et sur le point de se laisser choir sur les passants. (*Poisson*, sec. 3, p. 73). Un Génie apparut, d'une beauté ineffable, inavouable même. . . . Le Prince et le Génie s'anéantirent probablement dans la santé essentielle. ("Conte," *Illumin.*, p. 259).

Nous réduirons l'art à sa plus simple expression qui est l'amour; nous réduirons aussi le travail, à quoi, mon Dieu ? A la musique des corrections lentes qui se payent de mort. (*Poisson*, sec. 7, p. 82). Je suis un inventeur bien autrement méritant que tous ceux qui m'ont précédé; un musicien même, qui ai trouvé quelque chose comme la clef de l'amour. ("Vies II," *Illumin.*, p. 264).[26]

villes de fièvre sillonnées en tous sens par des femmes seules, villes d'abandon, de génie aussi, dont les édifices étaient surmontés de statues animées. . . (*Poisson*, sec. 20, p. 104). Ce sont des villes! . . . Les Bacchantes des banlieues sanglotent et la terre brûle et hurle. ("Villes," *Illumin.*, p. 276).

Les personnages de la comédie se rassemblent sous un porche . . . (*Poisson*, sec. 21, p. 105). L'Ancienne Comédie poursuit ses accords et divise ses Idylles. . . ("Scènes," *Illumin.*, p. 300).

Il y avait une fois un dindon sur une digue. Ce dindon n'avait plus que quelques jours à s'allumer au grand soleil et il se regardait avec mystère dans une glace. . . (*Poisson*, sec. 27, p. 119). Aussitôt que l'idée du Déluge se fut rassise, / Un lièvre s'arrêta dans les sainfoins et les clochettes mouvantes et dit sa prière à l'arc-en-ciel à travers la toile de l'araignée. ("Après le déluge," *Illumin.*, p. 253).

This is not to imply that *Poisson soluble* is a conscious imitation. Rimbaud's works, nevertheless, were sufficiently well known to the surrealists that one need only acknowledge that his style and themes were, so to speak, in the air for there to exist the possibility of influence. While Breton's work contains any number of allusions which have no parallel in Rimbaud or Lautréamont—for example, section 25 of *Poisson soluble,* which might have been subtitled "Reflexions on Eluard's Departure"[27]—it would not be excessive to say that if we were to extend the literary lines of Rimbaud and Lautréamont, the point at which they cross could be labeled Breton. If we cannot overlook Mallarmé's authority, especially during Breton's formative years, or that of Apollinaire or Valéry, Breton's style from late 1919 on everywhere looks back to the young poet from Charleville and his displaced Montividean contemporary, both with regard to the type of imagery and to its evanescent content. It is this intimate familiarity that undoubtedly simplified his early recognition of the false *La Chasse spirituelle* many years after he had "forgotten" the techniques so laboriously assimilated.[28]

Perhaps even more influential than Rimbaud, if we are to believe Breton, was the binding charm of *Maldoror*. "Nothing," says Breton, "not even Rimbaud, had up to that time affected me as much. Even today, I am absolutely incapable of coldly, analytically examining that astonishing message which, to me, seems in every way to surpass man's potential." And he goes on to quote Soupault: "It is not for me, nor for anyone else. . . to judge *M. le Comte*. One does not judge *M. de Lautréamont*. One can only recognize him as he passes and bow down," for Lautréamont, to all intents and purposes, is not of this world.[29] "We are opposed," Aragon, Breton, and Eluard wrote on another occasion, "we continue to be opposed to any attempt to bring Lautréamont into history, to assign him a place between X and Y."[30]

A disposition of this type, while unusual in sophisticated literary circles, has a long and honorable tradition among religious societies, in which the deity is carefully placed outside of historical time, and most peoples, primitive and other, have totems and taboos of various sorts to help them weather the storms of reality. To the surrealists Lautréamont had seen through the forest of symbols which surround us into the glory that lies just beyond the *dérèglement de tous les sens*. The *Chants*, however, are less visions of perfect moments, a preview of Proust's *moments privilégiés*, than scenes of unreal horror that might have been enacted by an early Caligari, scenes which, if Breton was willing to accept as authentic, he had no intention of imitating. Only Péret, of the early surrealists, rose to this challenge and attempted a synthesis of the technique of automatism, carefully controlled so as to give the desired end result, with the content of the Gothic novel: a combination of deliberate sensory and logical confusion with a matching subject. All this in an impeccable syntax.[31]

—Die, deaf horn!
—Die, eel soap!

—Die, head paper!

—Die, flighty elephant!

Such were the cries which echoed inside the tin tube where two virgins and their shadow were sleeping. With arms raised to heaven, they begged the arsonists to spare the roots of the beech tree which had given birth to them. The younger of the virgins, whose brow was a wine cellar reserved for the purest alcohols, those which the philosopher extracts from fur coats after they have shielded a woman's shoulders from indiscreet glances of a winter's night similar to a picture book Christmas when booted Russians hunt wolves in vegetable gardens bristling, for decorative effect, with frozen brushes and mannequins who nonetheless. . . .[32]

This is the wonderland of a child's picture book where reigns the wicked witch, a land where animal horns may turn deaf, eels wash (or [savon d'anguille] is it simply soap made of eels?), skulls are the source of paper (or [papier de crâne] is the paper *for* the skull?), and elephants are fickle. Not really very wicked or dangerous when compared with either of the world wars between which this falls, or when held up to the mischievous works of a Sade or a Lautréamont. On the surface this is far more a pampered child's version of what is dreadful in the world about him. For adults, on the other hand, Péret's tales are neither terrifying nor amusing. His chambers of false horrors are indeed so anodyne that there arises the suspicion he wanted it that way, that he was deliberately engaged in writing new fables for old children, as Desnos and Prévert were to do years later in their *Chantefables* and *Paroles*.[33]

### La Fourmi

Une fourmi de dix-huit mètres
Avec un chapeau sur la tête,
Ça n'existe pas, ça n'existe pas.
Une fourmi traînant un char
Plein de pingouins et de canards,
Ça n'existe pas, ça n'existe pas.
Une fourmi parlant français,
Parlant Latin et javanais,
Ça n'existe pas, ça n'existe pas.
Eh! pourquoi pas?

*Les Hiboux*

Ce sont les mères des hiboux
Qui désiraient chercher les poux
De leurs enfants, leurs petits choux,
En les tenant sur les genoux.
Leurs yeux d'or valent des bijoux,
  Leur bec est dur comme cailloux,
Ils sont doux comme des joujoux,
Mais aux hiboux point de genoux!
Votre histoire se passait où?
Chez les Zoulous? Les Andalous?
  Ou dans la Cabane Bambou?
  A Moscou ou à Tombouctou?
  En Anjou ou dans le Poitou?
Au Pérou ou chez le Mandchous?
  Hou! Hou!
Pas du tout, c'était chez les fous.

*La Cène*

Ils sont à table
Ils ne mangent pas
Ils ne sont pas dans leur assiette
Et leur assiette se tient toute droite
Verticalement derrière leur tête.

*L'Amiral*

L'amiral Larima
Larima quoi
la rime à rien
l'amiral Larima
L'amiral Rien.

Péret early struck this tone:

Un clou, deux clous, trois clous et voici notre maison bâtie. Devant elle se dresse une épée de sucre qui sous l'influence des rayons du soleil tend à devenir un monde nouveau, une planète de feuille sèche dont le désir de rotation autour d'un couple de hérons se manifeste par un léger hululement qui est le signal du départ pour les quarante-huit coureurs envoyés dans la course de Paris à l'étoile polaire en passant par tous les nouveaux cinémas des capitales européennes. Les voici partis, tandis que,

dans la course que nous voyons de temps en temps dans les
forêts de sel, les coureurs disparaissent un à un comme des
gouttes de rosée. Cette fois-ci ils se multiplient à mesure que
croît la distance qui les sépare de leur point de départ sans que
pour cela diminue celle qui les sépare de leur but.

For those tired of logic, of reason, of lockstep consensus, Péret offers
an enchanted land where houses are built in a twinkle, and one goes
from candy swords to prodigious bicycle races. Much may happen
in this aloof dream world, but it is all harmless, for it doesn't really
"engage" us as would, say, tangible reality. Things become people,
women are always at the ready, nothing is burdensome, and should
you be injured you can always change into something else.

Le vent se lève comme une femme après une nuit d'amour.
Il ajuste son binocle et regarde le monde avec ses yeux d'enfant.
Le monde, ce matin, est semblable à une pomme verte qui ne
sera jamais mûre, le monde est acide et gai. On dirait une pelle
neuve avec son manche blanc. Partout il y a des pelles et des
ustensiles de ménage, à croire que le monde a attendu ce jour-
là, aujourd'hui, pour s'installer, pour avoir son jardin et son
chien qui aboie dans sa niche parce qu'il a vu un million de
cloportes sortir du corps d'un lézard tué par le froid. Ce chien,
il faut que j'en parle et que je le décrive afin que nul ne puisse
le confondre avec un fraisier. C'est un bel animal énorme et
bruyant comme une pouponnière. Il saute, bondit à travers la
collection de timbres-poste de son maître. Il va du paratonnerre
au fond du puits plus rapidement qu'une pierre et se retrouve
de l'autre côté du mur toujours semblable à lui-même et à sa
porte cochère.[34]

In this dream world, which could serve as a model for a film to
delight the young and disturb the rest of us, the heart reigns
supreme. The standard tools of comprehension are of little avail.
Nonetheless, the human animal is sufficiently resilient to assimilate
even the strangest of human artifacts, however odd they may appear
at first sight. In a sense this is the glory of surrealism and its major
contribution to literature. Having obliged us to recognize the irrational in the world, it challenges the smug and obliges the sedate
to redraw the boundaries of reality. From the time of symbolism to
the present a certain type of art has become more and more of a
private affair, the author writing less for a public, even the restricted

one of fellow authors, than for himself. Art, at this point, becomes a form of self-knowledge requiring new techniques and a new logic, in much the same way that life then is identified with spontaneity and action, rather than with the idea of progress. Is this very different from Tristan Tzara?[35] For both Tzara and the old-line surrealists art-for-a-public was to be replaced by art-for-truth (subjective truth, *bien entendu!*), with each artist dipping his own siphon into the unconscious well and marveling at the bubbles which rose to the surface, individual bubbles reflecting a collective consensus. Where Tzara saw psychoanalysis as a "dangerous illness, [for it] puts the antireal penchants of man to sleep" and shores up a declining middle class, Breton perceived the possibility of turning psychoanalytic techniques away from integrating the "patient" into society and toward a new revolutionary self-awareness.[36] In Péret, as in Tzara before him, the content is sufficiently amorphous so that the reader is encouraged to restructure the poem (or story) according to the dictates of his ever-solicited caprices. The end result, as Breton foresaw, was "an unprecedented freedom of expression,"[37] one that, according to one critic, "does not aim to bridge the distance between the real and the surreal; it places us unequivocally in the realm of the latter."[38]

In Péret's universe, as occasionally in Mallarmé's, disembodied words have a reality all their own. Had not Breton insisted that "man was given language so that he might use it surrealistically"?[39] Péret would not have it any other way. The one pitfall is to *explain,* to reduce the complex unknown to a simple known, this in spite of the fact that "Thought is ONE and indivisible."[40] Although no mystic, Péret has a mystic's unconcern for categories: all is one and one is all. Where he differs is in placing the Godhead in poetry, surrealist poetry, to be sure. In that Wonderland where whim and chance are the reigning monarchs, Alice-Péret, the wanderer from beyond, will describe glass sternums polished by cellar sunlight and a turquoise titmouse beating its wings in cream.[41] As J. H. Matthews put it so nicely:

> Confusions in meaning and mingling of significances of this sort are representative of the metamorphic world of desire, as it is reflected in the work of Péret. Surrealism, as this poet indicates, resists immobility, in favour of an ever-expanding circle of possible meanings which, on occasion, may serve to erode or debase the true as we know it, but which certainly transform

it. Significances inter-act as they accumulate, and become inter-
dependent, in spite of the differences which would seem to
separate them.

It is in this connection, perhaps, that one may best consider
Péret's use of humour. Surrealist humour, defined by Marco
Ristitch in *Le Surréalisme au service de la Révolution* as "an
intuitive and implicit criticism of the mental process in its con-
ventionality," finds in Péret one of its finest practitioners. Re-
moving facts and phenomena from their normal context, Péret
involves them in the vertiginous play of unexpected relationships which is the surreal. Humour is thus, in Péret, corrosive
and destructive. It offers no concessions to convention, and
combats the conditioned reflex of social and moral attitudes. It
becomes the leaven of protest and revolt. Under its influence
reality exfoliates, and we are left to speculate regarding the
nature of the true. For Péret's subversive use of inverted logic
here takes its full effect, imposing conclusions our minds find
unacceptable, yet inescapable.[42]

Delusion or naiveté? Péret, and with him all the surrealist regulars,
assume that men and things can be described by what Camus termed
their "daily automatisms." But, as Camus so clearly saw, such a
world is a result of "a willful mutilation of reality," for it proposes
an imaginary man in an imaginary environment, abstract, gratuitous,
emptied of any content.[43] This is neither reality nor surreality, revolt
nor acquiescence. It is a game without end played by false innocents,
and, given the talent of some of the participants, it is not certain
whether laughter or lament would be more appropriate.

Placed in the context of what was later to be called an *absurd*
world, one in which man's desires are seen to be imprisoned by the
walls of reality, surrealist humor, *l'humour noir*, becomes a sort of
disdainful response to an imperfect universe. "There is nothing that
can happen to man," as Camus pointed out, "that scorn cannot overcome."[44] Breton had earlier come to a similar conclusion when he
defined surrealist humor as a "mental revolt," illustrating this with
an example drawn from Freud: the convict condemned to death
who, on being led to the gallows one Monday morning, is heard to
say, "This is a fine way to begin a week!"[45] The surrealists, in this
light, are absurd men laughing so that they will not cry, playing
comic roles to avoid acknowledging the pain of reality.[46] Where
Camus, conscious of the irreconcilable opposition between man and

the world, desire and reality, the call of the heart and the eternal silence of an indifferent universe, saw man as a "mime of the perishable," an "actor who moves and improves in the shifting world of appearances"—in short, as someone who has gone beyond the futility of despair toward an active commitment to life which, whatever its value, is all there is—Breton was regularly tempted by a leap into the irrational.[47] He believed in magic and in the ultimate resolution of mischievous antinomies *because* (to borrow a phrase from Tertullian) it was absurd. If Camus preferred action to inaction, creation to aloofness, it was because "to create is to live twice," and, having rejected a qualitative ethic, he embraced a quantitative one.[48] Thought alone, as he said, is incapable of transforming reality, it can only imitate it: beyond thought lies action, beyond the absurd, revolt.[49]

Péret, the long-time militant anarchist who, like Malraux, joined the Republican forces in Spain days after the outbreak of the Civil War, could have no quarrel with such sentiments.[50] Years before Aragon ran into censorship difficulties with his poem *Front rouge*, Benjamin Péret published what the normally blasé *Canard enchaîné* termed "this extraordinary *Je ne mange pas de ce pain-là*.[51] And it is.

> *Pour que M. Thiers ne crève pas tout à fait*
> Ventre de merde pieds de cochon
> tête vénéneuse
> c'est moi Monsieur Thiers.
> J'ai libéré le territoire
> planté des oignons à Versailles
> et peigné Paris à coups de mitrailleuses
> Grâce à moi ON a pu mettre
> du sang dans SON vin
> Ça vaut mieux que de l'eau
> et ça coûte moins cher
> Les perles de ma femme sont des yeux de fédérés
> et mes couilles de papier mâché
> je les dégueule tous les matins
> Si j'ai des renvois de nougat
> c'est parce que Gallifet me gratte les fesses
> et si mon ventre s'allonge
> c'est parce que j'ai fait danser
> l'anse du panier de
> la République

*Epitaphe pour un monument aux morts*
*de la guerre*

Le général nous a dit
le doigt dans le trou du cul
L'ennemi
est par là Allez
C'était pour la patrie
Nous sommes partis le doigt dans le trou du cul
La patrie nous l'avons rencontrée
le doigt dans le trou du cul
La maquerelle nous a dit
Le doigt dans le trou du cul
Mourez ou
sauvez-moi
le doigt dans le trou du cul
Nous avons rencontré le Kaiser
le doigt dans le trou du cul
Hindenburg Reichshoffen Bismarck
le doigt dans le trou du cul
le grand-duc X Abdul-Amid Sarajevo
le doigt dans le trou du cul
des mains coupées
le doigt dans le trou du cul
Ils nous ont cassé les tibias
le doigt dans le trou du cul
dévoré l'estomac
le doigt dans le trou du cul
percé les couilles avec des allumettes
le doigt dans le trou du cul
et puis tout doucement
nous sommes crevés
le doigt dans le trou du cul
Priez pour nous
le pied dans le trou du cul

*So That M. Thiers May Live a While Longer*

Belly full of shit pigs feet
poisonous head
it's me Monsieur Thiers.
I freed our country
planted onions in Versailles
and combed Paris with my machine gun

Thanks to me THEY have put
blood in HIS wine
That's better than water
and costs less
My wife's pearls are the eyes of rebels massacred in 1871
and my paper maché balls
I puke 'em up every morning
If I burp bits of nougat
it's because Gallifet [general who put down the 1871 Commune in Paris] is scratching my arse
and if my belly swells
it's because I've danced
with the ants in the
breadbasket of the Republic

> *Epitaph for a Statue to Our War Dead*

The general told us
with his finger up his arse
the enemy
is over there Go get 'em
It's for our country
We met our country
with its finger up its arse
The madame told us
Die or save me
With a finger up her arse
We met the Kaiser
with a finger up his arse
Hindenburg Reichshoffen Bismarck
with a finger up their arse
the Grand Duke X Abdul-Amid Sarajevo
with a finger up his arse
dismembered hands
with a finger up their arse
They kicked our shins
ate our stomach
with a finger up their arse
pierced our balls with wooden matches
with a finger up their arse
we croaked
with a finger up our arse
Pray for us
with a foot up your rear

It is clear, on reading the above, where Aragon found his inspiration for *Front rouge,* especially as that sort of violence is exceptional in his work.[52]

Breton himself has always been too restrained (bourgeois?) to use the type of vocabulary and situation that was normal to Péret.[53] Even his most radical verse sidesteps violence, his most erotic, any indecency.

### *Ode à Charles Fourier*[54]

Sur la brèche
Au premier défaut du cyclone
Savior *qui* reste la lampe au chapeau
La main ferme à la rampe du wagonnet suspendu
Lancé dans le poussier sublime

Comme toi Fourier
Toi tout debout parmi les grands visionnaires
Qui crus avoir raison de la routine et du malheur
Ou encore comme toi dans la pose immortelle
Du Tireur d'épine

### *L'Union libre*[55]

Ma femme à la chevelure de feu de bois
Aux pensées d'éclairs de chaleur
A la taille de sablier
Ma femme à la taille de loutre entre les dents du tigre
Ma femme à la bouche de cocarde et de bouquet
                    d'étoiles de dernière grandeur

. . . . . . . . . . .

Ma femme aux yeux de bois toujours sous la hache
Aux yeux de niveau d'eau de niveau d'air de terre et de feu

If there is anything in the *Ode,* Breton's longest and presumably most ambitious poem, that brings to mind surrealist admonitions which have accumulated over a period of forty years, it is the author's serene assurance that he has a message, a revelation which can change the course of human events: a peaceful, disciplined Fourierist utopia. The assurance is surrealist, but not the message. Fourier, in the Breton *Ode,* is less a source of solutions to twentieth-century problems than a pretext for a long look at a phalansterian heaven. The major novelty in "L'Union libre" is the style, with its repetition of a very limited number of syntactic constructions at the beginning of each line: *ma, à, de,* and *et* are the points of departure—the only ones—in some sixty lines, something he had never attempted before and was not to try thereafter.[56] Little in evidence—though by now it must be obvious that it rarely is otherwise—is the literary technique of least resistance. If Breton is far from embracing the prudent maxim that art is born of constraint, thrives on struggle, and dies of liberty,[57] he is no less far, in "L'Union libre," from the high road to the Unconscious.

I had suggested earlier that Breton's style was a cross between that of Rimbaud and Lautréamont, and while that is true *grosso modo,* due allowance must be made for contemporary influences such as that of Valéry, or even Claudel:

> En ce temps-là je ne te connaissais que de vue
>
> . . . . . . . . . . . . . . .
> Toi que ne parlais que de lier vois tout s'est délié
> Et sens dessus dessous on a redescendu la côte[58]

Had those lines been signed Claudel, scarcely anyone would give it a second thought. The words no longer make love[59]—always a highly cerebral affair to Breton—but instead knit a medieval tapestry of memories and myths. Is this philosophical whimsy Breton's answer to *Les Chants de Maldoror?* Hermetic phrases such as "Les attractions sont proportionnelles aux destinées" and "Je te salue du bas de l'echelle qui plonge en grand/ mystère dans la *kiwa* hopi la chambre souterraine et sacrée. . ." are little more than flat revampings of the, at least, colorful Lautréamont.[60] Revelation, which Péret termed the heart of all real poetry, is almost totally absent, as is any substantial insight into the philosophy of the nineteenth-century Fourier.[61] Or is perfunctory descriptive scholarship to be assimilated to poetry? If Péret is correct in saying that "poetry is the source and the crowning achievement of all thought," and that "there can be no thought without intuition, that is, without insight (*voyance*), and no intuition without thought," then it would be difficult to avoid classing Breton's last major poetry with Hugo's *Les Burgraves* as one of the striking literary failures of its time.[62] Breton's random reflections on the universe, lightly illustrated, are no more convincing than unsubstantiated affirmations ever are. Even more damning from the critic's standpoint, one has on occasion the impression that, to the ever-young surrealists, *everything* they did and said was a game, and not to be taken seriously.[63]

In the first three numbers, *La Révolution surréaliste* offered its readers a racy menu of surrealist dreams, dream-inspired texts, open letters, various pronouncements on life, love, and revolutions, a poll on suicide, and a glossary of puns—the lot interspersed with illustrations by Man Ray, Picasso, Ernst, Klee, Masson, Chirico, and others. But no poetry or other "literature-oriented" items. It is, therefore, with some surprise that we read in the fourth issue (July 15, 1925) that Breton will henceforth be the editor of the periodical so as better to protect the movement from any literary contamination.[64] The movement was also to be protected from political commitment, which too would sap the energy of the restless surrealists by distracting them from their primary goals: "Who dares speak of using us to improve our common earthly lot? We want, and will have, the 'beyond' in our lifetime. For that to come about we must give heed to nothing but our impatience and have complete confidence in our revelations."[65] Hardly a political program or an invitation to join some existing party. At any cost, it would seem, the movement had to be preserved from integration into society, from the dubious respectability of political or literary *engagement*. Nonetheless, immediately following Breton's text are the very first poems to appear in the magazine (by Aragon and Eluard), stories by Péret and Desnos, and the first part of Breton's series on "Le Surréalisme et la peinture." The change in orientation, despite Breton's disclaimers, was patently in the direction of literature and away from the artistic and intellectual isolation of the earlier numbers. Had the wolf been shouting "wolf"? Or is the paradox so little evident? The very next issue (no. 5, Oct. 1925), as if to compound the paradox, marks a decisive turn toward politics. Breton's review of Trotsky's biography of Lenin (p. 29), buried in reduced type in the hodge-podge section devoted to "chroniques," set a tone that has changed remarkably little in forty years; the equally important collective manifesto "La Révolution d'abord et toujours!" signed by the principal contributors to *Clarté, Correspondance, Philosophies,* and *La Révolution surréaliste* (pp. 31-32), does not even merit a place in the table of contents! Oversight? But Freud has warned us to be wary of oversights.[66] From this point on the secret collaboration of surrealist, poet, and revolutionary would take on the look of a three-way tug-of-war: the surrealist pulling in the direction of an ideal universe bounded by the twin poles of Armageddon and salvation; the poet attracted by the realm of Love, in whose center could be seen some semidivine androgynous couple lost in dream; the revolutionary, tired of the daily round, the mechanical grind, and the familiar habitat, rejecting the choiceless compulsion of an oppressively conventional milieu, moving in the direction of a limited commitment to reality. By late 1925, the heritage of Dada had apparently been completely liquidated.

In the history of surrealism Eluard's poetry is significant not because it is exceptional but because it is typical. His early verse is that of the perpetual adolescent singing the joys and sorrows of imagined simple virtues:

> *Fidèle*
> Vivant dans un village calme
> D'où la route part longue et dure
> Pour un lieu de sang et de larmes
> Nous sommes purs.[67]

The contact with Dada had little effect on his technique. When, in 1920, he brought out a small volume modeled after Apollinaire's *Bestiaire*,[68] there is nothing to indicate either technical experimentation, dream sequences, or the wryly cynical tendencies of Dada.

> *Poisson*
> Les poissons, les nageurs, les bateaux
> Transforment l'eau.
> L'eau est douce et ne bouge
> Que pour ce qui la touche.
>
> Le poisson avance
> Comme un doigt dans un gant,
> Le nageur danse lentement
> Et la voile respire.
>
> Mais l'eau douce bouge
> Pour ce qui la touche,
> Pour le poisson, pour le nageur, pour le bateau
> Qu'elle porte
> Et qu'elle emporte
>
> (*Les Animaux et leurs hommes*)
> (*Choix*, p. 28)

Had Apollinaire signed those lines, only the specialist would look askance—perhaps. In *Répétitions* (1922), the first of a half-dozen collaborations with Max Ernst, the veiled bittersweet quality we have come to associate with Eluard's poetry makes its debut. Here was, as one critic said, "a subtle, delicate poet, expert at capturing the faint waves which bind dream and reality together, the eternal lover of love and desire."[69]

*Max Ernst*
Dans un coin l'inceste agile
Tourne autour de la virginité d'une petite robe
Dans un coin le ciel délivré
Aux épines de l'orage laisse des boules blanches . . .

(*Choix*, p. 47)

*Lesquels?*
Pendant qu'il est facile
Et pendant qu'elle est gaie
Allons nous habiller et nous déshabiller.

(*Choix*, p. 50)

Not until 1929 would Eluard find a replacement for his principal source of inspiration, his whimsical wife Gala.[70] In the interval he perfected a highly personal form of free verse, half way between the classical alexandrine, with its obligatory rhymes and syllable counts, and the so-called prose poem, in which the first term describes the formal structure and the second the tone conveyed. The regularity expected of poetry becomes, in Eluard, a recurrence of one or a very limited number of rhythms, sometimes that of a twelve-syllable line, sometimes eleven, or ten, or eight—each line having sufficient rhythmic similarity to the others so that a given "beat" or rhythm is sensed, which is reenforced visually by lines of similar length, all beginning with the traditional capital. While no rhyme is aimed at,[71] there are recurring phrases which point to a unity of theme. None of this is in and of itself new. What is striking, however, is the economy of expression achieved in what is on first reading an informal "unpoetic" style, one which avoids both the recherché syntax of Mallarmé and the *précieux* tone of his lesser disciples. In "L'Amoureuse," for example we have a strikingly allusive sketch of the effects of love on two people:

Elle est debout sur mes paupiéres
Et ses cheveux sont dans les miens,
Elle a la forme de mes mains,
Elle a la couleur de mes yeux,
Elle s'engloutit dans mon ombre
Comme une pierre sur le ciel.

I see her though my eyes are
  closed
And her hair is mingled
  with mine,
She has the form of my hands,
She has the color of my eyes,
She is swallowed by my shadow
Like a stone in the sky.

Elle a toujours les yeux ouverts
Et ne me laisse pas dormir.
Ses rêves en pleine lumière
Font s'évaporer les soleils,
Me font rire, pleurer et rire,
Parler sans avoir rien à dire.[72]

Her eyes are ever open
And 'tis enough to banish
  sleep.
Her dreams in broad daylight
Make suns disappear,
Make me laugh, cry, and
  laugh,
Talk while having nothing to
  say.

Eluard's surrealist verse, passion oriented, is neither the love-sick sigh of adolescence or the professional smile of the Don Juan. It ignores politics as well as philosophy. If some of the surrealists can be called literary dilettantes—those who take themselves more seriously than they do their work—Eluard belongs to another, smaller group of those accepted (sometimes only temporarily!) for personal reasons, despite Breton's comment that Eluard wrote automatically.[73]

The *virtus* and the *studium* that in an earlier period were deemed capable of defeating the inimical forces about us became inspiration (or better, revelation) to the surrealists—and all merit was dependent upon it. For Eluard, as for Freud and Ficino before him, the pivot of all psychology was Eros. For the Renaissance philosopher it explained the universe; for the Viennese physician it was both therapy and theory; for Eluard it was the fountainhead of poetry. Woman, to the poet, was the means by which an erotically charged universe was rendered visible. Eros gave form and boundaries to a power otherwise masked in complexity or dissolved in infinity. All else is measured by this intangible. Wherever he turns, the poet discovers manifestations of its presence: in the shape of a tree, in a rock formation, a sunset—everywhere his imagination finds the contours, the splendor and power of his beloved.

*Amoureuses*
Elles ont les épaules hautes
Et l'air malin
Ou bien des mines qui déroutent
La confiance est dans la poitrine
A la hauteur où l'aube de leurs seins se lève
Pour dévêtir la nuit

Des yeux à casser les cailloux
Des sourires sans y penser
Pour chaque rêve
Des rafales de cris de neige
Des lacs de nudité
Et des ombres déracinées.

Il faut les croire sur baiser
Et sur parole et sur regard
Et ne baiser que leurs baisers
Je ne montre que ton visage
Les grands orages de ta gorge
Tout ce que je connais et tout ce que j'ignore
Mon amour ton amour ton amour ton amour.

(*La Vie immédiate*, 1932
*Choix de poèmes*, pp. 122-23)

Although Eluard broke with Breton in 1938 on the question of how best to oppose the Nazi menace, there is no radical change in the thematic content of his poetry.[74] The influence of the rupture appears, but in veiled terms only, as is almost invariably so when Eluard is dealing with persons and situations close to him. Whether this reflects an artistic attempt to universalize the particular or some deeper reticence at placing his sorrows and pleasures before a scandal-hungry public, or both, is not of major importance in this context. There can be no doubt that Eluard consciously refrained from revealing all, or that he modified his themes in the direction of comprehension (the subjective element is always under control), and that, as a matter of course, he rejected the fanciful structure of his more doctrinaire colleagues. While this in no way denies that the point of departure was some inspirational gift of the gods, the end result so clearly reveals an *intellectus agens*, a poetic vision deficient only for

being fixed in matter, that only rarely can it be termed even pass-
ably automatic.

Breton, on the contrary, regularly avoids either thematic or rhythmic unity.[75] Recurring partials are as rare in his verse as whimsical collocations are common. The sole necessity appears to be that
of a communication by the Unconscious over a line heavy with static:

Monde dans un baiser
Le joueur à baguettes de coudrier cousues sur les manches
Apaise un essaim de jeunes singes-lions
Descendus à grand fracas de la corniche
Tout devient opaque je vois passer le carosse de la nuit
Traîné par les axolotls à souliers bleus
Entrée scintillante de la voie de fait qui mène au tombeau
Pavé de paupières avec leurs cils
La loi du talion use un peuple d'étoiles
Et tu te diapres pour moi d'une rosée noire
Tandis que les effrayantes bornes mentales
A cheveux de vigne
Se fendent dans le sens de la longueur
Livrant passage à des aigrettes
Qui regagnent le lac voisin
Les barreaux du spectacle sont merveilleusement tordus
Un long fuseau d'air atteste seul la fuite de l'homme
Au petit matin dans les luzernes illustres
L'heure
N'est plus que ce que sonnent les pièces d'or de la bohémienne
Aux volants de coréopsis
Une écuyère debout sur un cheval au galop pommelé de boules
    d'orage
De loin les bras sont toujours en extension latérale
Le losange poudreux du dessous me rappelle
La tente décorée de bisons bleus
Par les Indiens de l'oreiller
Dehors l'air essaye les gants de gui
Sur un comptoir d'eau pure
Monde dans un baiser monde
A moi les écailles
Les écailles de la grande tortue céleste à ventre d'hydrophile
Qui se bat chaque nuit dans l'amour
Avec la grande tortue noire le gigantesque scolopendre de
    racines

World in a kiss
The player with wands sewn on his sleeves
Tames a swarm of young lion-monkeys
Who have noisily descended the coastal road
Everything becomes opaque I see the night coach pass
Pulled by blue-shod salamanders
Brilliant beginning to the assault that leads to the grave
Paved with eyelids and their lashes
The law of an eye for an eye wears out a star people
And you sprinkle yourself with black dew for my benefit
While the terrifying mental limits
With vine hair
Split themselves lengthwise
Letting pass some egrets
Who reach the nearby lake
The bars of the show are wonderfully twisted
Only a long spindle of air reveals the man's flight
In the early morning amidst the illustrious alfalfa
The hour
Is known only through the ringing gold pieces of the gypsy lass
With the aster flounces
A woman standing on a galloping horse dappled with small clouds
From afar her arms always appear stretched out sideways
The dusty underneath diamond brings to mind
The tent decorated with blue bisons
By the Indians of the pillow
Outside the air tries on mistletoe gloves
On a counter of pure water
World in a kiss world
Mine are the shells
The shells of the great heavenly tortoise with the
hydrophilus stomach
Who nightly has a love battle
With the great black tortoise the gigantic rootlike
hart's tongue.[76]

Eluard at this time was writing:

*Comme  deux  gouttes  d'eau*
. . . . . . . . . . . . . . . . . . . .
De tout ce que j'ai dit de moi que reste-t-il

J'ai conservé de faux trésors dans des armoires vides
Un navire inutile joint mon enfance à mon ennui
Mes jeux à la fatigue
Un départ à mes chimères
La tempête à l'arceau des nuits où je suis seul
Une île sans animaux aux animaux que j'aime
Une femme abandonnée à la femme toujours nouvelle
En veine de beauté
La seule femme réelle
Ici ailleurs
Donnant des rêves aux absents
Sa main tendue vers moi
Se reflète dans la mienne
Je dis bonjour en souriant
On ne pense à l'ignorance
Et l'ignorance règne
Oui j'ai tout espéré
Et j'ai désespéré de tout
De la vie de l'amour de l'oubli du sommeil
Des forces des faiblesses
On ne me connaît plus
Mon nom mon ombre sont des loups.[77]

*Like Two Drops of Water*
Of all that I've written about myself what remains
I have preserved false treasures in empty closets
A useless boat connects my childhood to my boredom
My games to my fatigue
A departure to my dreams
The storm to the arch of nights when I am alone
An island without animals to the animals I love
An abandoned woman to the woman ever new
In the mood to be beautiful
The only real woman
Here or elsewhere
Giving dreams to the absent
Her hand outstretched
Is reflected in mine
I say good day and smile
We don't think of what we don't know
And ignorance reigns

> Yes I've wished for everything
> And I've despaired of everything
> Of life of love of forgetfulness of sleep
> Of strong points and weak points
> No one knows me any longer
> My name my shadow are as wolves.

The Breton selection breaks with the linear, logical tradition of poetry in much the same way that a modern painting violates the spatial arrangements handed down from the Renaissance. Eluard, on the other hand, retains this perspective, up to and including the "vanishing point" of the terminal maxim—the "point" of the poem, where the despair of the outcast, alone, friendless, and without moorings of any sort is pinned to the wall for all to see. While the break with Breton was of major importance to Eluard emotionally, its influence on his poetry was minimal. Habits built up over a period of twenty years are not easily abandoned, and Eluard, after Aragon, was too fine a catch for the Communist Party for there to be any serious pressure on him to modify his style radically. Not that this was ever necessary, for there is little reason to think that Eluard was much addicted to the so-called "magic dictation" that Breton praised so often and used so little.[78] Besides, to the Communist Party, which could see what it wanted to see as easily as could Breton, Eluard was the committed author of "Critique de la poésie":

> C'est entendu je hais le règne des bourgeois
> Le règne des flics et des prêtres
> Mais je hais plus encore l'homme qui ne le hait pas
> Comme moi
> De toutes ses forces.
>
> Je crache à la face de l'homme plus petit que nature
> Qui à tous mes poèmes ne préfère pas cette *Critique
> de la poésie*.[79]

And with that to recommend him the rest could be conveniently forgotten.

Robert Desnos was early considered the most promising of the surrealists, "the one," according to Breton, "who has perhaps come closest to surrealist truth, the one who, in works as yet unpublished and throughout numerous experiments in which he took part, has thoroughly justified my hopes for surrealism and encourages me to expect much more of it. At the present time Desnos *speaks surrealistically* at will."[80] Paul Eluard, of all the surrealists the one most overtly and completely committed to poetry, referred to him as "the most spontaneous, the most free, a poet always inspired and who could speak as few poets can write."[81] What subsumed this attractive spontaneity was a verbal eroticism, a *joie de vivre* unique in the group, which was to Desnos what liberty was to Breton and fraternity to Eluard.[82]

The determining orientation in Desnos' poetry came in 1922, with his entry into the surrealist group, and specifically with the group's enthusiasm for the puns and spoonerisms signed Rrose Sélavy.[83] Axiomatic in form, they recall the inverted proverbs of Lautréamont's *Poésies,* especially at their most successful when they bring together wit and chance in an outrageous juxtaposition of terms disturbing in their implications and hilarious in their conclusion. Although rarely unconscious in inspiration, they cannot help but question the well-ordered world of convention:

> Rrose Sélavy demande si les Fleurs du Mal ont modifié
> les moeurs du phalle: qu'en pense Omphale?
> > (*Domaine public,* p. 39)

> Rrose Sélavy voudrait bien savoir si l'amour, cette
> colle à mouches, rend plus dures les molles couches.
> (P.40)
> Croyez-vous que Rrose Sélavy connaisse ces jeux de
> fous qui mettent le feu aux joues? (P. 41)
> Est-ce que la caresse des putains excuse la paresse
> des culs teints? (P. 41)
> Rrose Sélavy propose que la pourriture des passions
> devienne la nourriture des nations. (P. 42)
> Paul Eluard: le poète élu des draps. (P. 42)
> Rrose Sélavy n'est pas persuadée que la culture du
> moi puisse amener la moiteur du cul. (P. 43)

> La jolie soeur disait: "Mon droit d'aînesse pour
> ton doigt, Ernest." (P. 47)
> L'acte des sexes est l'axe des sectes. (P. 48)

By 1923 Desnos[84] had developed the play on words into an able confusion of Lear-type Wonderland nonsense with popular speech:

> Notre paire quiète, ô yeux!
> que votre "non!" soit sang (t'y fier?)

que votre araignée rie,
que vol honteux soit fête (au fait)
sur la terre (commotion!)
Donnez-nous aux joues réduites,
notre pain quotidien.
Pardonnez-nous nos oeufs foncés
comme nous part donnons
à ceux qui nous ont offensés.

Nounou laissez-nous succomber à la tentation
et d'aile ivrez-nous du mal.

Exhausser ma pensée
exaucer ma voix.

(*Domaine public*, pp. 57-58)

*Rrose Sélavy, etc.*
Rose aisselle a vit.
Rr'ose, essaie là vit.
Rôts et sel à vie.
Rose S, L, have I.
Rosée, c'est la vie.
Rrose scella vît.
Rrose sella vît.
Rrose sait la vie.
Rose, est-ce, hélas, vie?
Rrose aise héla vît.
Rrose est-ce aile, est-ce elle?
est celle
AVIS

(*Domaine public*, p. 70)

*C'était un bon copain*
Il avait le coeur sur la main
Et la cervelle dans la lune
C'était un bon copain
Il avait l'estomac dans les talons
Et les yeux dans nos yeux
C'était un triste copain
Il avait la tête à l'envers
Et le feu là où vous pensez

Mais non quoi il avait le feu au derrière
C'était un drôle de copain
Quand il prenait ses jambes à son cou
Il mettait son nez partout
C'était un charmant copain
Il avait une dent contre Etienne
A la tienne Etienne à la tienne mon vieux
C'était un amour de copain
Il n'avait pas sa langue dans la poche
Ni la main dans la poche du voisin
Il ne pleurait jamais dans mon gilet
C'était un copain
C'était un bon copain.

(*Domaine public*, p. 90)

Desnos' early importance was due principally to the ease with which he was able to drop off into a hypnotic trance and, while in that state, comment in sybilline terms on questions put to him. As Breton saw it, Desnos and others similarly endowed thus became recorders of the Unconscious oracle and as such capable of dredging up uncommon truths.[85] Whether these states were authentic is open to doubt. Blaise Cendrars, who knew Desnos after his expulsion from the surrealist camp, mentions that on the several occasions the subject was raised Desnos "merely winked and smiled knowingly."[86] When Desnos began using his "oracular" talents in the cause of literature, that is, when he began writing rhymed, coherent verse—and seeking publication to boot—the "literary alibi" and dream-work "stereotype" so feared by the surrealists as sources of counterrevolutionary activity made their unwelcome appearance.[87] Nothing could be more incongruous than a sometime revolutionary disbursing clichés molded in an alexandrine form, even if it were a Gothic cliché as seen by Rimbaud, or Fantomas.[88]

### The Night of Loveless Nights

Nuit putride et glaciale, épouvantable nuit,
Nuit du fantôme infirme et des plantes pourries,
Incandescente nuit, flamme et feu dans les puits,
Ténèbres sans éclairs, mensonges et roueries.
. . . . . . . . . . . . . . . . . . . . . . .
Appelle la sirène et l'étoile à grands cris
Si tu ne peux dormir bouche close et mains jointes

Ainsi qu'un chevalier de pierre qui sourit
A voir le ciel sans dieux et les enfers sans plainte.

O Révolte!

There is a certain irony that this friend of anarchists and presumably obscene author ultimately became one of the heroes of the French Resistance and, quite apart from this, popular for his children's rhymes.[89]

*La Fourmi*
Une fourmi de dix-huit mètres
Avec un chapeau sur la tête,
Ça n'existe pas, ça n'existe pas.
Une fourmi traînant un char
Plein de pingouins et de canards,
Ça n'existe pas, ça n'existe pas.
Une fourmi parlant français,
Parlant latin et javanais,
Ça n'existe pas, ça n'existe pas.
Eh! pourquoi pas?

*Le Pélican*
Le capitaine Jonathan,
Etant âgé de dix-huit ans,
Capture un jour un pélican
Dans une île d'Extrême-Orient.

Le pélican de Jonathan,
Au matin, pond un oeuf tout blanc
Et il en sort un pélican
Lui ressemblant étonnamment.

Et ce deuxième pélican
Pond, à son tour, un oeuf tout blanc
D'où sort, inévitablement,
Un autre qui en fait autant.

Cela peut durer pendant très longtemps
Si l'on ne fait pas d'omelette avant.

The Desnos that came to surrealism in September 1922, shortly after the Breton-Tzara rupture, brought with him a mild interest in radical causes, a vague acquaintance with Louis de Gonzague-Frick, and a strong interest in literature.[90] Hypnotic seances and the use of semiautomatic techniques gave his work a new orientation without in any way modifying his goals. To Breton, Desnos' ability to plunge to the depths of the unknown and surface with a treasure trove of popular phraseology, café puns, and an occasional meaningless phrase was ample proof of the validity of his theories. Even if they were a bit too pat, too clever, Desnos' revelations had an uncommonly convincing point of departure—much more so than, say, Eluard's. Regardless of its literary quality, however that be judged, *his* verse was surrealist, and as such was of inestimable value as an example of the reality that lay behind convention.[91]

In February 1944 Desnos was arrested by the Gestapo for his Resistance activities, eventually sent to Buchenwald and from there to the concentration camp at Terezina, in Czechoslovakia, where he died of typhus on June 8, 1945, only days after the liberation of the camp. His last poem, with its play of light and shadow, dream-thought and action, fatigue and hope—devoid of rhetorical frills and the clever search for *le mot juste*—merits a place apart.

> *Le Dernier poème*
> J'ai rêvé tellement fort de toi,
> J'ai tellement marché, tellement parlé,
> Tellement aimé ton ombre,
> Qu'il ne me reste plus rien de toi.
> Il me reste d'être l'ombre parmi les ombres
> D'être cent fois plus ombre que l'ombre
> D'être l'ombre qui viendra et reviendra
> dans ta vie ensoleillée.
>
> (*Domaine public*, p. 408)

All language has its own rhetoric, its own commonplaces, but Desnos' last poem has so thoroughly integrated them that they are one with the sentiment, almost a language of soul to soul, as Rimbaud might have said, for we sense an enormous affection which the words themselves point to but do not exhaust.[92]

If Breton was the theoretician, Eluard the professional poet, and Péret and Desnos the gifted practicing surrealists, Aragon was potentially the most talented of the group with a gift for insight and innovation the fruits of which might be borrowed but never matched. At the height of Dada he summed up its "lettristic" essence with uncommon efficiency and elegance:

*Suicide*
a b c d e f
g h i j k l
m n o p q r
s t u v w
x y z.[93]

Shortly thereafter, as the Breton group moved away from Dada and closer to poets such as Apollinaire, Aragon proposed the following epitome of the *calligrammes*:

*Persiennes*

|  | Persienne | Persienne | Persienne |
|---|---|---|---|
|  | Persienne | Persienne | Persienne |
| Persienne | Persienne | Persienne | Persienne |
| Persienne | Persienne | Persienne | Persienne |
| Persienne | Persienne |  |  |
|  | Persienne | Persienne | Persienne |
| Persienne?[94] |  |  |  |

With the changes necessitated by flourishing surrealism, Aragon, whose verse of the period was more witty commonplace than un-conscious revelation, offered a laconic résumé of his past, one which could with equal justice be applied to the group as a whole:

*Ancien combattant*
J'ai fait le Mouvement Dada
Disait le dadaiste
J'ai fait le Mouvement Dada

Et en effet
Il l'avait fait[95]

These lines, clearly not derived from any mental substratum, nor especially concerned with dreams, love, or liberty, reveal the Dada constant in the surrealist equation.[96] Two additional examples, both from the same collection, *La Grande gaîté*, strengthen the conviction that while Dada may have changed its name and added to its goals it never really died. The first, "Berceuse," sets a tone not far removed from that now associated with Jacques Prévert; the second further reenforces the impression of a highly conscious technique which amalgamates the universal with the unique and the vulgar with the pretentious for the purpose of highlighting the effrontery of the lat-ter in each category and the fundamental decency of the former.

*Berceuse*
Chie chie chie chie donc chie
Ecoute la voix de ta mère
Petit enfant chie
Comme les grands de la terre . . .

(*La Grande gaîté*, p. 13)

*Ramo dei morti*
A force de s'en foutre
Ça finit par vous démanger
Je ne peux plus supporter le son des
      cloches
Cloches cloches ma vieille Poë
Il y a des particuliers qui trouvent
      ça poétique
Moi je n'aime pas qu'on me fasse entrer
      par les oreilles
La sottise parée absurdement de croix
On ne me trompera plus avec des sonnettes
Ça veut dire ce que ça veut dire
Je suis d'humeur à m'expliquer
. . . . . . . . . . . . . . . . . . . . . . .
A en croire les journaux d'aujourd'hui
On a tué l'Ennui l'Ennui est mort
Il n'est plus question de l'Ennui
C'est très mal de s'ennuyer
C'est dégénéré pas moderne déjà connu classé
      pourriture bourgeoise
Toc démodé fin de siècle nous sommes
      heureusement nous avons heureusement
Dépassé ce stade dépassé
Le progrès toujours le progrès
Tout le monde s'ennuie d'abord c'est une crise
Et puis la vie
Il y a un mot que je ne comprends pas ici

Le phonographe tourne j'aime ce râclement
Ainsi ON ce géant aux lunettes de fer
Ne s'ennuie plus
L'Ennui
Est
Mort

(*La Grande gaîté*, pp. 100, 105-6)

It is scarcely surprising that dandies of the twentieth century should pour their hearts out in twentieth century confessions. Desnos did just this in his "Confession d'un enfant du siècle," before he captured the epic tone of "Le Veilleur du Pont au Change."[97] Aragon, on the other hand, too reserved for the confessional genre and more convinced by surrealist doctrine than capable of exemplifying it in his poetry, was responsible for the most effective nontheoretical prose produced by the group, in which—to paraphrase Péret, in another context—we sense a breath of freedom which ultimately will bring about the liberation of man in his totality.[98] On occasion Aragon brings to mind a highly sensitive litmus paper. When the unrestrained joy that was Dada was at its height, he brought out his unrestrained tale of a shoddy Rimbaud stumbling from one Chaplinesque adventure to another.[99] The following year, in *Les Adventures de Télémaque,* he spelled out the themes that were to be dominant—almost to the exclusion of all others—until his commitment to the Communist Party in the thirties: writing, love, and those "two unknowns, man and woman."[100] For the surrealists, writing at that time was essentially a method of fixing inspiration in semipermanent form, synthetic rather than analytic, impressionist in technique as much as anything else: "The deficiency of analytic techniques is especially evident," wrote Aragon, "when compared with a surrealist text like *Les Champs magnétiques.*"[101] Nevertheless, in addition to being one of the first and staunchest of Breton's allies, Aragon was also one of the earliest to express serious doubts about the techniques advanced: "I have often seen," he pointed out prior to the first Manifesto, "the style of those who gave themselves over to surrealism become quite stereotyped."[102] Is this why he never completely abandoned his interest in nonsurrealist literature, exemplified at one extreme by "Lorsque tout est fini. . . ," a moral tale of sorts, and on the other by his 1924 article in praise of Barrès?[103] Curiously enough, these excursions beyond the surrealist pale never met with the strictures of the type applied to Soupault and later to Desnos. Was it because Aragon was so close to Breton that he could do much as he wished, as could Eluard? Breton certainly had no objection to borrowing from Aragon, or at least (if "borrowing" is too strong) in following in his footsteps.[104]

Several months before surrealism was to receive the consecration of the first Manifesto, Aragon opens his volume *Le Libertinage* with the comment, "The most beautiful story in the world does not merit being told"—a phrase the now-dispersed Dadaists would have applauded.[105] From its plays to its anecdotes, there is nothing in this random collection to suggest that its author belonged to a group devoted to Love (as contrasted with sensuality, its less ethereal counterpart), Liberty, and Poetry. If all that remained of Aragon's writings were his early prose tales—*Anicet* (1921), *Les Aventures de Télémaque* (1922), *Le Libertinage* (1924), *Le Paysan de Paris* (1926), and *Le Traité du style* (1928)—it is difficult to see in what way they would recall surrealist theory, unless it be in their rejection of bourgeois society, but then that rejection was not limited to the surrealists. *Le Paysan de Paris,* for example, is a superb impressionistic biography—Aragon would say "synthetic" biography—of what Matthew Josephson, years later, was to call *Life Among the Surrealists.*[106] Life, as Aragon describes it, is a sticky gray dream occasionally enlivened by imperious needs, most of which can be satisfied by a brief trip to a brothel.[107] There is the great mass of people whom we never see and then the small group of privileged observers who drift through the Certâs of the city, devoted to capturing the essence of reverie-provoking ephemera:[108]

ÉPHÉMÈRE

**F. M. R.**

*(folie - mort - rêverie)*

*Les faits m'errent*

LES FAIX, MÈRES

Fernande   aime   Robert

pour la vie !

O   ÉPHéM̀ERe   o

ÉPHÉMÈRES

Impelled by boredom, "the absurd specter of my destiny," Aragon had committed himself completely to the "vice called Surrealism. . . the undisciplined and passionate use of the drug *image*," or rather to the eliciting of images both for their own sake and also for the purpose of observing how they metamorphose reality.[109] And this in spite of his awareness that this "vice" might well lead its victims to "ocean depths where swim the sharks of madness."[110] With all its risks surrealism was the one sure way of banishing boredom. One lived from day to day, constantly *disponible*, as Gide might have said, awaiting the gifts of Chance, the descent of Gods unknown, or the revelation of some fanciful woman.[111] It has some of the characteristics of an overly long drunk, according to Aragon, with this one difference: he didn't care for the "drink" in question, nor of course did he relish the subsequent depression.[112] This *enivrement*, as with Baudelaire, was the very antithesis of *ennui*, a concrete miracle of sorts: "Finally we were going to destroy boredom [*l'ennui*]; we had before us the possibility of a miraculous hunt, an experimental area where it was impossible not to encounter the unknown many times over and, who knows, perhaps even a wondrous revelation which would transform our life, our destiny."[113] "Man lives with his eyes closed in the midst of magic precipices."[114] Everything is fantastic, as Aragon reiterates, for if reality is defined as the apparent absence of contradiction, "revelation [*le merveilleux*] is the contradiction which appears in reality."[115] For every thesis, it would seem, Aragon can find a verbal antithesis. Such is the world of hope, where surprises of all sorts await the press of a button or a leap through the looking glass. As Aragon observed, in a phrase that Camus was to modify, "There is no rest for Sisyphus, but his rock instead of falling rises, and never ceases to rise."[116]

*Le Paysan de Paris*, the book Arnold Bennett once claimed he would like to have written,[117] can also be considered the first of a two-part surrealist autobiography. The second, *Le Traité du style* (1928), is even less concerned than its predecessor with the physical atmosphere and far more with the intellectual itinerary of its protagonist, and if only for that reason merits the attention normally reserved for Breton's *Manifestes*. Where Breton labors over doctrine, its purity and implications, his principal ally is occupied with something more mundane, *happiness*, which is variously labeled an illusion and an empty (if consoling) word.[118] Proust, finding the present intolerable, may have sought his salvation in the past; for Aragon, however, either there is no paradise or they are all artificial, that is, self-induced (dreams, drugs, fatigue, etc.). "The foolish search for happiness" is futile; even drugs have no durable effect: "they change you less than a new suit," for they cannot change your dreams which offer "always the same merchandise."[119] In a word, "life with or without opium is unbearable."[120] What is only too evident in this last prose surrealist-inspired work of Aragon is an enormous emptiness not significantly different from what we find in the early days of Dada: Tzara taking up literature in an attempt to banish boredom, and Breton picking up the refrain note for note.[121] In post-Dada days Breton avoided the question of happiness by conjuring up a wonderland of shifting forms; Aragon faced it and found it a trap: "a miserable postulate," "the pursuit of a habit" no more necessary than a drug.[122]

Le Paysan de Paris is at bottom the work of someone at peace with his world. When he is nostalgic, there are friends to share his memories; when he wanders through the city, we sense that his friends are not far off. Le Traité du style, in contrast, stabilizes and magnifies the passing bitterness of the earlier work. His long-time friends are no longer quite so receptive: "Will it ever again be possible," he asks, "to suggest an image, nothing but an image, that doesn't seem to you thoroughly ridiculous?"[123] The surrealists consciously falsify reality. "The stupidity, the monstrous stupidity of it all," he says in what can only be an indirect allusion to his fellow surrealists who, if they have not taken a paradox and turned it into a principle, as Dada had done, were nonetheless guilty of stifling any creativity they might have.[124] Years before Jean Paulhan, Aragon denounced the new literary terror that would replace sense with nonsense, order with disorder, literature with surrealism. "Yes, I read. I have that failing. I like fine poems, striking lines, and everything that lines of verse bring to mind." And shortly thereafter, lest there be any doubt as to what he enjoys reading: "Here is Vauvenargues. . . . Here is Benjamin Constant's outstanding contribution to the study of religion."[125] Style is the touchstone; not the Unconscious, the uninterrupted flow of language, but style. When he does speak of the Unconscious, it becomes the lamentable source of idées reçues. "The ideas of a period," he points out laconically, "are crudely synthesized in certain automatic crystallizations. That is what constitutes its intellectual historical development; that is what is meant when people speak of progress, civilization, clarification."[126]

When Aragon describes the unsavory world of 1927, he has ample opportunity to allude to a possible cure, which to the surrealists of the day lay in alignment with the Communist Party; but no such allusion is present.[127] The *Traité du style* is an *art poétique* crossed with a vague history of literature, all in the form of a subjective *critique synthétique*. Aragon is no prophet of the possessed any more than, say, Camus was a prophet of the absurd: the role of prophet in both cases goes to others. The author of the *Traité* had no intention of turning fantasy into reality. Life was meaningless and death horrible, but with it all there was always the possible escape via suicide.[128] Yet, as with Camus after him, Aragon prefers the concrete to the uncertain: "Life is a fact and as such indisputable."[129] Suicide, nonetheless, along with other evasions, *is* a possible solution to life, a rejection of present dross in favor of some hypothetical paradise.[130] Where Camus, faced with the absurd, declines suicide for the new trinity of revolt, liberty, and passion, Aragon can only envisage escape to heaven, but for him there is no heaven.[131]

It may seem odd to refer to Camus rather than to other surrealists when speaking of Aragon, but Aragon, for all the years spent with Breton, has few affinities with his manifesto-oriented colleague. If he refuses the escape from reality offered by death, religion, and travel, it is surely not for any belief in his present earthly happiness. In a phrase which recalls later existential utterances, Aragon philosophizes aloud: "If happiness exists, in the true sense of the word exist, it manifests itself. Where does it manifest itself?"[132] Implicitly, nowhere. . . and we are consequently plunged ever deeper into the anguished world of the absurd, with its foundation of quicksand, nausea and its horizon of barren futility. Dada was no solution, nor was surrealism.[133] The latter, however, did propose a defense against the meaninglessness of it all, not a solution but a defense: humor. Humor, as the author of the *Traité* conceived it, is pure poetry, an open-ended game with no terminus in sight.[134] Formed of an image and provoking a cataclysm of surprise—or laughter—humor has the supreme merit of clearing the land of all that is unpoetic.[135] In its novelty poetry is humor, and thus inevitably has but a brief existence. Each generation must make its own, for that of the past— almost of necessity—has lost its provocative character. Humor needs style, as does inspiration, as do dreams.[136] Not everything that flits through the mind merits telling, nor should these whims be a pretext for a literary exercise—and here he would seem to have several of his colleagues in mind: "We cannot permit the dream to become the blood brother to the prose poem, a distant cousin of nonsense or the brother-in-law of the haiku."[137] Even surrealism, the highest form of inspiration, must have an acceptable style. "Surrealism is inspiration recognized, accepted, and practiced. No longer as an inexplicable visitation, but rather as a faculty which is exercised."[138] In a word, there is good surrealism and there is bad surrealism. The former is vigorous and full of surprises, the latter tired and repetitive: "Shocking though it may be to some, there is a way of distinguishing among surrealist texts. By their strength and by their novelty."[139]

Surrealism, in this sense, is an *approach* to the unknown, a way of dealing with it; but both approach and technique must be molded by style, must be shaped to a given form before its spectrum can effectively overcome the reader's resistance. Or as Aragon put it, "surrealism is not a refuge from style."[140] Creative and original, Aragon's language is closer to that of the slumming aristocrat than to that of the cautious bourgeois or the snobbish *précieux*. The latter two would find a revolution in any area repugnant, whereas for the gutter elite, uprooted by definition, it spelled salvation. George Meredith, and Sir Lewis Namier after him, thought it an "ironical habit of mind to believe that the wishes of men are expressed by their utterances." [141] With this no surrealist could disagree, but to Aragon the style of the utterance could serve to bring together the complimentary and communicating vessels of dream and reality.[142]

What we have said so far scarcely scratches the surface of what could be said if we were to attempt to map the numerous deviations from the main surrealist party line. Philippe Soupault, Breton's early friend and collaborator, was also the first to leave the movement, for literature in the traditional sense was his (as it was Apollinaire's) primary goal, his career. The first indication that all was not well between the two authors of *Les Champs magnétiques* came with Breton's taking over, alone, the editorship of *Littérature*.[143] In November 1922, in his lecture at the Ateneo of Barcelona, Breton inserted a melancholy reference to his one-time colleague: "At the present time only Philippe Soupault has not lost hope in Dada, and it is quite moving to think that perhaps until the end of his days he will remain the plaything of Dada as we have previously seen Jarry in the grip of Ubu."[144] Nor would Soupault take issue with the substance of that remark, not recognizing that his eclecticism would lead to his expulsion. "It is very difficult at the present time," wrote Soupault in concluding his first novel, *Le Bon apôtre* (1923), "to speak of Dada. Perhaps no one can know what it represented. Its features were never fixed. It was our mirror, and probably for that reason we were hopelessly attached to it. To scandalize. Why not admit that we were passionately committed to fomenting scandals? It was a reason to live. (Count them.) The time was poorly chosen, but we weren't interested in success. . . . In its own way the public scandalized us. It sought to understand without ever succeeding. What madness! . . . Bit by bit. . . we lost contact and became frightened. The necessary *esprit de corps* is ever more rare. . . . It's all over now. I write novels; I publish books. I keep myself busy. And what the hell!"[145]

Years later, Soupault would attribute his departure to several other causes: love of a woman, which presumably kept him from attending group meetings; love of revolt (scandal?), which Breton preferred to avoid; and, finally, Breton's inordinate interest in things political.[146] Whatever the specific reasons for his departure, "with neither sadness nor bitterness," as he later commented, he was sufficiently outside the movement by 1926 for Aragon to speak disparagingly of his most recent publication, the collection of poetry entitled *Georgia*.[147] It may be, as Soupault contends, that he has never ceased being a surrealist, but only in the sense that surrealism, as Dada before, felt that one of its primary functions was "to combat the religion of literature, or, more exactly, the confusion of literature considered as a religion."[148] Nevertheless, when we consider that for a number of years Soupault held an editorial position with *La Revue européenne* and in 1924 almost won the *prix Goncourt* for his novel *Les Frères Durandeau*, one cannot help wondering if his interest in "l'insolite" was not subordinate to his desire for success.[149] If his poetry, with the exception of his contribution to *Les Champs magnétiques*, is not especially representative of surrealism either in technique or content, his critical comments, free of the gibberish Breton often used to mask his thoughts,[150] permit a clearer appreciation of what the movement attempted. "It is important to remember," Soupault wrote years after having left the movement, "that thanks to surrealism it is now possible to come up with a more sincere and less confused definition of poetry, and, moreover, we can now clearly distinguish its powers. Its principle feature is authenticity."[151] In a word surrealism is honesty, as he sees it, and a refusal to be limited by appearances: "Poetry is above reality," unless, presumably, one takes reality to include the superimposed lands of dream and desire.[152]

Soupault left, or was expelled, because of his attachment to

Dada and also, paradoxically enough, because of his interest in literature. Pierre Naville left for political reasons, seeing in the movement no real attempt to come to grips with the social problems of the day.[153] While the first Manifesto does propose an absolute (if amorphous) nonconformism in the social realm, and the early Dada-surrealists were indeed extravagantly concerned with distinguishing themselves from their Boeotian brothers, this attitude begins to change by late 1925 and is significantly modified in the next few years. By 1930, the surrealists—or what was left of them, what with Artaud's departure because of their insufficient stress on the *sur* part of surrealism, the gaps left by Soupault, Drieu La Rochelle, Naville, and Vitrac, not to mention Desnos' increasing commitment to journalism and Ernst's passing "error" in preparing the sets for the ballet *Roméo et Juliette*—had consolidated their position both in literature and politics.[154] But that is a discussion we will have to leave for another chapter. One final author, however, should be mentioned here: Tristan Tzara.

Tzara's connection with surrealism is both close and tenuous. If surrealism is understood as serious-Dada, a position intelligently defended by Michel Sanouillet (*Dada à Paris*), then Tzara can lay claim to being its natural father. If serious-Dada is felt to be a contradiction in terms, for scandal for the sake of scandal was endemic in Dada, then some other descriptive phrase will have to be found. As far as literature is concerned, the written records left by both groups are sufficiently similar to enable us to speak of filiation. It is incontestable that the early surrealists were all former Dadaists and that the later Dadaists were surrealists who would not accept Breton's leadership. The differences that exist are found in a context of similarities. Eluard's poetry did not change when he became a surrealist, nor did Tzara's when he refused to. The major influences on both men, and on their colleagues, antedate the surrealist rupture. Tzara's *L'Homme approximatif* (1929-31), for example, presents a syntax and imagery not significantly different from *La Première aventure céleste de Monsieur Antipyrine* (1916).[155] The novelty of *L'Homme approximatif*, Tzara's first contribution to the "new" surrealism, lies in two other areas: vocabulary and poetic technique. By 1931, his command of French had improved to the point that he could undertake to rival Mallarmé in his use of *précieux* terminology and not rely exclusively on unexpected juxtapositions to breech the wall of smugness which was stifling contem-

porary poetry. Some examples may help illustrate this development:[156]

### La Première aventure céleste de M. Antipyrine

si l'on peut demander à une vieille dame
l'adresse d'un bordel

oi oi oi oi oi oi oi oiseau
qui chantes sur la bosse du chameau
les éléphants verts de ta sensibilité
tremblent chacun sur un poteau télégraphique
les quatre pieds cloués ensemble
il a tant regardé le soleil que son visage s'aplatit
oua aah oua aah oua aah
M. le poète avait un nouveau chapeau
de paille qui était si beau si beau si beau . . .

The simplicity of the above Dada exercise is in sharp overt contrast
with Tzara's later manner, but once the surface is scratched an
underlying identity becomes manifest.

### L'Homme approximatif

la coqueluche des montagnes calcinant les escarpements
    des gorges
aux pestilentiels bourdonnements d'aqueducs automnaux
le défrichage du ciel gratuit qui fosse commune happa
    tant de cristallines pâtures
les langages des nues les courtes apparitions des
    messagers
dans leurs touffes annonciatrices de suprêmes
    clameurs et obsessions
les inquiètes usines souterraines de chimies lentes
    comme des chansons
la rapidité de la pluie son fourmillement télégraphique
    cru de coquille ruminant
les crevaisons à vif des pics d'où émergent
    les moutonnantes lessives
rompu à tous les paysages et aux ruses des
    goguenardes vallées tentatrices de patries. . .

If the *effect* of the second passage is not substantially different from
the first, the vocabulary appears to be drawn from quite another
stratum of the language. A second innovation is in the area of poetic

technique, specifically the repetition of the initial part of the line, thus suggesting a beginning rather than an end rhyme. Of the approximately hundred lines which appeared in the 1929 issue of *La Révolution surréaliste*, the majority begin with *le, la, les, et, où, un(e), lorsque,* and *au(x)*, which not only establishes a given series of litany-type rhymes but also requires a similar series of syntactic constructions. That Breton appreciated these innovations, especially the incantatory quality of the repetitions, is evident from his poem "L'Union libre" (1931), where the recurring "Ma femme. . . " with the majority of lines introduced by "A(ux). . . " to carry on the image, would seem to owe something to Tzara.

Breton, with the others in his group, was an Outsider—in the Colin Wilson sense[157]—seeking a reality that forever eluded him. But the Outside is a lonely place littered with the remnants of free-floating anxiety and displaced nausea. Not many had the staying power of Breton. He and those of like mind longed to capture the infinite within the finite, to find on earth what they knew was not there but what they could not, in the deep yearning of their hearts, stop looking for. Breton more than the others made of his love a woman after his own will. A Pygmalion enamored of his own creation, he continually improved on her until, in the later stages of his devotion, his hommage becomes the adoration of a myth and she the embodiment of her lover's most secret desires. This is the one theme that Breton did not banish from surrealist literature, for the mainspring of love lies in the Unconscious. The shadowy world of dreams was to give form and meaning to the disorder and absurdity about us. It alone could serve as a touchstone enabling man to distinguish the authentic from the inauthentic, and to deny to the latter a role in life. Cut off from any possibility of divine benevolence, the surrealists refused to be reeds overwhelmed by the cold winds of the external world. In some ways theirs is a baroque view of reality, for they recognized, with Racine, that man is controlled on the outside, seething and tormented on the inside. The task, for them, was to bring the torment to the surface in a form that would contain it, and there can be little doubt that they succeeded.

# IV: In the Arena: Surrealism and Politics

There are *three* major goals in surrealism: the social liberation of man, his complete moral liberation, and his intellectual rejuvenation.

—A. Breton, "Comète surréaliste" (1947), in *La Clé des champs* (Editions du Sagittaire, 1953), pp. 104-5.

We can have no difficulty in recognizing the fact that the Outsider and freedom are always associated together. The Outsider's problem *is* the problem of freedom. His preoccupation with Ultimate Yes and Ultimate No is really a preoccupation with absolute freedom or absolute bondage.

—Colin Wilson, *The Outsider* (Boston: Houghton Mifflin Co., 1956) p. 113.

"The greatest influence I underwent," remarked Breton early in his career, "was that of Jacques Vaché."[1] At first reading, an observation of that type, if accurate, would seem to make any chapter on surrealism and politics of very doubtful value. But, as I hope to show, it is *because* that statement is accurate that such a chapter is crucial to an understanding of the movement.

The little we know of Vaché can be rapidly summarized. Breton tells us he met him in Nantes in early 1916. They were both twenty-year-olds, Breton, an intern in a military neurological center, the other, wearing an aviator's uniform ("we never did find out what service he was in"), being treated for a slight wound in the calf. "We were gay terrorists," wrote Breton, "scarcely more sentimental than anyone else; in short, promising youngsters."[2] Vaché had no use for the war—for either side—nor any interest in the causes that led to it or the type of changes it might bring about. In contrast to Breton, who was at that time a fervent admirer of the poet-patriot Apollinaire and the anglophile Mallarmé, he was content to parade through the war as one might through a *bal des quat'-z-arts*. "Handsomer than a child's reed-flute," Vaché had spent just enough time at the Ecole des Beaux-Arts to develop a taste for the *recherché*: "Every morning (in the hospital) he would spend a full hour arranging, on a lace-covered table within arm's reach, one or two photographs, some bowls and some violets."[3] As with all dandies, the *image* was far more important than the reality behind it—"he was the first to stress the importance of the gesture, so dear to André Gide"—and yet, "he was past master in the art of 'attaching very little importance to anything.'"[4] This was the man, says Breton, who convinced him that he should abandon literature and who transformed the bourgeois medical student into a *révolté*.[5]

Vaché's distinctive temper is reflected in two gestures of defiance: he would shake hands neither on greeting nor on taking leave of one—a terrible affront in France, comparable to telling someone what you think of him; and he kept a mistress, a young girl named Louise, with whom he claimed never to have made love, and whom he apparently treated with both extravagant respect and insolence.[6] He would require her to sit motionless in a corner for hours on end while he chatted with Breton, but he would kiss her hand when she served 5 o'clock tea—of such stuff were these lost souls. This was the man—whose suicide shortly after the armistice may just possibly have been a "final joke"—who was Breton's touchstone of human integrity on the eve of his conversion to communism.[7] It is significant that when Breton first became aware of Tristan Tzara's existence, not long after Vaché's disappearance, he saw in him a reincarnation of his former friend: the same cynicism, the same extravagance; where one affected uniforms, the other preferred monocles; where Vaché would wave a revolver in a crowded theater, Tzara would shoot syntactic blanks at an audience of complacent Insiders.[8] The principal difference between the two lay in their solutions to the absurdity about them, to the intrinsic meaninglessness of life: where one could see no way out of the jungle (art and literature were senseless pastimes), and took his own life as a consequence, the other actively sought an escape in one revolt after another.

Since Freud's time, at least, we have known that dreams and cravings projected into the void tend to gather round some figure: for Breton that figure was Vaché. As late as 1940, years after he had left the amateurish circularity of Vaché's *ennui*, Breton saw fit to applaud his careful indifference and the clever scandal of the ambiguous suicide which put an end to his life and that of a friend.[9] This in spite of the fact that the studied "world of games" was to Vaché an end in itself, and one from which he early withdrew, while to Breton the game rapidly became a means to something else.[10] Everything we know of that latter-day dandy fits into an early Dada-surrealist pattern, from the "good" family background (in the news story announcing Vaché's death, his father is described as "un honorable officier supérieur"), to the rejection of that background and the society it reflects; from his calculated attack on convention to the exclusive interest in his "image." Interestingly enough, the pattern is as applicable to the romantics with their foppish attire and manners—the scarlet waistcoat, the lobster on a leash, the rejection of a middle-class military home (remember Baudelaire?)—as it is to their avatars. What adolescent has not said "ART IS STUPID," where art might be replaced by any one of a number of civilized pursuits, or mocked the greats of a previous age, as did Vaché: "I know nothing of MALLARME, no insult meant—but he is dead—We no longer recognize Apollinaire or Cocteau—For—We suspect them of being too arty, of patching up romanticism with telephone wire and knowing nothing about dynamos."[11] It is both too easy and pointless, for however accurate or profound such an insight may be, it mirrors a fundamental immaturity, as does the view that true art, or true anything, lies in some untapped dynamo just the other side of the looking glass. Vaché turned Breton from literature; Breton returned the compliment by using Vaché, and Tzara after him, as points of departure toward a new, expanded, and more unified concept of literature—one which would eventually include the possibility of social commitment. If Breton had lived by the example and precepts of Vaché, he would never have left the merry-go-round that was Dada for the high seriousness that was surrealism or the roller coaster of intellectualized social revolt.

At no time prior to mid-1925 is there any indication that the surrealists, either individually or as a group, had any interest in things social or political. "The further I go," wrote Eluard, "the more obscure do things become," and this might serve as an epitaph for those formative years when, having shaken loose from the absurd world of Dada, the new clan moved haltingly and almost blindly toward a surrealist salvation.[12] Breton himself, in a little known interview from the post-Dada period, confided that he was sick of it all, that nothing had worked out as he would have wished, that "literature was as little interesting as politics."[13] Only the hazy vision of some ultimate reality beyond consciousness still attracted him, a reality beyond the patch of land cleared by reason and logic. *There* was reality, here was only a wasteland:

> I see crowds of people walking round in a ring.
> . . . . . . . . . . . . . . . . .
> He who was living is now dead
> We who were living are now dying
> With a little patience.[14]

"This is the dead land," observed T. S. Eliot, "This is the cactus land," and his solution was:

> Teach us to care and not to care
> Teach us to sit still
> Even among these rocks,
> Our peace in His will.[15]

Except for the final line, the sentiment expressed accurately describes the atmosphere of the surrealist group in 1923. But two events were to change matters: The *soirée du Coeur à barbe* of July 6, 1923, and the opening to the left, instigated by the magazine *Clarté*, beginning in mid-1925.[16]

The *soirée du Coeur à barbe* was Tzara's last serious attempt to make a place for himself on the Paris literary scene. His Pyrrhic victory in the ill-fated Congrès de Paris of the year before had permanently split Dada into two opposing camps consisting of (1) those who considered the movement an intellectual machine gun to be fired at random against the complacent yea-sayers of the world, and (2) those who, like Breton, purportedly wished to replace the machine gun with a cannon and blast away at a limited number of (literary) targets. Tzara had won that battle with the aid of Ribemont-Dessaignes and Eluard, and also thanks in part to a number of tactless statements by Breton.[17] The year's lull had helped neither side, although Breton, having a periodical behind him, was in a far better position to attract new adherents in search of a literary alibi and thus to attempt a poetic comeback. Tzara had neither a periodical nor the funds to start one. Nor could he move in the direction of a new series of Dada matinees, as no theater owner would rent to him, given the strong likelihood of the spectacle ending in a riot.

Determined to hold a *soirée Dada*, Tzara resolved the problem by using another group as a front, and thus was able to rent a hall. This strategy brought its own problems, and the program which resulted was a tissue of compromises: music by Georges Auric, Darius Milhaud, Erik Satie, and Igor Stravinsky; poems by Apollinaire, Cocteau, Soupault, Eluard, Jacques Baron, and Tzara; dances; three short films by Hans Richter, Man Ray, and Charles Sheeler (a friend of Man Ray); a lecture by Georges Ribemont-Dessaignes; a zaoum poem by Ilia Zdanévitch (Tzara's front for the occasion); and Tzara's three-act play *Le Coeur à gaz*, first performed some two years previously (June 10, 1921). There was a bit of everything on the program: modern music, literature, poetry, and some Dada provocation. The specific pretext for surrealist intervention was the conjunction on the program of the names of Cocteau, the *bête noire* of the surrealists, and Eluard. Eluard found this sufficiently objectionable to call upon his surrealist brothers to stand up for their principles, which they gladly did. Breton at one point, for example, went on stage and, aided by Péret and Desnos, succeeded in fracturing Pierre de Massot's arm (he was a disciple of Picabia). Enter the police, exit the three culprits. At the beginning of Tzara's play, Eluard rose to denounce the expulsion of Breton and to ask Tzara to defend himself; after the uproar (more police intervention) had quieted down somewhat, Tzara appeared on stage only to be interrupted and struck by Eluard, who also took this occasion to strike René Crevel (not yet a surrealist partisan). Because of the disturbance which followed, and in which Eluard was badly manhandled, the remainder of the program perforce was canceled.[18]

If this imbroglio did little to enhance Tzara's literary reputation, it did permit Breton to consolidate his grip on his small, relatively homogeneous band of dissidents. Dreams that money could not buy, but which presumably could be fixed in automatic writing, were their stock in trade. The seance, "rediscovered" in 1922, was the latest of a series of keys which would open the doors to artificial paradises—replacing Baudelaire's hashish, Rimbaud's voluntary visions, Mallarmé's formal gardens, Jarry's perfect clown, and Vaché's uniforms and opium. For some two years the game went on, with each issue of *Littérature* bringing its quota of puns and surprises, both pictorial and verbal, and with the number of subscribers regularly falling. The first inkling that all was not well with the movement comes with the gap of almost one year between *Littérature*, no. 11-12 (Oct. 15, 1923), an issue devoted to poetry, and the final no.

13 (June 1924).[19] This is the period when the movement's literary orientation, in spite of Breton's avowed decision to abandon literature, becomes ever more pronounced.[20] How could it be otherwise? The Dada cover had been added to a literary base: having abandoned Dada only literature was left. The critics, eager to eradicate the blot that was Dada, come to the rescue: Jean Paulhan, writing in *La Nouvelle revue française* is favorably impressed with Breton's collection of poetry *Clair de terre* (1923), despite his feeling it is all a deliberate mystery;[21] Marcel Arland, some months later, is even more lavish in his praise of Aragon's *Le Libertinage*.[22] From 1923-25, Breton, Aragon, Crevel, and Desnos appear in the pages of the highly unsurrealistic *Paris-Journal*.[23] Aragon, having vacationed in Berlin in 1922, returned with a 32-page bit of erotica, *Les Plaisirs de la capitale*;[24] one year later Eluard goes to Rome to meet Chirico;[25] Soupault, meanwhile, is helping edit *La Revue européenne*.[26] With Tzara caged as a result of the *Coeur à barbe* fiasco, the way was clear for a major advance. But in which direction? For all their travels, politics and the social turmoil of the time seem to have made little impression on the inner circle. The signing of the Soviet-German treaty at Rapallo in April 1922 finds no echo in their publications, nor does Mussolini's march on Rome in October of that year. France occupied the Ruhr in early 1923, in the midst of a galloping German inflation, but though Ernst was German and Aragon might visit the capital, there is a remarkable silence with regard to what was going on. This is equally true of the Fascist coup in Spain by Primo de Rivera in September 1923 (less than a year after Breton had delivered an address at the Barcelona Ateneo), the collapse of the separatist insurrection in Germany the following month, the Hitler putsch in Munich in early November, and the death of Lenin in January 1924. A long incubation period would be necessary before events of that type would appear as significant as the in-fighting of the *procès Barrès* or the grandiose schemes of the *Congrès de Paris*.[27] In a sense Abd-el-Krim fathered this new orientation when he invaded French Morocco in April 1925, *Clarté* was its midwife several months later, and Trotsky its godfather.

In February 1925, Victor Crastre, a relative newcomer to the editorial board of *Clarté*, inserted an unsigned editorial on "Le suicide est-il une solution?" in which he stressed certain points of contact between surrealists and *clartéistes*, in a tone designed to bring the two groups closer together. If this show of good will elicited no reaction from the surrealists, the Communist Party was sufficiently aroused at this breach of seriousness to take the offending editorial to task publicly.[28] Shortly thereafter, in May of that year, Crastre returned to the attack with an article (dubbed "essai" by a cautious senior editor, Marcel Fourrier) on the "Explosion surréaliste," in which he attempts to awaken his unsuspecting readers to the revolutionary potential of this parallel movement. His evident good intentions were rewarded with a card: "André Breton would like to thank Victor Crastre very much for his article 'Explosion surréaliste.' "[29] When Jean Bernier, the second senior editor of *Clarté* and its financial mainstay, returned from one of his numerous vacations, he offered to introduce Crastre to Aragon: "This unreal magician [who] showers us with flowery bouquets of kind words and happy gestures. . . . I see in this true Proteus [Aragon] such a gift for transformation, such an extraordinary aptitude for playing the most different roles, that I wonder if the real Aragon is no more than that: one of the finest actors of our time?"[30] While a step in the direction of social *engagement,* this meeting produced nothing substantial. The surrealists may have been intrigued by what they heard from Aragon, but they were still unswerving in their commitment to an ideal solution, one based on Hegel's "absolute idealism," which would permit the resurrection of a paradise of infantile joys and mysteries.[31]

Several months before, when Anatole France, humanitarian and sometime Socialist had died (Oct. 1924), a state funeral was decreed, much as had been given Victor Hugo in 1885. For the surrealists this was an admirable opportunity to demonstrate further their radical disagreement with the literary and social Establishment. Hence, at about the time Breton's *Manifeste du surréalisme* was coming off the press (achevé d'imprimer Oct. 15, 1924), and just days before France was to recognize the Soviet Union (Oct. 28), the surrealists honored the memory of the deceased national hero with *Un Cadavre*.[32] For Philippe Soupault, Anatole France was an egocentric clown interested primarily in his public image; for Eluard, he represented the worst aspects of *l'esprit français,* "scepticism, irony, [and] cowardice"; for Breton, he was a policeman who "bedecked his smiling inertia with the colors of the Revolution"; for Aragon, he recalled all that was "mediocre, limited, and fearful in man, a constant compromiser," admired alike by "the tapir [Charles] Maurras and the imbeciles in Moscow."[33]

The supple character of the general vision of surrealism is nowhere evident in *Un Cadavre*, rather do we suspect a group of men enrolled in some holy cause, whose goals are not overly clear. It is therefore not surprising that Aragon's friend, Jean Bernier, took him to task in the pages of *Clarté* (Nov. 15, 1924). Aragon's reply, which we can assume reflects equally well the attitudes of his colleagues, leaves little doubt as to the orientation of the surrealists at that time: "I have always placed the spirit of revolt well beyond mere political action. . . . As for the Russian Revolution, that leaves me cold. On the level of ideas, it is no more than a vague cabinet crisis. . . . The fundamental problems of human existence were not faced by that little miserable revolution which took place somewhere east of us. Let me add that it is only by stretching the term excessively that one can call it a revolution. . . . My eyes are fixed on a point so distant that no one will ever excuse my silly pretentions."[34] Marcel Fourrier, in commenting on this letter, properly referred to Aragon as a "pure anarchist," while Bernier, with greater insight, recognized in his tone the fanaticism common to certain religious cults.[35] It is against this backdrop of mutual recrimination that Crastre published his article on surrealism ("Explosion surréaliste") and subsequently made contact with the group.

There the situation might have remained, on the one hand, those convinced of the irrelevancy of human action in determining man's fate, on the other, those determined to prepare a political and social revolution in the here and now. But the Bureau de Recherches surréalistes was getting out of hand, what with cranks and curiosity seekers invading the premises; Naville refused to recognize painting as a legitimate surrealist occupation; Soupault and Desnos were turning ever more in the direction of literature; in short, the movement was losing what little direction it had.[36] It was at this point, in the late summer of 1925, that Breton came across the recently translated biography of Lenin by Trotsky:

> From certain allusions in this journal and elsewhere [wrote Breton in his review of that work, published in Oct. 1925], there are some who may have gotten the idea that we surrealists had a poor opinion of the Russian Revolution and of the mentality of the people who led it. . . . For my part I absolutely refuse to be a party to any condemnation of communism, regardless of the reasons underlying such a condemnation, even the apparently legitimate one of the refusal to accept work. It alone has enabled the greatest social upheaval ever to come about. . . . For us revolutionaries it is of little importance which

conception of society is preferable. . . . Our general attitude, if it is aimed at anything it must be in the direction of a *revolutionary reality*, and must take us there *by any means and at any price*.[37]

Rejected is the free-floating surrealist (and Gidean) liberty on which Aragon had written so persuasively in just the preceding issue of *La Révolution surréaliste*.[38] Rejected also are those passages in Aragon's open letter to Drieu La Rochelle in which he had promised to shout "Long Live Lenin" *because* it was forbidden:

> That is not an adequate reason, for it can only help our detractors, who are also Lenin's, to have them think we act in that way only for defiance's sake. Long Live Lenin, on the contrary, *because he is Lenin!*[39]

From the tone of the articles one would imagine that Breton had long been interested in the Soviet leader, but in the ten months since his death—ten months and three numbers of *La Révolution surréaliste*—this is the first inkling that the surrealists considered Lenin a *passant considérable* (Mallarmé's phrase with reference to Rimbaud). And Trotsky too, even if he does not "believe in eternity, as we do."[40]

What had certainly helped further this new political orientation was the ever-increasing intimacy between surrealists and *clartéistes*, especially since the summer of 1925. Toward the end of that summer the two groups were sufficiently sure of one another to delegate Aragon and Victor Crastre to draw up a declaration which would seal their union.[41] The surrealists, without specifically rejecting their past, agreed henceforth to subordinate the "disinterested, detached, indeed despairing" elements of their revolution—its "surrealist illumination" and its "new mysticism"—to more immediate goals.[42] Whereas earlier they had debated "whether their actions should be guided by the surrealist or the revolutionary principle" of their movement, they now conclude, in the broadside *La Révolution d'abord et toujours!* (Oct. 1925), that their "love of the Revolution and [their] desire for results" require, among other things, that they call for unilateral disarmament and the cessation of the French police action in Morocco against the forces of Abd-el-Krim: "this Revolution," to which they are now presumably converted, "we conceive of it only in its social form."[43]

"Tu causes, tu causes. . . ," as the parrot in Queneau's *Zazie dans le métro* put it so nicely. Years before, Dada, too, had called for a revolution, though not specifically a social one; and the Dada spirit in 1925 is regularly shooting bubbles to the top of the surrealist pot. There is, for example, *l'affaire du Vieux-Colombier* (early June 1925), in which the antiliterary surrealists had no objection to having an Aragon play performed at the *Théâtre du Vieux-Colombier*, but found intolerable that it be preceded by a lecture on the "Average Frenchman."[44] Catcalls were followed by surrealists taking over the stage, which of necessity led to police intervention and to another victory for—what exactly? For the Exceptional Frenchman? Or was this but another attempt on the part of the surrealists to convince themselves they were alive (and important) by forcibly bringing themselves to the attention of others? Perhaps the explanation is too existential, or childish, but traditional logic is of little avail here. Aragon could have withdrawn his play, proposed a change in speaker to the management, or drafted an open letter; but that assumes the group was not restless for a pretext to demonstrate.

The scandal at the Closerie des Lilas (a well-known Paris restaurant) was of the same order.[45] After a long absence from the Paris literary scene, the old-line symbolist poet Saint-Pol-Roux was invited by the editors of the *Mercure de France* to a banquet in his honor (July 1, 1925). Unfortunately for the decorum of the customary meal and speeches, the surrealists took the opportunity to arrive early and slip under each place setting an open letter to Paul Claudel, who in an interview some two weeks before had lumped both Dadaism and surrealism together as "pederastic" movements.[46] The surrealist answer is of interest not only for what it says—that the then ambassador to Japan is more of a filthy scoundrel than a poet, that beauty is a concept worthy of a bygone age, that salvation is impossible and patriotism reprehensible—but also for what it does not say. If the surrealists attack Catholicism and the Greco-Roman tradition, they do so for moral reasons and *not* with reference to any Marxist or Communist guidelines.[47] To top off the festivities at the banquet, they took offense at a remark made by Mme Rachilde, the wife of the editor of the *Mercure de France*, and

> Suddenly a fruit. . . flew through the air and struck one of the officials, in the midst of shouts "Long live Germany." The disturbance soon became generalized and turned into a riot. Philippe Soupault, hanging from the chandeliers, knocked over plates and bottles. Outside, the curious gathered. Everyone was fight-

ing. . . . The poet of Camaret [Saint-Pol-Roux], like the pilot of some ship caught in the middle of a storm, horrified by what he saw, tried to re-establish order. He is ignored by his friends on the planning committee. The opportunity to crush these *provocateurs surréalistes* is just too good. And as they can not carry it off, they call to their aid those natural defenders of poetry scorned, the police. . . . In the midst of shouts "Long live Germany! Long live China! Long live the Riffs!" Michel Leiris, opening a window facing on the boulevard, yells "Down with France!" Invited by the crowd below to come downstairs and say that, he doesn't hesitate a moment: the battle continues on the Boulevard du Montparnasse. Continuing his defiance of both police and crowd, Leiris is almost lynched. Taken to the police station, he is thoroughly worked over.[48]

"The scandal," as Nadeau points out, "was enormous."[49] *L'Action française*, viewing the surrealists as tasteless publicity seekers, suggested that they be quarantined behind a haughty wall of silence, or preferably prosecuted as "criminals."[50] And yet, with it all, there is no record of anyone at the Closerie des Lilas shouting "Long live the Soviet Union," or "Long live the workers' paradise." Revolutionaries, yes, but not yet Marxists or Trotskyites: that would come later in the long hot summer with Breton's reading of Trotsky and the drafting of *La Révolution d'abord et toujours!*

By October 1925, the surrealists had traveled somewhat more than one-half the distance toward Communist affiliation. Their unity affirmed and their purpose strengthened by the melees at the Vieux-Colombier and the Closerie des Lilas, their self-esteem flattered by the attention accorded by *Clarté*—which for a while they took to be a Communist Party publication[51] (Communist oriented, yes; but then so was Trotsky!)—they entered into a short-lived marriage with the *Clarté* activists whose immediate goal was to obtain the withdrawal of French troops from Morocco, where the Riff war had appreciably intensified. "The progress of the Moroccan War," wrote Fourrier in November 1925, "literally threw us together."[52] But half way was not far enough for the surrealist Naville, who more than most of his colleagues was attracted by the possibility of direct political intervention. Barely months after the united front of "intellectual revolutionaries" and "para-communists" had been formed, he undertakes to analyze the basic paradox of such a union and openly transfers his allegiance from the first to the second.[53] Breton has no quarrel with the *theoretical* basis of Marxism, nor with Naville's interpretation of it in his 1926 manifesto *La Révolution et les intellectuels*.[54] But he does not care for Henri Barbusse or his dull-witted daily, *L'Humanité*.[55] If he looks forward to the eventual "transfer of power from the bourgeoisie to the proletariat," he has no desire to join a party only to find himself immediately relegated to the Opposition![56] Join he would; but as a man of principle he would do so only on his own terms: he would be a fullfledged member of the Party, a leader among leaders—they revolutionizing the outside world, he the inside. "While waiting for the Revolution [in France] to succeed," wrote Breton, "it is imperative that the [surrealist] experiments dealing with mental activity be permitted, and with no outside control, even Marxist control."[57]

This is far too individualistic an attitude for Naville. The time for waiting, regardless of Breton's quibbles, is long since past: "We affirm our absolute solidarity with the worldwide Communist movement, and we dedicate this brochure to those who place before all else the battle for the complete liberation of the proletariat."[58] Naville does not question the subversive potential of surrealism, but, having joined the professionals, he finds his former friends politically naive: "the bourgeoisie doesn't fear them. It will easily absorb them."[59] If the Party isn't perfect, it is at least, according to Naville (who here prefigures Sartre), an efficient weapon for reform, which surrealism, with its basis in anarchism and its flighty, romantic attitude, clearly is not.[60] On the surface the discussion seems futile, as is inevitable when two adamant faiths are confronted. Both speak of paradise, but the paths to salvation are not the same. Both work on man and seek to reveal his true condition, but some simplify (and by so doing distort), while others do not seek evidence as much as confirmation. The friendly polemic between Breton and Naville had, however, one thoroughly unexpected result: the surrealists joined the Communist Party. Or was their change of heart due to the defection-expulsion of Soupault and Artaud? These two—one privately wealthy, the other poor as a church mouse—had for some years been the nucleus of the literary coterie in the movement, and, Artaud especially, had bitterly opposed any political commitment as diminishing the spiritual potential of the movement.[61] With these two gone, the way was clear for the brochure *Au grand jour* (*Out in the Open*, [May] 1927), which affirmed the general similarity in aspirations of Communists and surrealists and announced to the public at large, "we have joined the French Communist Party."[62]

The five letters which make up *Au grand jour* present as many variations on the theme "Why?" To their Belgian colleagues they say they joined for the purpose of attacking more efficaciously the complacent society about them. To Marcel Fourrier, they defend their political orthodoxy while questioning his. To their fellow French surrealists who were aware of their intentions but who did not join them in this step, they defend the logic of their move as one deriving from surrealism itself: a "pure protest," they insist, echoing Naville, is pointless when divorced from any effective means of *acting* on it. To Pierre Naville, the financial backer of the new series of *Clarté*, "who, with no risk to himself, travels in ideological areas where we might be lost were we to move with his haste," they wonder aloud at his lack of sympathy with their new position, which he was the first to suggest. To their new camarades in the Communist Party, they reiterate their complete acceptance of the party line: "We insist with all our strength that we have never dreamed of asserting ourselves as surrealists."[63] In spite of their protestations, however, the surrealists were uncertain allies; nothing they did could make the Party forget Freud and Trotsky, their bourgeois background, and their equally disturbing magazine, *La Révolution surréaliste*, with its curious subject matter and even more curious illustrations. Together with the fatiguing experience of being constantly obliged to defend himself before Party committees established for the sole purpose of determining his orthodoxy, Breton found himself unable to accept the routine of the "cell" to which he was assigned. Whether real or imagined—and it was probably real—the "hazing" and "persistent hostility" to which he felt he was subjected led to his withdrawal from the Party (along with Aragon and Eluard) less than one year after joining.[64]

For the Communists the real nerve of the controversy lay in determining whether the surrealists in joining the Party intended to remain surrealists first and be Communists only thereafter (assuming surrealism had a political component), or be surrealists in art and literature and Communists in the realm of politics, or renounce their past and commit themselves totally to communism. The surrealists, on the other hand, saw this as a false dilemma, but were never able to convince their opposite numbers. Having come to the Party of their own free will, rather than through any inexorable material reasons, they found the mindless discipline (the party line came from unknown sources in Moscow) and the disciplined suspicion intolerable. Why, for example, the obligation to withdraw *Légitime défense* from circulation?[65] Hadn't those early uncertainties been resolved in *Au grand jour?* Breton saw surrealism as expanding the revolutionary potential of communism; nascent Stalinism could view it only as another expansive deviation, comparable if not identical to Trotskyism. Both parties were probably correct, but they could not coexist: traumatic is the marriage of the yogi and the commissar. When Breton opened the pages of *La Révolution surréaliste* to the deviationist Naville in October 1927, the die was cast. To claim "the *right to criticize*" recalled only too clearly what the Opposition was saying in Moscow: Breton would have to leave, and leave he did the following month.[66] Revolutionary fervor was fine in its day, but the time had come to settle down to ordered purges. What the surrealists considered the most urgent problems were not to their fellow travelers the most fundamental. While both sides recognized the existence of a divided culture, their techniques for unification were radically dissimilar; where one feared inspiration and the fireworks of spontaneity, the other lived by it. Artaud's view, expressed shortly after the publication of *Au grand jour*, that surrealism was "a new type of magic" and that the early surrealists considered "individual liberty far more important than any conquest of a more relative (material) sort" was undoubtedly not far removed from that held by the Party hierarchy when they discreetly eliminated the sectarians from their midst.[67]

Although the surrealists lost their political virginity in 1927, and some of their illusions with regard to the Party hierarchy, they did not lose their taste for politics. This was to be their new vice, one which would further confirm their position as Outsiders, for they were now even outside of the clique of Party Outsiders. Theirs was a lonely path: intellectual Trotskyites obliged to avoid references to the fallen idol (he was exiled to Siberia in January 1928) lest they permanently close the door to collaboration with the Party, they could serve the cause, but would never be part of it. Not until 1938, after the degrading spectacle of the second series of Moscow "trials" (1937), would Breton take the logical step of allying himself with the titular leader of the IV[th] International.

From 1928 to 1938 the history of surrealist involvement in politics resembles that of a mad tea party: the Communist Party's directives were also those of the surrealists, as long, that is, as they in no way interfered with surrealist practices and were not contrary to their theories. They were consummate fellow travelers, but only of a parallel star, and were constantly surprised when they stumbled: it is not easy to march to two drumbeats, one distant and the other

unconscious. For all their verbal brilliance the surrealists were political amateurs who used the dialectic as they previously had used
automatism—as a technique for arriving at greater self knowledge,
or Truth, such as that may be in matters human. Had Péret, their
principal activist, been present during the critical years following
the surrealist departure from the Communist Party, it is just possible
that the course of events might have been modified—but not significantly: the surrealists were too few in number and had access
neither to the sources of political power nor to any large revolutionary following.[68] This, indeed, they seem to have recognized, for
their sorties into the political arena are remarkably irregular and
discontinuous, given the turbulence of the period. They were far
more concerned with *big* questions than with little ones, with theory
than with day to day practice, with being correct than with being
in control. Neither Dada nor surrealism had ever evolved a systematic, coherent political philosophy of its own. Their revolution
was of another order: total rather than social, looking inward more
than outward. They came to politics because of outside temptations,
and the guidelines they chose to follow meshed only imperfectly with
the Ariel-like principles of early surrealism.

The initial disillusionment produced by their Communist experience led to a certain amount of retrenching. The sixty-four pages
of the October 1927 *Révolution surréaliste* (no. 9-10), of which approximately one-third was devoted to political theory and polemic,
become forty pages in March 1928 (no. 11), none of which alludes
to their recent interests. Antonin Artaud and Roger Vitrac, long excluded from the magic circle, make an unexpected appearance in
that same March issue, in what can only be an attempt (unsuccess-
ful) at fence mending. Jean Genbach, defrocked abbé and mystical
surrealist, who for a time appeared to be Artaud's replacement, is
also there after almost a year's absence.[69] A *rapprochement* with
the Belgian surrealists proclaimed by a brief *Avis* (signed by Breton,
Aragon, Goemans, and Nougé in March 1928) marks still another
attempt to consolidate their shaky position, as does the return of
Tzara to the fold the following year. From the political point of
view, the period 1928-29 is one of transition. Breton brings out his
*Surréalisme et la peinture* and *Nadja* (both 1928), a new edition of
the first *Manifeste "augmentée d'une préface et d'une Lettre aux
voyantes"* (1929), a first version of the *Second manifeste* (in *La
Révolution surréaliste*, Dec. 15, 1929), and, with Aragon, *Le Trésor
des Jésuites* (first published in *Variétés: Le Surréalisme en 1929,*

June 1929, but not performed until March 17, 1935, in Prague);
Aragon is not far behind with his *Traité du style* (1928), the translation of Lewis Carroll's *La Chasse au Snark* (1929), and the collection of poems *La Grand gaîté* (1929); for Eluard there is his
*Défense de savoir* (1928) and the appreciably longer *L'Amour la
poésie* (1929); while Péret has his inimitable tales of *Et les seins
mouraient* (1928), *Le Grand jeu* (1928), and the first "semester" of
1929 (photographs by Man Ray; the second "semester" was prepared
by Aragon—published clandestinely in 1929). Politics was clearly
not uppermost in their minds at this time.

When the Soviet Union expelled Trotsky on January 31, 1929,
it inadvertently offered Breton the opportunity to tighten the reins
on his wandering band of literary revolutionaries. Scarcely days after
the news of Trotsky's expulsion was confirmed, a letter (dated Feb.
12) was addressed to some seventy-three persons sharing at least
in part the surrealist "liberal" attitude, and who might be interested
in consolidating their efforts.[70] On the basis of the replies received,
a second letter was sent (this one dated March 6) calling for a meeting on March 11, at 8:30 P.M., at the Bar du Château, 53 rue du Château, where the principal subject of discussion would be an "analysis
of what has recently happened to Leon Trotsky."[71] What conclusions
could these part-time revolutionaries, having no information other
than that published in the newspapers, possibly hope to arrive at?
Had they been seriously concerned about Trotsky, a laconic statement, or petition, signed by several hundred "intellectuals" would
have been quicker and might perhaps have had some slight effect. As
it stood, the meeting and the subject to be discussed had all the ear-
marks of a pretext—which is what it turned out to be. With Max
Morise presiding, the numerous replies to the original letter of
February 12 were read, at which point the assembly rapidly degen-
erated into a series of personal attacks on those who for one reason
or another had failed in their revolutionary ardor or compromised
their integrity.[72] Needless to say, no conclusion was ever reached
with regard to Trotsky, nor was any necessary, for it was clear from
the very first that the entire assembly was horrified by his treatment
at the hands of Stalin. What was heralded as a cross between a
manifestation in favor of the exiled Soviet leader and a new Congrès
de Paris, turned rapidly into a noisy surrealist purge. With their
allies exhilarated and their enemies confounded in this new version
of the *procès Barrès,* the new believers could now continue on the

circular tightrope, faceless, but juggling so adeptly the two masks of saint and wily revolutionary that one blended into the other.

And there matters remained for some two years. Although outside the Party, the surrealists never ceased considering themselves Communists. Although Trotskyites by persuasion, they never ceased to condemn all deviations—except those endorsed by Trotsky himself.[73] The group was now more numerous and more diversified than it had been since the heyday of Dada: Tzara was back; there was the young Georges Sadoul and the politically inclined André Thirion; the poet René Char and Maurice Heine with his rehabilitation of Sade; Dali and Buñuel, as well as Tanguy, Man Ray, Maxime Alexandre, René Crevel, and the several others who had escaped unscathed from the 1929 purge of the rue du Château and the subsequent *Second Manifeste*.[74] The political position of the group was, nevertheless, highly unstable. They might reply, as they did, when asked by the Russian Bureau International de Littérature Révolutionnaire what their attitude would be should the Soviet Union be attacked: "We will abide by the orders of the Third International," but they were still suspect to the Party.[75] Aside from the obvious fact that the commissar can never trust the dilettante (it would be both simple and amusing to plot the dialogue of a top-level Party discussion of the surrealist dandies), there was reason to suspect that the surrealist answer to the questionnaire was motivated as much by practical considerations as by political conviction.

Aragon, for example, would shortly be leaving for the Soviet Union accompanied by Elsa Triolet (soon to be his wife), and if the proper cards were played he might receive an invitation to the Second International Congress of Revolutionary Writers, to be held in Kharkov, beginning November 6, 1930. (At the last minute his surrealist colleague, Georges Sadoul, who was then appealing a three-month prison sentence, decided to follow them.) This apparently anodyne trip, suggested by Elsa Triolet, whose overt purpose was a family reunion with her sister, was to have repercussions which would ultimately oblige Aragon to leave the group and thus still further exacerbate relations between the surrealists and their sometime Communist allies.[76] Aragon had met Elsa—whose sister, Lili Brik, was an intimate of the Russian poet Vladimir Mayakovsky—some two years before, in a Montparnasse bar, in all probability thanks to the intervention of Mayakovsky.[77] Aragon at that time had just gone through a major emotional crisis, one which led to the destruction of a novel, *La Défense de l'infini*, and had brought him to the brink of suicide.[78] Bitter and depressed, to which the final poems in *La Grande gaîté* attest (they were written in the summer of 1928), unhappy in love and uncertain of his future, Aragon was very much ready for a "conversion."

Very little information is currently available on the reasons *for* this trip, as contrasted with what occurred *during* it. Nonetheless, given its uniqueness (no other surrealist before or since has made the pilgrimage) and its two major effects (the exclusion of Aragon from the surrealist movement and the heightened awareness by the surrealists of the deviousness of Soviet practices), it may be worthwhile to examine the subject with greater care than it is usually given. Aragon had no compelling reason to visit the Soviet Union. The one Russian writer he knew slightly, Vladimir Mayakovsky, had committed suicide earlier that year (Apr. 14, 1930). As a gesture of respect the trip would appear somewhat excessive, but as a pretext it would do as well as another: Elsa was returning home and was eager to show her friend the wonders of the new régime; to her admirer, *le paysan de Paris*, it was an exceptional opportunity to see what his Russian counterparts were doing. As Breton summed it up: "Looking back, there is every reason to think that the change in Aragon's orientation was due primarily to her [Elsa's] influence."[79] Given the difficulties between the French Communists and the surrealists it was obviously out of the question for any surrealist to be officially invited to attend the International Congress, due to open on the eve of the thirteenth anniversary of the Russian Revolution. But should someone qualified happen to be in the vicinity of Kharkov, then he might well be invited to sit in on some of the meetings, if only in an unofficial or advisory capacity. That is what the surrealists had banked on, and that is what happened.[80] Aragon had gone to Russia to be with Elsa and, if possible, to strengthen the surrealist position with the Party. If his happy association with Elsa succeeded in opening doors in Leningrad and elsewhere that, without her, would surely have remained closed, his attempt to convince the Congress that the surrealists in France should be given free rein to operate as they saw fit without outside interference was doomed to failure from the very beginning: the spectre of a leftist deviation recalling both Trotsky and the Constructivists of an earlier period was not designed to quiet Stalinist apprehensions, while those who might secretly have sympathized with them could not fail to be put off by the heady perfumes of uninhibited dreams, formalized eroticism, artificial paradises, and the uncertain loyalty of this close-knit confederacy. Yet for all this, Aragon was one of the major writers of the younger generation, and his good will was vouched for by Elsa. Giving ground on small points—for example, the limited condemnation of *Monde*—the organizers of the Congress succeeded in obtaining from the lonely Frenchman a last-minute rejection of (1) Breton's *Second Manifeste,* "where it conflicts with dialectical materialism," (2) Freud's "idealistic ideology," and (3) Trotsky's "counterrevolutionary ideology."[81] Aragon was neither ideologue nor leader. His strength had always been Breton; alone, as it turned out, he was no match for the combined arguments of love (Elsa), prestige (the chance to work with the party of the future), and friendship (Sadoul, recently condemned by a French tribunal for having insulted a Saint-Cyr cadet, saw his vindication more in the Revolution than in the Unconscious, the latter being powerless to overturn his conviction).

When Aragon returned to France, prudently stopping first in Belgium so as to permit Sadoul to prepare Breton and the others for the unhappy news that the surrealist cow had been inexplicably bartered away for a handful of magic beans, he not unexpectedly found that his Paris friends would have none of it. But youth being the season of generosity, and Aragon not being in a position to deliver the surrealists (as Jack had at one time delivered the cow), the "deal" could not be concluded. There might things have remained, with Aragon once again taking his place at the right hand of Breton, had not the government indicted his poem "Front rouge."[82] Why the government felt that a poet's call to shoot down in cold blood Léon Blum, Boncour, Frossard, and Déat (among others)—however objectionable the idea might be—was anything more than misplaced poetic frenzy is difficult to understand. But under the dominion of fear, authority does not always behave rationally or with restraint. Determined to defend his wayward friend, Breton fell back on the one argument that could not help but alienate such sympathizers as he might have both in and out of the Party: "Front rouge" was essentially a poem, not a political tract, and could only be fully understood when placed in a purely poetic tradition. "The poem," wrote Breton in *Misère de la poésie,* "cannot be judged on the basis of the successive images which it conjures up," for these "are only a point of departure. The scope and sense of the poem lie *beyond* the sum of its component parts. . . . If this were not so, the language of poetry would long since have been swallowed up by that of prose. Its survival among us is our best guarantee of its necessity."[83] Instead of accepting this statement at face value—that poetry has an incantatory power which the sum of its images can neither exhaust nor define, the righteous and the hasty saw Breton relegating poetry to some formalist dungeon and denying to it any social relevance. The poet, to hear them, should have the courage to stand behind each and every one of his phrases—something Breton never denied, but refused to limit to phrases or poems out of context.[84] Breton, however, had reckoned without Aragon. When faced with the decision of choosing between surrealism and communism, between Breton and Elsa, an artificial paradise and *le monde réel*, he in every case abandoned the former for the latter.[85] Ironically enough, the first formal announcement that Aragon had changed camps came from the Association des Ecrivains Révolutionnaires, an organization for which the surrealists had been pressing and which had been secretly formed by the Party without their presence.

It would be nice to say that Aragon's departure from surrealism was due to ideological differences lately realized, but carefully examined. That this is not so is evidenced by his year-long hesitation and, even more convincingly, by the annotations on Eluard's private copy of the brochure *Paillasse! (Fin de "l'Affaire Aragon")*, a far more compelling bit of testimony than Eluard's more formal *Certificat* because it was never meant to be made public.[86] Several of those marginal notations are given below. (The emphasis in each instance is on the Eluard copy.)

| *Eluard* | *Paillasse* (page references to Nadeau, *Histoire du surréalisme*) |
|---|---|
| absurde | Ou Aragon *était d'accord avec ce papier qu'il a signé* (in which he rejects Trotsky, Freudianism, and those sections of the *Second Manifeste* which presumably conflict with dialectical materialism). . . . (p. 358) |
| excessif | De retour à Paris . . . sa signature, se plaint-il, lui a été *extorquée*. (p. 359) |
| bien | Parce que dans cette lettre Aragon apprécie faussement la position d'observation adoptée par Breton par rapport au trotskysme à la fin de 1929 et se refuse tout à coup de reconnaître |

les découvertes de Freud sous le pretexte im-
bécile qu'elles ont donné suite à une idéologie
idéaliste (freudisme), nous exigeons une recti-
fication. (p. 359)

faux
à ne pas dire

On a pu voir s'accomplir au sein du
surréalisme *une évolution profonde* QUI NOUS
A PORTÉS sur le plan du matérialisme dialectique. (p. 360)

? ? ?

Nous saluons comme un témoignage capital
de la probité révolutionnaire et de la *clairvoy-
ance théorique* d'André Breton la publication
de *Misère de la poésie.* (p. 360)

nul et
incorrect

Décidés à poursuivre le mouvement dont le
*Manifeste du surréalisme* marque la naissance
et le *Second manifeste du surréalisme un point
de son évolution. . .* (p. 360)

What emerges, if we follow Eluard, who was one of Aragon's
most intimate colleagues, is that (1) it is inconceivable that Aragon
agreed with the statement he was asked to sign in Moscow in December 1930; (2) he did not sign because of any overt pressure, in
spite of what he claimed; (3) he inadequately understood Breton's
position with regard to Trotsky and Freud; and (4) while the two
Manifestos may have fixed certain aspects of surrealism, the basic
changes in the movement, conscious and reasoned rather than inspired, antedate the Manifestos. In a word, banal though it may
sound, the major inducement for Aragon's departure was internal
rather than external, emotional rather than rational: his love for Elsa
Triolet. It can scarcely be stressed too much that surrealism is not
a dispassionate pastime like astronomy, which springs from the contemplation of things at a distance, and that after years spent toying
with dreams, love, and spontaneity it is not surprising that one of
its adherents embraced *l'amour sublime* when he had the opportunity to do so. What I am saying is that on the basis of the limited
evidence available it would seem that Aragon left surrealism less
for communism than for Elsa—a very surrealistic gesture, though
only obscurely sensed by the participants at the time.

One might assume at this point that the surrealists, having

played the *vierge folle* to the Communists' *époux infernal* for some seven years, would take the hint and close the door softly behind them. For how many years can one suffer the indignity of being considered a pornographer, a decadent petit bourgeois, and a counterrevolutionary—both in private as well as in public? But there are few things in history more common than oppression, and the surrealists evidently had strong backs (and thick skins). Reluctantly accepted into the Communist-dominated Association des Ecrivains et Artistes Révolutionnaires shortly after the Aragon affair—how could he be refused, since he was a revolutionary of a sort and wanted to join?—Breton was the first to be summarily expelled, after having graced its roster for little more than a year. The pretext, as petty as one might wish for, was a letter from a then unknown provincial commenting critically on a Russian film, which letter Breton saw fit to publish in *Le Surréalisme au service de la révolution*.[87] This might almost be a reenactment of the La Fontaine fable of "The Wolf and the Lamb":

> —Si ce n'est toi, c'est donc ton frère.
> —Je n'en ai point.—C'est donc quelqu'un des tiens;
>     Car vous ne m'épargnez guère,
>     Vous, vos bergers, et vos chiens.
> On me l'a dit: il faut que je me venge.
>     Là-dessus, au fond des forêts
>     Le loup l'emporte, et puis le mange,
>     Sans autre forme de procès.

But Breton was determined to reform the Party from the inside, and, especially in the thirties, the Party regularly needed all the support it could get: so the wolf and the indestructible lamb were destined to live in vindictive harmony for several more years.[88] For a moment after the rightist putsch which flared in Paris on February 6, 1934, it seemed that the two groups might once again join forces, and so they might had the surrealists not published a collective manifesto protesting France's expulsion of Trotsky from the country.[89] To protest or not to protest? Surely Breton must have known after so many past difficulties that whatever good will he might have accrued through his liberal posture in the February riots and the March aftermath he would fritter away in defense of the Russian exile. In the conflict between the principled rebel and the revolutionary so thoroughly committed to his ends that the means lose all im-

portance, the former is at a notable disadvantage. Breton was no
fool, but he was not a Stalinist either, and the Party knew it and distrusted him for it. Politics, like art, lives by convention, which means
occasional factual distortion for the sake of some larger truth. This
Breton had difficulty accepting. "For the surrealists," as Camus
pointed out, "revolution [and here he is speaking of *political* rev-
olution] was never an end to be sought in daily action but rather a
myth, both consoling and unquestioned."[90] The *surrealist* revolution,
with its ethical, psychological, and aesthetic components, had transformed the guts of its adherents into something so ethereal that, except on rare occasions, they were incapable of coping with the
roughage of "practical" revolutionary drudgery. This is what Henri
Pastoureau, who came to the movement from communism at about
this time, had in mind when, looking back, he wrote that the most
serious reproach which could be directed against surrealism, from
a Communist point of view, was that it "diverted from revolutionary
activity intelligent, sensitive youths who would probably have done
better to become political agitators or union administrators than
bourgeois writers."[91] But that was written after he became convinced that Breton's ambitions were more literary than social.

On August 17, 1934, some three days after Breton's second
marriage, Andrei Zdanov opened the first Pan-Soviet Literary Congress in Moscow and officially propounded the theory of socialist
realism in literature and art.[92] What few illusions Breton may have
had about being reinstated in the good graces of the Communist
Party should at that point have been dashed, but they were not; so
still another dreary page in the on-again off-again relationship of
the two groups was prepared. And as before, it was an excruciat-
ingly petty incident that most stirred the summer passions.

An International Congress for the Defense of Culture (Congrès
international pour la défense de la culture), Communist-sponsored,
had been proposed in the spring of 1935. The surrealists in their reply of April 20 agreed to take part, with the understanding that
certain questions which they felt to be basic would be discussed,
specifically, the rationale of defending the culture of a capitalist
society, the right of the writer and artist to seek new means of expression regardless of initial public reaction, and the protection of
the writer (and artist) from governmental interference.[93] Needless
to say, on the eve of the Stalinist purges the demand for ever greater
liberty was anomalous, if not ridiculous. As for the first point—why
defend a capitalist culture when it was doomed to be replaced in

short order—that was answered by the unexpected Franco-Russian mutual aid treaty of May 2, 1935.[94] French culture was to be defended because France was now an ally of the Soviet Union. Not without difficulty did the surrealists obtain the assurance of the organizing committee that one of their number, Breton, would be permitted to speak at the Congress. However, shortly before the Congress opened in late June, Breton by chance encountered Ilya Ehrenburg on the streets of Paris, remembered he had been insulted by him in a recently published book, and proceeded to answer the insults with a public thrashing. Only later, after his name was summarily removed from the program, did he learn that Ehrenburg was a member of the official Soviet delegation to the Congress. There matters might have remained had not René Crevel, who had only a short while before moved from surrealism to communism without, however, abandoning his first love, insisted upon Breton's appearance and, failing to convince his superiors, committed suicide. While Breton's "Discours" was subsequently reinstated, it was placed at the end of the program and read to an almost empty hall by Eluard (less objectionable than Breton).[95] This series of comic-tragic events culminated in the publication of Breton's *Position politique du surréalisme*, only months after the storm had subsided. After attacking Stalin for abandoning the "principles which led to the Revolution"—which in 1935 was tantamount to bidding a permanent farewell to any future collaboration with the Stalinist-controlled Party—Breton reiterates that "over and above the considerations which follow and which are the result of ten years of thought and effort, i.e., to reconcile surrealism as a *method of creating a collective myth* with the much more general movement concerned with the liberation of man, which requires first of all a fundamental modification of the bourgeois form of property, the problem of *action*, of what to do next, remains ever pertinent."[96] And so a year that had begun very auspiciously, with trips to Prague and to the Canary Islands to inaugurate surrealist exhibitions and spread the word of happy collaboration between the political and artistic avant-garde, came to a more somber close: between the parties of dream and action there would be no alliance, at least not while Stalin reigned.[97]

Breton was a novice in politics, as were the great majority of those about him. While he recognized the danger of Nazi Germany, it appeared to him no greater than that of any other imperialist nation. This is why he could support the statement of the Comité de Vigilance des Intellectuels (March 25, 1935) that there should be no attempt to establish a series of alliances, a sort of *union sacrée,* aimed at Germany, for that could only antagonize a people still capable of taking a revolutionary posture. This is also why it appeared to him "particularly painful" when Stalin, on May 15 of that same year, publicly supported France's first steps in the direction of rearmament, although those steps—limited for all practical purposes to the establishment of two years of military service—were in direct response to German rearmament, about which Breton had nothing to say.[98] Literature is a game played with words, and there Breton was the equal of any; but the rules of politics are other, and there he combined the tact of Polonius with the insight of Caliban and the happy assurance of Bottom. Were it not for the repeated interventions of the surrealists into the political arena, and their notable revolutionary good will, the whole sorry spectacle might best be forgotten.

When 1938 rolled around, Europe was on the brink of catastrophe. Germany, thoroughly Nazified, had occupied the Rhineland on March 7, 1936, Italy had succeeded in conquering Ethiopia (Oct. 1935-May 1936), France was plagued by a series of sit-in strikes following the victory of the Popular Front at the polls (May 1936), the Civil War in Spain was in progress (July 18, 1936-March 1939)— Péret had gone there almost immediately after hostilities had broken out, the infamous Soviet purge trials of 1936 and 1937 had just drawn to a tentative close, and the Munich Pact bringing "peace in our time" was to be signed on September 30, 1938. The surrealists, meanwhile, excluded from the councils of political power, were obliged to limit their activities to matters literary and artistic, best exemplified by their contributions to the luxurious art periodical *Minotaure* and, to a lesser extent, the *Cahiers d'art.*[99] In London, in June 1936, in the depths of the depression, they gathered their forces for an International Surrealist Exhibition.[100] A year and one-half later, in January 1938, the first such exhibition to be held in Paris was opened at the Galerie des Beaux-Arts. Surrealism had become a force to be reckoned with in art and literature, if not in politics.

As a consequence, when Breton was offered the opportunity to lecture in Mexico under the auspices of the French Cultural Services, he accepted with alacrity: not only did he need the money (he was now married and had a daughter), but in Mexico he would find Trotsky.[101] From 1925 on, from the time he first came under the influence of the former Soviet commissar through his numerous run-ins with an ever more inflexible Party, Breton's political orientation had paralleled that of Trotsky. In Mexico, for the first time, they would have an opportunity to confront their views, dovetail them if possible, and proceed together in their minority assault against the established bastions of the capitalist world. So it was. After several months of friendly contact, the two men drafted a manifesto, "Pour un art révolutionnaire indépendant," calling for the creation of a Fédération internationale de l'art révolutionnaire indépendant (F.I.A.R.I.).[102] Perhaps the best indication of how similar the views of the two authors were is that either one of the two could have signed this call for an untrammeled revolutionary art alone, and few would have taken it amiss. Fundamental to the manifesto is its terminal statement:

> What we want is:
> *the independence of art—for the revolution; the revolution—for the definitive liberation of art.*[103]

So important for both was the concept of artistic liberty that when, in an early draft, Breton had proposed the maxim, "complete freedom in art, except against the proletarian revolution," it was Trotsky who crossed out the second half of the phrase, saying it could lead to abuses.[104] In a magnificent act of faith—or is it rather a redefinition of art?—they agree that all authentic art in the modern world must be revolutionary, for it alone can "aspire to a complete, radical reconstruction of society."[105] Every true artist is thus seen as a critic, in much the same way that Plato saw the poet more than two millennia ago; but where the Greek's republic was forever perfect, and hence had no need of critics, the classless society envisaged by the two strangers in Mexico was but one point on the road toward that ever-receding perfect horizon, and the artist, if only in theory, would always be welcome. While the means of production in a truly revolutionary society should be socialized according to some overall plan, "with regard to intellectual creation the revolution must from the very beginning establish and assure an *anarchist* regime of individual liberty."[106] An incredible statement, given what we have seen of "revolutionary" regimes in the not-so-distant past. Yet lest there be any residue of disbelief, they reiterate: "No authority, no restriction, not the slightest trace of compulsion!"[107] Can Trotsky really have signed this document? Or did he realize, as he must have, that in actual practice the state (which would control the "means of production") would be in a position to pick and choose what it would print? A milder form of censorship than that which obtains in some societies, but quite real nonetheless. That the two artists were not unaware of the paradox between artistic freedom and social control is evident when they take pains to stress that they have no desire to resuscitate any so-called "pure" art:

> No, we have far too high an opinion of the function of art to refuse it an influence on the fate of society. We believe that the supreme task of art in our time is to participate consciously and actively in setting the stage for the revolution. Nonetheless, the artist can help advance this battle for freedom only if he is subjectively imbued with its social and individual content, only if his very nerves have assimilated its meaning and drama and if he freely seeks to give an artistic incarnation to his internal world.[108]

The paradox is double. While the artist is expected to further the revolution, it will be a politician who will determine if he has succeeded. The artist's internal world, moreover, is presumably a source of revolutionary fervor, or at least of inspiration which is capable of being directed toward revolutionary ends. But if the politician is not sufficiently artistic, or if the internal world in question is insufficiently revolutionary (and by what standards all this!), what then? Is the artist still a member of the club, or is he expelled as were Soupault, Artaud, Desnos, and how many others? And where to, then, in a state whose "means of production" are centralized? The most convincing explanation—however disturbing—would seem to be that in the New Society only those artists who were properly *engagés* would be considered artists, and the rest could go hang, or be barely tolerated. How this relates to preserving the "integrity of artistic research" or the injunction that art must be considered an end in itself and "should under no pretext become *means*" is difficult to see.[109] What is probably true is that at one and the same time Breton held to both views: the authentic artist *must* be socially committed, and the commitment *must* be made freely; art, however, is an end in itself and must *never be made* to serve any external cause. The *true artist* (in existential fashion) will do so freely, and it was clearly he whom Breton and Trotsky had in mind.

When Breton returned to France in August, he learned that during his absence Eluard, the last of the old guard, had moved tentatively into the Stalinist camp. The reasons are unclear: perhaps a desire to be a member of the major revolutionary party of the day and have access to its publications, perhaps more subtle, personal reasons. In any case, as Breton wrote years after the fact, after a fruitless meeting "we never again saw one another. Thus, abruptly ended a friendship which for years had never stopped growing."[110] If a serious blow internally, the departure was scarcely noticed beyond the precincts of the two groups involved, implying that an exceptional amount of discretion was shown by all concerned, or that the tensions of the prewar period so dominated the scene that an *affaire Eluard* was out of the question. Europe, after all, was preparing for Munich, the dismemberment of Czechoslovakia, and the collapse of the Western alliance against Hitler. Some three days before the Munich Pact was signed, the "surrealist group" brought out a tract denouncing both the forthcoming war and the vacillating peace. As neither of the two antagonists adequately represented the forces of democracy, justice, and liberty, it would be impossible to support wholeheartedly one against the other: "The States which. . . identify themselves with those concepts [democracy, justice, liberty] have acquired their wealth and consolidated their power through tyrannical, arbitrary, and bloody methods."[111] They presumably permitted Ethiopia to fall for fear of encouraging colonial revolts; Spain was refused arms for fear of establishing a revolutionary government in the West; imperial Japan was preferable to revolutionary China, and so on.[112] Rejecting at one and the same time the totalitarian regimes of the West, the Europe of the treaty of Versailles, and the scandalous regime of the Third International, there was not, unfortunately, much left—except some highly hypothetical "forces destined to rebuild Europe from top to bottom by means of a proletarian revolution."[113] These forces, to be grouped around the newly proposed F.I.A.R.I., never materialized, but the war did, and both surrealists and members of the short-lived F.I.A.R.I. were dispersed to the four winds.[114]

Barely one year after Breton's return from Mexico, his worst fears were realized in the signing of the Russo-German nonaggression pact (Aug. 22, 1939): the general mobilization that followed and various "security" measures taken against foreigners and others put a temporary end to any organized surrealist activity in France. On September 1, Germany invaded Poland. Days later Breton was observed in an officer's uniform at the Café de Flore.[115] From September to Christmas 1939 and from May through mid-June 1940 Ernst was interned as an enemy alien.[116] Paris was occupied on June 14; a week later the Franco-German armistice was signed. In July, Péret was released by the Nazis from a military prison in Rennes, where the French had confined him for "dangerous" political activity.[117] Trotsky was assassinated on August 20. (Freud had died peacefully in London on Sept. 23, 1939.) By the winter of 1940 an ever-increasing number of intellectual "undesirables" had headed for the Free Zone, specifically Marseilles, in an attempt to avoid almost certain harassment by the authorities. By mid-1941, Péret was in Mexico, Breton and Ernst in New York, where they found Tanguy, who had arrived in December 1939.[118] "A photo, taken March 1942 at the Pierre Matisse Gallery in New York, shows a group of 'artists in exile': Matta, Zadkine, Tanguy, Ernst, Chagall, Léger, Breton, Mondrian, Masson," and others.[119] Both tactical considerations (they were foreigners subject to deportation) and the muddled world situation militated against any further revolutionary activity, except in the relatively harmless areas of art and literature.

When in June 1942, Breton, as one of the three editorial advisers of the luxurious bilingual periodical *VVV* (the other two being Marcel Duchamp and Max Ernst), helped draft the new magazine's statement of principles, there was nothing to recall the ardent founder of the F.I.A.R.I., the enemy of Stalinist Russia and of capitalist imperialism.[120] The way of the exile is never easy. "My position as a refugee," as Breton told his audience at Yale University in December 1942, "does not permit me to be more explicit on this point"—with reference to the causes of the war.[121] So studiously did he avoid the realm of politics that his summation of surrealism is fundamentally distorted—unless one assumes that the entire social aspect of the movement was a profound aberration best forgotten:

> Persistent faith in the value of automatism as a probe; persistent hope that the dialectic (that of Heraclitus, of Master Eckhardt, of Hegel) will resolve the antimonies which crush mankind; recognition of objective chance as one indication of a possible reconciliation between the goals of nature and those of man, at least in the eyes of the latter; the firm intention to make *black humor,* which alone at a certain temperature can play the role of escape valve, an integral part of the psychic apparatus; practical preparation for *intervention into man's myths,* where the first order of business would seem to be to clear out

the dead wood; these have been, and still are at the present time, the basic guidelines of surrealism.[122]

All this has a disturbingly modern (literary) sound to it, in spite of the quarter of a century that has elapsed. In the "Prolegomena to a Third Manifesto or Not," which appeared several months later, he fills in the missing gaps somewhat: "Not only must the exploitation of man by man cease, but also that of man by the so-called 'God,' of absurd and provoking memory. . . . Man, with his arms and equipment, must join the army of Man."[123] Man is more important than ideas, more important than success or favor, however appealing they may be: "Now after twenty years, as in my youth, I am obliged to denounce all conformism, and specifically an overly obvious surrealist conformism. [. . . ] In 1942 more than ever, the principle of *opposition* must be strengthened. All ideas which triumph are doomed."[124] Even to the apocalyptic tone, the Breton of the war years was what he had always been, only now he had a more frightening setting, and the death of Trotsky and Freud to look back on, and the evident dissolution of a once close-knit group.

Within days after the close of the New York International Surrealist Exhibition (Oct. 14-Nov. 7, 1942), Germany put an end to the fiction of an independent France by occupying the Free Zone.[125] "With few exceptions," wrote Tristan Tzara after the war, all surrealist activity in Paris came to a halt in 1943: unity was achieved, but "in the ranks of the Resistance."[126] The war years in France were hardly the time to plan utopias or elaborate revolutionary projects. With the liberation of Paris in August 1944, Breton along with thousands of other refugees made plans to return and pick up such pieces as still existed. A Brave New World was waiting just beyond the horizon. That is what Breton had always preached, and in his own way had striven for. Perhaps it was now at hand.

*Qui vive?* But there was almost no answer. Several painters, notably Ernst, and a handful of little-known writers. The old guard was gone, some dead in the war, such as Desnos and Pierre Unik, others now firmly committed to other masters. A new movement now held the stage, it too, as Dada and surrealism before it, a product of war. It, too, spoke with deep feeling about the corruption of the past and the necessity for commitment. But where surrealism had sought its inspiration within, existentialism had its eyes firmly fixed on the world of external reality. Anguish was something to be overcome, not cultivated: it was a sort of initiation rite through which every bourgeois would have to go before he could attain the peace that came with revolutionary commitment. Liberty was another peculiarity of man. He was condemned to it; but the simplest solution to *that* problem was to place the liberty on the altar of some cause, preferably the Revolution. That would take care of both liberty and anguish, and make you feel good all over. It is all so true, even if the inner man tends to be overlooked and there is some question as to which revolutionary party merits your support. But Sartre and Camus had spent the war in France, and their voices were those of the younger generation. After some two months in Haiti, where his friend Pierre Mabille was cultural attaché, Breton arrived back in France in the spring of 1946, prestigious but alone.[127] Opposed to him politically, as ever, was the victorious Communist Resistance organization (Aragon, Eluard, Tzara, et al.); philosophically, there was the rising existentialist current; poetically, there was an understandable public indifference to prewar experimentation—except as a historical phenomenon. In a sense Breton represented "the good old days." It would take a while before that image could be corrected.

For the first year after his return to Paris, Breton was as unarmed and defenseless as ever he had been in the New World. In financial straits, having neither organization nor periodical at his disposal (it was out of the question to resuscitate the ephemeral F.I.A.R.I.), his principal supporter, the surrealist activist Benjamin Péret, obliged to remain in Mexico until late 1947 (he lacked sufficient funds to leave), Breton was scarcely in a position to make his voice heard. All the more welcome, therefore, were periodicals such as *Les Quatre vents*, which helped keep the names of surrealists and sometime surrealists before the public eye, and the occasional manifestation, whatever its purpose, that would bring together the literary lights of *Tout Paris*.[128] The old idealism, however, and the tartness of expression which regularly gave the movement its distinctive form were not long in coming to the fore. The guidelines followed were in a sense prewar, in a larger sense as old as the history of man: liberty from oppression (man-made or divine); the intrinsic fraternity of all men everywhere against their common enemies (the human condition, bounded by a double eternity, is no respecter of color, religion, or national origin); and the inviolable right of the individual to speak and write as he sees fit, under the sole direction of his conscience and intelligence (what Gide had termed *authenticity*).

In April 1947, some four months after the negotiations between France and the newly proclaimed government of Vietnam had collapsed, the surrealists once again raised their voices to oppose colonialism in the tract *Liberté est un mot vietnamien*. The names might change, Ho Chi Minh replace Abd-el-Krim, but the situation was essentially the same as it had been some twenty years before: the Brave New World had a curiously familiar face.[129] Independence is met with pacification, liberty with property rights—and for eight years the battle would rage. To their amused and cautious peers the surrealists offered the curious picture of spectres from a bygone age propounding moral verities to a society imbued with the logic of the *raison d'état*: they were morally right, but the world was not, never had been, and was not likely to be. The surrealist revolution of dream in action, transforming both the inner man in the direction of ever greater awareness of his potential and the outer world to an acceptance of individual and collective experimentation, was an apocalyptic menace to the status quo.[130] Fortunately, they were few and unarmed. The Establishment had seen their kind before in the group around Charles Fourier, for example, in the previous century, and no harm had come of it.

Hounded by the twin horror of ineffectualness and compromise, the fear of becoming a debating society with high principles and the parallel fear of being obliged to compromise those principles for the sake of some effective action, the surrealists rapidly found themselves isolated from their more practical cousins in politics, for whom compromise was a way of life.[131] Their disclaimers notwithstanding, they were a small group of *purs* in an impure world, calling the tired masses to join them in principled revolt. As might be expected, the Communists were their principal *bêtes noires*, representing as they did not only a rival force but also a constant temptation to compromise their principles for the sake of some questionable short-range goal. Given the troubled climate of the times—the cold war, the threat of the bomb, Europe on its knees economically, and France still fighting in the jungles of Vietnam—it was almost inevitable that the surrealists would reach for straws.

One of those straws was Garry Davis' Citizens of the World movement.[132] On May 25, 1948, the twenty-six-year-old ex-G.I. Garry Davis, then living in France, renounced his American citizenship to become, as he put it, a citizen of the world—and, worse yet, invited others to join him. People are good, he seemed to say; only governments are bad. If enough people could get together and refuse to follow the dictates of narrow nationalism, then indeed we might have the Brave New World for which so much blood had been shed and which the cold war was daily making less likely. When his visa expired in August of that year, the French government quite happily asked him to leave: if he was going to cause an international scandal, let him do it in the U.S.A. Davis, however, had other views, and dressed in his military field jacket and armed with a sleeping bag he took refuge in the United Nations headquarters (the Palais de Chaillot) in Paris, where he stayed until he received assurance that he would not be summarily expelled from the country. One of his more publicized exploits was his interruption of the proceedings of the General Assembly (November 19, 1948) to bring his message directly to the attention of the delegates gathered there: internationalism would have to replace nationalism if the world was to be spared another holocaust. It was apparently this gesture—a dream in action—that convinced Breton and his group to lend their support.[133] Nor were they alone, for at one time the movement numbered some 400,000 members![134] Inevitably, in a group so numerous and so widespread—requests to join had come from throughout the world, including from countries behind the Iron Curtain—conflicting attitudes were not unknown. What finally drove the surrealists from Davis' entourage—if we exempt his inability to exercise any effective control over the unwieldy mass—was an apparently minor detail, minor to anyone but a surrealist. Davis had gone to the Cherche-Midi prison, in Paris, to protest the imprisonment of a conscientious objector, a certain Jean-Bernard Moreau. With sleeping bag and field jacket he intended to repeat his gesture of the Palais de Chaillot. Attempting to wrest from the French government a law recognizing conscientious objection was, however, quite a comedown from the exemplary call for World Citizenship of the previous year, and even more troubling, he willingly accepted the support of a number of ministers. This is why when Breton was asked to speak at a meeting called by several left-wing groups to protest the government's policy of imprisoning conscientious objectors, he took the opportunity to warn those assembled against Garry Davis' recent activities. So strong was the feeling for Davis that when the anarchist weekly, *Le Libertaire*, printed the text of Breton's intervention several days later it felt obliged to precede it with a disclaimer.[135] The marriage of World Citizen and surrealist had lasted less than a year, with no indication that either side had had any enduring effect on the other. If there is serious doubt that Davis would ever have become a so-called tool of the reaction, which was what Breton feared, there can be no doubt that their views on organized religion were radically dissimilar.[136] One of the underlying resemblances between the surrealists and Garry Davis' movement was their inability to keep their attention fixed on any immediately accessible, short-range goal. While the surrealists could publish tract after tract, and Davis sleep-in night after night, they were both easily distracted. One broadside per subject seemed to suffice for Breton, and then his attention was claimed by other matters, which in their turn would each receive a personal pat on the back. Davis, too, if we can believe Breton, rapidly lost track of the main issues, the "big" issues, and was sidetracked into the back alleys of conscientious-objection-for-religious-reasons. Neither was ready for the plodding, organizational work necessary to establish any mass movement. Breton, especially, preferred the rarified atmosphere of proclamation and pronouncement, and then, like some nimble mountain goat, on to another peak. The world, as far as he was concerned, had been no gainer by its drudges.

The major tenets of surrealism, both in the social arena and in literature, were fixed before World War II. While a given situation might require a restatement in somewhat different terms, the underlying principles remained unchanged. What had changed, radically, was the society in which they operated. Before the war they were the young mavericks of good family speaking up, in the best verbally revolutionary tradition. After the war they were upstaged by the new generation of existentialists and *lettristes*.[137] The *engagement* of the former recalled Gide's and the surrealists' *authenticity*, but put to the acid test of immediate commitment. In this, Sartre brings to mind Pierre Naville of an earlier day, with all due regard for the new philosophical superstructure. The *lettristes*, on the other hand, were the new literary experimenters, and they had the firm intention of replacing their now established elders at the very tip of the avant-garde.[138] Politically, Breton had nothing to offer that was not also available elsewhere, other than his own personal leadership and the assurance that his movement was not exclusively political. It would thus appeal, in theory, to those who liked their politics in a surrealist casserole, a small casserole, where each bean knew its neighbor. As Camus once put it: "Unlimited revolt, complete insubordination, systematic sabotage, humor and the cult of the absurd, surrealism is fundamentally the continual questioning of everything."[139] This is fine, he implies, but it is not enough.[140]

Following a brief association with the weekly *Arts*, the surrealists—still lacking a magazine of their own—moved over to *Le Libertaire*, a publication of the Anarchist Federation. There, between mid-October 1951 and the end of January 1953, they kept their name before the public by means of a weekly "billet surréaliste." The subjects treated, which ranged from art to literature and philosophy, included a series by Péret on "La Révolution et les syndicats" (June, July, Aug. 1952).[141] The collaboration ceased shortly after they succeeded in founding their own review, *Médium, informations surréalistes*, in November 1952, under the direction of one of their younger members, Jean Schuster.[142] By this time the crisis occasioned by the so-called *affaire* Pastoureau (or Carrouges), which had flared briefly the previous year and had led to a number of defections, had quieted down to where the group could once again concern itself wholly with external matters.[143] Against all odds, against enemies literary and political, and in a rapidly changing world which seemed to mock their principles, the surrealists continued to propound to an ever-growing audience their sybilline message of a generation ago: "Surrealism," wrote Breton at the end of 1953, "is the meeting point of the temporal aspect of the world and of eternal values: love, liberty, and poetry."[144] One year later, in the last of his "manifestos," he opens with the phrase, "It is now public knowledge that surrealism, as an organized movement, was born of a major attack on language."[145] Social involvement and the attitude of permanent political nonconformism came later. Perhaps nowhere, however, are the bursts of surrealist enthusiasm and suspicion more evident than in the area of politics. When Pierre Mendès-France, for example, was attempting to put into action his pragmatic policies—the armistice in Indo-China, independence for Tunisia, and the rest—the surrealists saw in him an anachronistic phenomenon, albeit a sympathetic one, for his conservative background was not designed to cheer the true revolutionary.[146] Had he mouthed revolutionary slogans—and failed—he would undoubtedly have had their wholehearted support. The true believer sees enemies everywhere outside the chosen clique.

But the surrealist fervor, suspicious though it might on occasion be, was very real. The Algerian crisis, which came to the surface on November 1, 1954, only months after the Indochinese conflict appeared to have been settled, offered them still another opportunity to demonstrate this, as did the Hungarian uprising of October 1956. If they were far more convincing in their defense of the Hungarian rebels, it was because the situation seemed far simpler: freedom fighters against Soviet oppression.[147] The Algerian conflict presented no such clear-cut opposition. On the one hand it was a national war of liberation, on the other it was a "pacification" of a rebellious part of France. While "pacification" was anathema to the surrealists, so was a narrowly conceived nationalism. If that were not sufficiently disturbing, there were two other factors to be considered, one historical, the other human. Algeria had never been a nation and had no national tradition, as did, say, Tunisia and Morocco. While this did not exclude the possibility (or desirability) of her becoming a nation, the argument for "liberation" was not thereby strengthened. On the human side, opposite eight million Moslem Algerians there lived more than one million indigenous Europeans—one of whom, incidentally, was Camus—who had been there for generations and considered Algeria their home, and *they* had no desire to break away from France. It was civil war in two senses: the Algerian territory against the central power, and Algerian against Algerian. This is why, when the surrealist group denounced the Algerian war, they hesitated to offer a solution. They might call for a cease fire, or say "all honor to Messali Hadj" (one of the moderates! not Ben Bella, the leader of the F.L.N.), but would go no further.[148] Even the famous *manifeste des 121*, of which Breton was one of the original signers, with Sartre and others, called for nothing more than a form of passive resistance; it did not propose any specific solution.[149]

In the past decade the surrealist revolution has been well served by its periodicals. From the striking *Le Surréalisme, même* (Oct. 1956-Spring 1959), to the modest *BIEF* (Nov. 1958-Apr. 1960) and the more substantial *La Brèche*, which ceased publication in November 1965, politics has been as vital a part of the movement as poetry—perhaps even more so, if one is to judge by the space alloted.[150] If it is less the practice of politics than the theory, indeed less theory than exhortation, that is because the surrealists are not a political party and have no intention of becoming one. But as a self-proclaimed moral force they will be heard, in politics as elsewhere. Part of the explanation for this continuity of political interest lies in the composition of the present group. The original surrealists had, almost without exception, come to the movement from a literary background: they had been poets before they became surrealists, and they were surrealists before they turned revolutionaries. The new group, in the main, appears to have come to surrealism from a desire for social reform, a sort of Camus-like *révolte*: poetry, to them, is an afterthought rather than the point of departure it was to their elders. I think here of Jean Schuster, Gérard Legrand, José Pierre, Robert Benayoun, and Jean-Louis Bédouin, and of the second series of *Médium* (Nov. 1953-Jan. 1955), composed of games, interviews, criticism, announcements and pronouncements, but no poetry. There are, of course, those who are primarily creative writers, such as André Pieyre de Mandiargues, Joyce Mansour, Jean-Claude Barbé, but they are clearly exceptions not only in number but also in frequency of appearance. What was once the movement of a group of writers disillusioned with literature has become the movement of a group of intellectual independents disillusioned with the present social scene. While both used literature, it was a vital arm for one, and it is no more than a useful adjunct for the other.

Marxist in orientation, openly favorable to Trotsky since 1938, but critical of the several other groups which also claim to derive from this *passant considérable*, the surrealists, in their integrity, have drawn swords against every major political party in France. Having no large following and refusing to proselytize, at best they could function as gadflies—and gadflies are rarely welcome. Invariably in the minority and having no effective power, they were never responsible for decisions taken elsewhere by others. While their signatures might be useful on some joint declaration, there was little reason to consult them on major policy decisions. In literature they had shot their bolt; in politics they never had one. What one can say in their defense is that they early recognized their limitations and tried on numerous occasions to ally themselves with the major party having revolutionary pretensions. Rebuffed, they sought in vain some more hospitable haven. Dante once addressed to Francesca a line not inappropriate to the surrealists: "Francesca, i tuoi martiri / A lagrimar mi fanno tristo e pio" (*Inferno, V*).

# V: In the Critical Eye

O wad some Pow'r the giftie gie us
To see oursels as ithers see us!
—Robert Burns, "To a Louse."

To put it quite simply, art is only a stepping-stone to reality; it is the vestibule in which we undergo the rites of initiation. Man's task is to make of himself a work of art. The creations which man makes manifest have no validity in themselves; they serve to awaken, that is all.

—Henry Miller, *Sunday after the War* (New York: New Directions, 1944), p. 155.

"The most revolutionary poetic experiment in a capitalist régime [has] been unquestionably, in France and perhaps throughout Europe, the dada-surrealist experiment, in that it has tended to destroy all the artistic myths which, for centuries, permitted the ideological and economic exploitation of painting, sculpture, and literature. . . . "[1] Such was the view of at least certain members of the Communist-dominated Association des Ecrivains et Artistes Révolutionnaires in early 1934, during one of the brief reconciliations between the surrealists and their sometime Communist allies. When due allowance is made for the ideological bias of the speakers, there can be little question about the underlying accuracy of that statement. In surrealist hands the myth of the talented artist gives way to that of the "exteriorization of libido"; the surrealist painter, instead of fixing his attention on external reality, looks inward for inspiration, where the camera cannot reach; the writer's task is no longer to add beauty to the world but rather to turn his desires into reality.[2] Their increased consciousness will show us the way to expand ours and thus eventually transform the humdrum into the ideal. To the surrealists an objective reality lies just beyond revelation, and it is senseless to be paralyzed by the endless relativity of conventional illusions when a provocative world lies on the other side of the veil. Whereas the artists had formerly been slaves to reality, they were now pioneer explorers of the unknown, pushing aside the dry leaves of conformity. If there are but "two ways of life in the world," as one historian claimed, "two existential situations assumed by man in the course of history," one *sacred* and the other *profane,* Breton and his followers have clearly chosen the former, the way of the Outsider, despite a tradition many centuries old in the West favoring the latter.[3] To this, in part, must be attributed the remarkably bad press surrealism has had almost from its inception.

Much of the criticism recalls the stunned silence of the adolescent who fears for his idols: it affords more information about the person affected than about the prime mover. And as such it is futile criticism, for it neither holds a mirror to the phenomenon nor does it cast any light. This we shall ignore.[4] Some critics, however, among them Sartre, Camus, Robbe-Grillet, and the sociologist Roger Caillois, with the objectivity which distance often lends, have highlighted what is valuable in surrealism, what has entered the mainstream of French culture, and what has not. With this we will concern ourselves.

"Literature as Absolute Negation becomes Antiliterature," says Sartre with reference to surrealism, "which is the most literary form writing can take."[5] This may be so, but it is not self-evident, and it would be a mistake to confuse the evangelical rhetoric of an official existentialist with literary realities. For Sartre literature can have only one function, to serve in the war of liberation against social injustice and class oppression, and only one attitude, total, responsible commitment to the revolution.[6] The controversy is not over goals but between modes of attack: Sartre's objectives are also Breton's, but while one limited his attention exclusively to the social revolution, assuming that the inner transformation would come about inevitably, rationally, and in due course, the other could not so easily abandon the yearnings in his heart for the strictures of his mind. Yet the two are remarkably close on many points. When Sartre speaks of man as being "condemned to liberty," he is advancing one of the three major tenets of the surrealists.[7] When he regularly uses the love situation to illustrate his characters' "authenticity" (a combination of sincerity, honesty, and responsibility), he inadvertently acknowledges that his predecessors were quite right to stress the importance of passion and its revelatory potential. Where he parts company with them is in his refusal to attribute to poetry the same values they do.[8] On closer examination, however, his objections appear to be founded on a misconception of what surrealist poetry is. Sartre's view is the fashionable one, though rarely phrased so baldly: literature must *lead somewhere,* must serve a purpose in improving society; poetry, on the other hand, is usually concerned with the individual. The complex design of intentions and effectiveness is here reduced to a familiar if not terribly consoling simplicity. Moreover, the objection does not apply to a goodly portion of surrealist writing. One of Breton's basic propositions has always been that "poetry must lead somewhere," must have a purpose—and that purpose is regularly defined as the transformation of both the individual and society.[9] If this is not always illustrated as clearly as it might be in surrealist poetry, it is because theory and practice never completely overlap: not all experiments are successful. The surrealist attempts to plumb the depths of the unconscious in search of some concealed verity did not all succeed, any more so than, say, Sartre's own novels are adequate illustrations of his literary theories. Sometimes gains in range and daring are offset by a loss of surefootedness. Nor is Sartre especially convincing when he says that the typical poetic attitude is to consider "words as things rather than as signs."[10] For a surrealist such a distinction would be inconceivable, as all words, all phrases, are two-sided: from one angle they are opaque, "things," from the other they are transparent, a window on another reality. Word-juggling, for example, is at least as peculiar to Nathalie Sarraute and Robbe-Grillet as to anyone else. What Sartre has succeeded in doing is to propose a partial analysis of poetry—an analysis appropriate to symbolist poetry, especially as typified by Mallarmé—for a complete one. While symbolist and surrealist poetry often resemble one another in their hermeticism, that is at best a negative similarity. It is probably a good thing that Sartre did not join the movement in the late twenties, as he must surely have been tempted, for he would have quickly been expelled as a deviationist![11]

When Camus suggests that "the absurd is the confrontation of the irrational and man's tremendous desire for clarity," he underscores the opposition between a social reality which resists reduction to a series of hard and fast propositions and man's longing for order. He is also, perhaps unwittingly, rephrasing an older surrealist antinomy between the individual's desire for perfection and an imperfect world which refuses it.[12] "The absurd," as he later remarks, "depends for its existence as much on man as on the world"; "it is in neither of the two elements being compared but is rather a product of their confrontation."[13] A dreary succession of just wars and of high-minded pacifications has done nothing to weaken that statement. Nor is it without interest that Camus' meditation on the absurd in human existence leads him to a tripartite conclusion: the necessity of revolt against a status quo which would reduce man to a cog in the social machine; the importance of remaining sufficiently free to adapt to rapidly changing situations; and, of no less moment, the significance of passion, without which the first two would become bloodless and turn man into an inhuman *cogito*.[14] What is lacking in both Sartre and Camus, if one wished to fit them into a surrealist mold, is the stress on *revelation* and on the power of *poetry* to elicit it. This is not to say that they have imitated or borrowed from their predecessors, but rather that concepts first developed by surrealists had to such an extent become part of the culture that extremely sensitive writers could reflect surrealist attitudes without being consciously aware of it.

It is common knowledge that for a Communist of the Zdanov and post-Zdanov period "literature is morality in action."[15] Its goal, the amelioration of man's lot, happiness for one and all in a classless society.[16] At no time should literature be an escape from reality, even under the pretext of seeking some "higher reality."[17] In simplified form, one either writes for the revolution or (perhaps unconsciously) against it; one either directly attacks the problems of reality or one's writing is frivolous, not to say counterrevolutionary. Aragon stated this very succinctly shortly after he joined the Party:

> It is time to put an end to the look-at-me-how-sad-I-am style of writing. It is time to put an end to both individual and group hallucinations, to the partiality shown the subconscious over the sense of sight, hearing, smell, taste and touch, to sex as a system and to delirium as a representation of reality. It is time to put an end to the baroque, the "modern style" and the flea market— the final resources of sophisticated boredom and of the pessimism derived from too much leisure. It is time to put an end to phony heroism, fake purity, the tinsel flashiness of a poetry more given to finding its material in the aurora borealis, agates, statues in parks, parks surrounding castles, castles of bibliophilic Lords-of-the-Manor. . . . What we need is a return to reality.[18]

It is difficult to believe that this is the same person who had earlier written "Une Vague de rêves."[19] Had Aragon in some strange fashion forgotten what he once knew, or had this new commitment suddenly

made everything he had once believed in seem shabby? A new perspective will occasionally work wonders—as will a new boss.

Alain Robbe-Grillet is in some ways more sophisticated than either
his existential or Communist contemporaries—especially in his literary criticism. But he is not beyond giving the impression of opening up virgin territory by discarding "the old myths of psychological
analysis."[20] Years before, however, the surrealists had rejected that
type of causal explanation, "the reign of logic," as offering only
partial, tendentious truths.[21] "Imagination," suggested Breton, "is
now perhaps almost ready to take over."[22] Not any imagination, but
a *verbal* one, for as Aragon had pointed out, "all of surrealism sup-
ports the proposition that there is no thought outside of language."[23]
Robbe-Grillet's insistence upon presenting only the facts, only what
is actually seen, heard, and touched—a sort of ultimate reality—inevitably brings to mind the surrealists' scorn of the conventionally
ordered, carefully explained novels of the day, and the urgent need
they sensed to unveil a new concrete reality, one in line with their
"absolute nominalism."[24] While Robbe-Grillet's amorphous characters
do act out a story, that story no longer has "the certainty, the assurance, the innocence" of comparable works of the past.[25] If his tales
have any subject, as he took pains to point out, it is the play of the
*imagination*, the delight in *invention*: They thus offer in nondoctrin-
aire fashion a surrealist revelation, *le merveilleux*.[26] Robbe-Grillet
would of a certainty object to this identification, for it assumes that
man is at the center of the world, a view he finds untenable. The
surrealists, on the other hand, never questioned this possibility: they
*were* at the center of the world (as was everyone else), striving to
resuscitate that mythical time when being and reality were one.
Theirs was a cosmic responsibility, in contrast with the narrowly individual one of their contemporaries. Yet, oddly enough, Robbe-
Grillet's distant objectivity brings him to within a hairsbreadth of
surrealist subjectivity.

   Several examples may make this clearer. His affirmation that the
principal condition of art, without which art could not exist, is its
*freedom* (for which read noncommitment, or Gide's *disponibilité*)
is not without recalling his transcendental forerunners.[27] When
he remarks that at the source of all literary creation is a "rhythm, a
general plan, words and grammatical constructions," he brings to
mind a statement made years before by Breton's one-time mentor
(Valéry) and later given more stylish trappings in the surrealist

definition of objective chance.[28] What if we were to suggest that "the true writer has nothing to say," Robbe-Grillet puckishly asks, "but only a way of saying it?"[29] A surrealist would not find that offensive, for at the origin of all art (as he sees it) there lies nothing more than a chance encounter or a formless desire to plumb the unknown. That, to the surrealists, was the way of invention.[30]

Where Robbe-Grillet and the surrealists part company is on the question of the image. Almost from the very beginning the surrealists saw in the metaphor the key to *le merveilleux*: its proper use could wrest revelation from indifferent matter. "The less the two items compared have in common and the more precise they are," wrote Breton, following Pierre Reverdy, "the more powerful will be the resulting image."[31] The analogy had almost magical properties. It was "what made the world go round. . . [especially when] it was unexpected, a surprise."[32] Marinetti had earlier said much the same thing when he defined the analogy as "the deep love that brings together distant things, things apparently disparate and hostile," and offered as examples the comparison of a fox terrier with the telegraph, or with boiling water.[33] It is sometimes overlooked that, several years before Apollinaire elaborated his theory of surprise, his friend Marinetti had given it a place of honor in the Futurist pantheon: "We detest what is old and already known. We love only what is new, unexpected."[34] In this he follows Baudelaire who in order to heighten the sensation of beauty was not above adding "an element of surprise."[35] With a little effort, as Baudelaire and Swedenborg recognized, all things could be transformed: a color might evoke an aroma, or a woman an angel. Breton, combining Charles Fourier and Baudelaire, considered the extravagant image to be an objectivization of the Unconscious, a gift of the nether gods. This is what Michel Beaujour saw so clearly (and surrealistically) when he spoke of "the new cosmogony, where the anthropocentric view of the world is bypassed for an analogic vision whose principal purpose is to encourage a humanized nature and a 'naturalized' man to converse together, free from hindrance, in exalting clarity."[36]

To Robbe-Grillet, however, this confusion of man with nature is deliberate deception and nothing good can come of it. "The metaphor, whose sole purpose is presumably to express a simple comparison, in fact does something more: it surreptitiously introduces into the text a breath of sympathy (or antipathy), which is its real purpose. . . . The descriptive value of an image is a mask behind which its real meaning hides."[37] What Robbe-Grillet has in mind is that a phrase of the type, "The village was *huddled* in the valley," says far more about the village and its inhabitants than "The village *was* in the valley"—and that were it not for the availability of the term "huddled," the location of the village might never have been specified. This type of pathetic fallacy, if we can believe our critic, is far more common than a summary examination would reveal. We end up, ultimately, describing ourselves rather than the rest of the world, our own subjectivity rather than *things*.[38] How simple it is to see a consoling bond between man and things, to have the secret of the universe in our hands, when our very language encourages it. There is no longer a *human* nature peculiar to man, but a *universal* nature common to all things, animate and inanimate, past and present alike —and why not future? This unity, to borrow a term from Camus,[39] is exactly what the surrealists had proclaimed. With the advent of the concrete metaphor they would all turn into concrete angels.[40] Robbe-Grillet, undoubtedly influenced by his existentialist contemporaries, preferred to distinguish people from things, and to distrust any theory which posited a universe governed by the pathetic fallacy. "All analogies are dangerous," according to Robbe-Grillet, "and perhaps the most dangerous are those in which the human parallel is not explicit."[41] The surrealists, in the other camp, have no fear of seeing man everywhere: the stars beckon to him, the Tarot cards speak to him, all Nature awaits his glance. This metaphysical pact between Man and the Universe circumscribes the surrealists' activity and, while suggesting that his desires have a reality quite as substantial as the things which surround him, prevents him from *using* the world as it is.

The overt humanization of Nature may in origin have been no more than a series of rhetorical figures (although there is little evidence for this assumption), but constant reiteration has succeeded in giving them demiurgic solidity. If all is one and one is all, as the romantic surrealist suggests, then the impossibility of joining the *disjecta membra* of reality into an all-encompassing ecstatic atom becomes tragic. The oracularly inclined invoke the androgyne, but man and woman remain stubbornly apart; the rebel assures his audience that he will walk the streets till he encounters and wins the mysterious *femme-enfant* (or *sorcière*), be she called Mélusine or something more modern.[42] Should the mysterious *femme-enfant* maliciously refuse to drop into the wavering net of chance, it is a tragedy, and the disappointed fisher will check his surrealist guide to be sure he has not inadvertently violated some basic rule. Where the surrealist sees universal tragedy, Robbe-Grillet sees only the wrong questions being asked. "Where is Mélusine?" might better be replaced with a more fundamental question, "Is there a Mélusine?"[43] The tragedy of her disappearance would then be reduced to its proper dimensions, quite as poignant, but clearly based on an illusion. When an invocation goes unheeded, it may indeed imply a tragic (if provisional) solitude, or it may simply be that there is no one on the other side of the wall. In spite of numerous proclamations on the importance of liberty, the surrealists would bind man to dreams as others would to machines, and it is not clear which in the long run would prove more depressing. (The supply of well-preserved medieval ideas in surrealism is close to inexhaustible.) What they succeeded in doing was to increase arbitrarily the interior distance between desire and realization. No realization was *the* Realization, hence the search could continue indefinitely. Perhaps the best reply to this attitude was offered by Robbe-Grillet when he proposed less metaphysics and more description, but *precise* rather than metaphorical description, for all comparisons contain an element of error (except a mathematical proportion) and their virtue is more persuasive than factual.[44]

In one of his more recent articles, Robbe-Grillet turned his attention to Raymond Roussel, whose influence, he reminds us, has exercised a strange fascination on several generations of writers and who, he adds, is one of "the direct precursors of the modern novel."[45] Given the surrealists' canonization of Roussel some forty years ago,[46] Robbe-Grillet's comments on the same gentleman may well repay examination. He recognizes that by all conventional criteria Roussel "has nothing to say and says it poorly," his writings have no story line, and the style is both flat and colorless.[47] A work, in a word, likely to be opaque and unrewarding. But this opaqueness can with equal justice be termed *transparence*, for his style has no hidden meaning, offers no symbol—is pure description.[48] In a sense it is this very lack of meaning outside the context of the spectacle that makes Roussel so difficult to follow. His works are self-contained; they are an "ideal" world having no need of any other reality. Or as Robbe-Grillet put it so nicely, Roussel's writings on occasion recall "a meaningless gesture."[49] We know, of course, as does Robbe-Grillet, that Roussel considered writing a game, the purpose of which was to get from the opening sentence to the final one (the two being phonetically identical except for one element, which element would significantly change the meaning of the two sentences) by means of stories whose sole function was to fill the gap between A and Z.[50] This experimentation in poetic futility, evoking both *Les Champs magnétiques* and the *lettristes,* is what so appeals to Robbe-Grillet.[51] Only one of Breton's group, Benjamin Péret, moved with some consistency in that direction. His work recalls that of Roussel in overt density (his words mean exactly what they say in context, only there is no meaningful context) and in its lack of a story line that purports to reflect reality. Like Roussel, Péret has created a universe parallel to the one in which we live; it rivals it without either illuminating or reproducing it. The Roussel-Péret world represents a new type of creation, in much the same way that a nonrepresentational painting or free-form sculpture does. What must not be lost sight of, however, at the risk of being thought "deader than a fossil" (Rimbaud's phrase),[52] is that mundane reality is sufficiently flexible to assimilate these unlikely forms, so that the context-free surrealism of yesterday has become the context-sensitive realism of today.

The most cogent, if sympathetic, criticism of surrealism came from Roger Caillois, a one-time member of the group.[53] His is the conventional wisdom, theirs the bold hypotheses about shrouded occurrences. Where Caillois saw an extravagant lyricism composed of naive confessions, forced imagery, and pretentious terminology, the surrealists beheld a self-granted mandate to transform man and his world, a mandate whose source and wisdom could not be questioned.[54] Where Caillois saw sincerity replacing effort and merit, and inspiration (the call of the prophet) supplanting the discipline of the poet, Breton could counter that literature was less his goal than was knowledge, than was the discovery of the "point where life and death, the real and the imaginary, past and future, the communicable and the incommunicable, high and low cease to be seen as contradictory."[55] Where Caillois stressed the need for discipline—"intelligence and will," in his definition—and insisted that poetry is not "magic, mysticism or music,"[56] Breton could reply that from time immemorial poetry has vaunted its oracular pretentions. On the seas of chance, and given the zigzag paths of human possibility, the surrealists found more profound truths in dreams than in lucidity. In some ways theirs was the faith of a latter-day "natural man" divested of the sophistication of centuries. Too impatient to seek truth along well trod paths, they preferred to elicit revelation (and shake their boredom) by means of disconcerting dreams and problematic images. They went hunting these wearing the mask of an outcast, but all the while sure that a halo rested on their brows. The mask they wore soon grew to fit them, just as the goals they sought soon took on the shape of wisdom born thousands of years before the oldest Frenchman.

Without its saving empiricism, surrealism would rapidly have become an empty ideology. Thanks to it, Breton and his fellow adepts succeeded in opening (and keeping open) a number of windows on the unknown which more disciplined authors were incapable of forcing. Such creatures of habit are we. What is principally objectionable to Caillois is less surrealism as such than the possibility of fake surrealism and the quantity of doubtful literature bearing the movement's *imprimatur*.[57] To this there can be no answer, for the risk is always there. Nor would it do to quote Melville that "failure is the true test of greatness," for failure is other things too.[58] Breton, however, like Camus' delicate murderer, would prefer to honor the daring failure over the (unprincipled) safe success. Continual success indicates that a man knows his powers, and perhaps knows them to be small. This sort of myopia was never one of Breton's weaknesses.

The Communist, the existentialist, the formalist, and the former surrealist do not exhaust the range of attitudes toward surrealism, but they can serve as a first step toward seeing the movement as others saw it. In the early chapters we tried to keep to a surrealist perspective, to see the whale from the inside, with only occasional excursions outside to check our bearings. Here the *modus operandi* is reversed, and we must expect that the picture will be somewhat different, especially when personal or theoretical rivalries are also at issue. The cosmic liberty of the surrealists was but so much talk to the suspicious Communists, who saw bourgeois idealism at the turn of each phrase. Breton, like Phèdre, carried with him the burden of a limiting past. Though nonbelievers, the surrealists were not without a religious behavior pattern, sometimes seen in their obeisance before the *deus absconditus,* the hidden God of mystics and mysteries, sometimes seen in their nod in the direction of the *fixed point,* the golden moment of truth which lies at the end of time. Their descent into the Unconscious was a latter-day initiation, a plunge into a personal Hell to do battle with personal monsters for the golden fleece of Truth. None of this was designed to change the Communist view that the surrealists were amateur revolutionaries and uncertain allies.

Much the same could be said for the existentialist reaction, if for the sake of simplicity Sartre and Camus may be lumped together. Those who see themselves destined to struggle against overwhelming odds in building a more just world are unlikely to be entranced when the Prophet of the Possessed arrives with suggestions for simplification and improvement. The way to cast light on the human predicament, as far as most revolutionaries are concerned, is to examine its intellectual—not its psychosexual—antecedents. Yet, as one of this century's most distinguished historians noted:

> One inevitable result of heightened psychological awareness is. . . a change of attitude toward so-called political ideas. To treat them as the offspring of pure reason would be to assign them a parentage about as mythological as that of Pallas Athene. What matters most is the underlying emotions, the music, to which ideas are a mere libretto, often of very inferior quality; and once the emotions have ebbed, the ideas established high and dry, become doctrine, or at best innocuous clichés.[59]

The world of values is a timeless world, hard, fixed, dead—something like a Tanguy landscape. Breton preferred the chaos of *sincerity*, the touchstone of surrealist experience as it is of religious experience. The surrealists hungered for sincerity—an inner response which is seen by others as authenticity—in an age which discourages it; their heroism as a consequence was thought to be a sham, the comic posturing of a slightly daft fool.

Art is normally considered a response to a desire for order and clarity, for permanence. It reflects a very special reality, one from which man is never completely absent. The very terms we use imply this: composition, style, arrangement, presentation, unity. Long before Robbe-Grillet, the surrealists refused the distortions of traditional order in their quest for a hidden reality. But true objectivity cannot exclude Man who is an integral part of the real world. The village the new novelist sees is a human village which cannot be reduced to its stones and streets. The reader, who sees himself in all the heroes and heroines, in all the weeping trees and stony silences, knows this. Take out the adjectives and he is still there—and the adjectives too, for the reader will insert them. Anthropomorphism lies impacted in the heart of every culture, of every complacency, a pocket of consoling reality. It is as much a part of life as the hunger for heroism, or the desire for escape. Objectivity will not remove the God Within who daily creates anew the world in His image. As

Colin Wilson put it, "One cannot *talk* about the real issues of life: one can only *show* them"—and that is what the surrealists attempt to do.[60]

In that web of fantasy and tongue-in-cheek sincerity that is Lautréamont's *Poésies,* the surrealists found two phrases which they chose to take at face value: "Not all the water in the ocean will remove a spot of intellectual blood"; "Poetry should be a communal affair, not an individual one."[61] The first, in its deliberate ambiguity, can be taken both as a rallying cry for intellectual honesty and as a warning to those who would tamper with the artist's freedom; the second, assuming it was meant to be taken seriously, permits a multitude of meanings ranging from communal writing of poetry (like the surrealist *cadavre exquis*) to the use of communal themes, or themes common to all mankind (like those found in the Unconscious), or even a Valéry-type interpretation: the poet may write what he wishes but it is the public who will determine what meaning his poetry will eventually have. In a sense all of surrealism is contained in those two phrases. While it would be repetitious to elaborate on them at length, a brief commentary may clarify some surrealist attitudes that are superficially contradictory. Lautréamont suggests that the poet occupies a unique position, that nothing can absolve him should he betray his trust. Nor can any crime committed against him be pardoned. He is, in a word, a man apart. Yet notwithstanding this uniqueness he is as nothing in the universe, for true poetry is not an individual matter. His poetry is not his, and hence should not concern him overly. Its sources are many; its themes universal; its style due to several hands. Stripped of all pretense, the way of poetry becomes the way of knowledge: it is not art and frivolity but science of a sort, like that later developed by Freud:

> To put it quite simply, [wrote Henry Miller, who was never formally a surrealist] art is only a stepping-stone to reality; it is the vestibule in which we undergo the rites of initiation. Man's task is to make himself a work of art. The creations which man makes manifest have no validity in themselves; they serve to awaken, that is all. And that, of course, is a great deal. But it is not the all. Once awakened, everything will reveal itself to man as creation. Once the blinders have been removed and the fetters unshackled, man will have no need to recreate through the elect cult of genius. Genius will be the norm.[62]

*That* is pure surrealism.

The Lautréamont-surrealist-Henry Miller type of universe is unlikely ever to materialize for reasons which have nothing to do with
the soundness of its theory or its desirability. It represents, after all,
one extreme of the pendulum's swing—in a way, the classical extreme, if one takes classicism to be the imposition of an internal vision on the outer world. The outer world is the raw material shaped
by a series of inner revelations. It goes without saying that only the
rare academic critic (and no surrealist!) would find this paradoxical
identification of surrealism with classicism acceptable; the majority
would claim quite properly that the products of surrealism are too
*agitated*, reflect too starkly the constant buffetings of the winds of
reality and revelation, and lack the harmony and factitious conclusions of what is normally called classical writing. Classicism, wrote
Henry Miller, "seeks the elevation of good taste, which is the apoth-
eosis of negation."[63] "The true poet is an awakener; he does not
promise bread and jobs. He knows that struggle and conflict are at
the very core of life; he does not offer himself as a balm. All ideas
of government fail insofar as they exclude the poet and the seer who
are one."[64] It would be difficult to find a surrealist who would disagree. Miller's quarrel with surrealism lies in another area; it is a
quarrel not with the theory but with the practice: surrealist works
lack "*guts and significance*."[65] Although the movement has a clear
revolutionary potential, it has never really been effective; if the surrealists write stimulating works, they have too much metaphysics in
them and not enough life.[66] Conscience-soothing fantasies, whether
of an absolute God or an absolute Unconscious, whether of the
brotherhood of man or some more elaborate political doctrine, cannot take the place of a full, forceful, effective life.[67] As Miller says,
"Below the belt all men are brothers," and it is presumably this
region—not the head—that should be cultivated.[68]

Automatic writing, perhaps the most controversial of surrealist
techniques, is both a means and an end. This duality has on occasion
given rise to confusion. It is a means toward a greater creative facility
in that it permits a close examination of the Unconscious, which to
the surrealists is the source of all inspiration. Whatever is dredged
up is valuable, regardless of its literary merit, for the primary purpose
of the technique is *to see what lies below*. Needless to say, this in
no way precludes *using* the finds of automatism—say, in a painting
or a poem. Any work so produced, in addition to whatever other
virtues it may possess, will be a mirror on the unknown. The sur-

realists, however, were not limited to this technique, nor were they obliged to use it in any given way or to any given degree. Even a critic like Rolland de Renéville, who is normally quite sensitive to things surrealist, was at one point led to see a change in the orientation of the movement because the text he was examining lacked the qualities he associated with pure automatic writing.[69] But unlike others, he was never tempted to toss the surrealists in the same hopper with Mallarmé, Proust, Gide, Valéry, and Giraudoux and charge them all with promoting the triumph of "the concept of pure literature"![70] If Breton sometimes writes like a Valéry gone beserk in the direction of a Madame Blavatsky, he at no point moves toward the art-for-art's-sake concept implied by "pure literature." Automatism was a science as much as an art form, and its practice had the double merit of revealing man to himself and casting light on a shifting substratum whose features were presumably common to many men. What artistic merit it had was *en plus,* if not *de trop.* Valéry claimed to feel aloof from his poetry *once it was written*: "My lines have the meaning the reader gives them. . . .It is an error contrary to the nature of poetry, and which would even be fatal to it, to claim that for each poem there is one and only one real meaning, corresponding or identical to some idea of the author."[71] Breton could answer with Rimbaud's phrase, "Je est un autre."[72] There is a difference between *transcribing* what you find (or pretending to), like Rimbaud and Breton, and admitting that a given artifact can have several meanings. The automatic poem has no meaning, any more than the meteor from outer space has one: they are marvelous relics from another world. If you know their language you can "read" them, or at least determine their component parts. Their "message" is their presence, and if they cannot be fitted into any existing frame of reference, it is the frame that will have to adjust.

Almost all ideologies overrate man's capacities to foresee the consequences of ideals imposed on reality. Surrealism was no exception. In literature, in politics, wherever it moved, the "organization"—to use Breton's Mafia-sounding term[73]—found it would have to compromise to exist. When obliged to modify a course of action, the group did so only with reluctance, normally refusing to admit that any change had occurred or discovering a justification for it in one of their early writings. They were touchy and proud, very sensitive to criticism, which is exactly what one would expect of a close-knit pioneering group. (Admissions of error are extraordinarily rare in their publications.) While it is true that surrealism—born of disappointment and disillusion, embracing the uprooted of all persuasions, driven by half-conscious desires, fears, and gusts of whimsy—was the movement of men seeking a new rallying point and new attachments, this information cannot be used to determine the value of what they attempted or accomplished. They reacted against cruelty, injustice, oppression, and nonsense, and that is to their credit. Their nostrums for freedom and the full life, while a very different matter, are by no means devoid of merit. They tried to understand, rather than accept things blindly like so many sheep. As an eminent Dutch historian commented: "To understand is a function of the mind which not only enriches the life of the individual, it is the very breath of the civilization we are called upon to defend."[74]

The surrealists were seekers more than finders. If a civilization is indeed known by the questions it asks and the clichés it coins, then the surrealists will have left an enduring mark. They delved into the Unconscious and its shifting swamps; they questioned the basic postulates of rationalism and humanism as few had done before; they attacked with both conviction and virulence the contemporary lack of candor, fake piety, pretentious rhetoric, evasive double-talk and innuendo; they took as their allies—their greatest cunning—virtue and sincerity, far more effective than vice and evasiveness in subduing the world and its principal stay, the moral code. What their works lack in traditional cadences and soothing images, they make up for in surprise and stimulation: the well-trod paths of the Luxemburg Gardens are abandoned for the rain forests of the Unknown. All is not ordered in their works—certainly not by traditional standards. Much is resistant to any conventional analysis or grouping. But the new, the different, the challenging have regularly been termed futile, meaningless, and immature—until such time as the novelty wore off and the web of civilization stretched to make room for the newcomers. In great part this has now taken place. Madison Avenue has popularized in thousands of variations the dreamlike insights of Dali and others. The movies and television have borrowed what they dared. The carefully worked plots of an earlier period are with greater frequency giving way to "pointless" autobiographical sketches—like *Le Paysan de Paris,* an exemplary travelogue in a surrealist church, where all the places visited have a certain sacred character, but where nothing *happens.* Baudelaire proposed a motto for this type of existence many years ago—as did Camus more recently—when he said that the only important thing in life was "to be a great man and a saint *to yourself.*"[75] The surrealists added to this Baudelaire's view on the "eternal superiority of the Dandy" who always faces outward and never forgets his public.[76] In this way their inner assurance of being at the center of the world would be constantly confirmed by the admiring glances of their audience.

It is a commonplace that, to a mystic, absolute liberty goes hand in hand with the destruction of the contingent world. The only way the individual can realize all his desires is to do away with the world as we know it, governed as it is by natural and social laws which invariably stand in the way. (Even the Indian mystic, who progressively eliminates his desires, eventually dissolves reality in Nirvana.) The surrealists, however, never ones to be chary of a paradox, claimed to walk in both directions at the same time. This in itself should have alerted those critics who saw the surrealists as sometime mystics or philosophical primitives that something was wrong.[77] There can be no doubt that the surrealists believed in liberty, which they sometimes termed absolute, and that they strove with all the means at their disposal for ever-greater freedom of expression. There is equally no doubt that they never *behaved* as mystics. If their opposition was to the *real* world, it was not with a view to replacing it with some world beyond. They sought a golden age, an Eden before the Fall, but in the here and now. Sex was sanctified, both for itself and for its presumed liberating powers: the taboos Freud, Sir James Frazer, and Havelock Ellis had so carefully described all apparently had a common source. The freedom they pursued was absolute only in that it would cut the bonds of custom and taboo, and enable man, released from the impedimenta of personal repressions and social prudery (prudence?), to materialize his desires. The Revolution would help by placing in positions of power those who (in theory) had most to gain from a change in regime. Once the economic bonds were loosened, could the others be far behind? Down would go the political and social myths propounded by a corrupt bourgeoisie; down would go the religious myths which lent divine support to oppression, guilt, and fear. And in their place would arise a new "collective myth" which, if nothing more, would at least have some "poetic justification" and aim at "the complete utilization of our psychic strength."[78] As far as Breton was concerned, man's role is to defend man, not God or the defunct social order.[79] If there is an absolute it is the individual man, and what he can become when he wrests from a reluctant society the liberty to move in the direction of Poetry and Love. The *real* life, the only one worth living, thus becomes the *surreal* life, founded on freedom and propelled toward a very special sort of goal, one which Nietzsche would have had little difficulty recognizing.[80]

The intimate sense of this goal—Poetry and Love—is not always easy to understand; and the present analysis is likely, at best, to be more convincing than conclusive. Freedom in the abstract is meaningless. Where there is no purpose, freedom is an empty word. In this sense Sartre is correct: freedom takes on shape only when you commit it. It is a coin on which is stamped, paradoxically enough, *engagement*. Surrealism's aim was for increased consciousness, the abolition of the frontiers between dream and reality *in favor of the latter*. In some ways it reminds one of Goethe and Nietzsche, Camus and Malraux. Not long ago, Colin Wilson put it this way: "I thought I had seen the final truth *that life does not lead to anything; it is an escape from something,* and the 'something' is a horror that lies on the other side of consciousness."[81] Having recognized the problem, the surrealists went on to propose a solution: rip away the veil that cuts the mind in half and by so doing transform the horror into revelation. But the veil has been there for quite some time, and while they might peer through it, they were never able to pull it aside completely. On the basis of what they saw, however, they were persuaded that Freud's description of the Unconscious was correct: it was a city dump of desires and libidinous caprices, the whole lot infested with the maggots of guilt. These couldn't be destroyed, but they were regularly pushed aside, forgotten. Both as an individual, and as a public health measure this forgotten area had to be cleansed, its relics aerated and subjected to a tonic sunbath. When the boundaries of the imagination were effectively pushed back, we would have a new world to examine and profit by. Love would no longer be a phenomenon regulated by society, but one affecting solely the individuals concerned. Poetry would be Play, by turns formal and investigative, whimsical and carefree, but always open to the revelations of chance. It is scarcely surprising that the society of the day took a dim view of the whole project. One could laugh or be shocked (both titillating experiences) at their play-paintings or play-sculpture; one could only mutter at the opaqueness of some of their writings. The former can be *seen* to be appreciated, for meaning has never been an indispensable part of painting or sculpture; the latter must be *understood*. But how does one understand *le merveilleux?* Expecting a description of the outside world, the public was quite unprepared for the surreal one with its regular confusion of dreams and reality, past and present, intention and accomplishment. It was, in fact, another world. And yet, where surrealism appears to be less informative, it often turns out to be more meaningful.

The surrealists joined the Communist Party because they saw in it an adjunct to their own revolutionary movement: the Party would prepare the terrain which they could then utilize. Once the social opposition to their goals were crushed, and the party of freedom installed, then, they felt, they could proceed with their investigations far more effectively. The true revolution, the radical one, the permanent one, was the surrealist revolution: the other, while important, did not really get to the heart of the matter. The proletariat could not be said to be truly liberated until it had also thrown off the binding dogmas of the bourgeoisie. A revolution whose sole purpose was to raise the proletariat to the economic level of the bourgeoisie would be tantamount to replacing one group of robber barons with another. This, to the surrealists, would be a false revolution and a complete misreading of the intentions of its founders. But by the time the surrealists came to the Party, the total revolution had become primarily social and its leaders more than slightly suspicious of deviationists. While the Party may have needed all the support it could get, these tireless experimenters with their claims of privileged irresponsibility (intellectuals, to boot) were hardly to its taste. In a nutshell, the surrealist commitment to the revolution was real, but misunderstood and, as a consequence, ill-appreciated. Politics, for Breton, was never the art of the possible. He was blatantly against his class, stridently opposed to the Church, and uncompromisingly hostile to his country's leaders and most of their policies. His allies were few, fewer still feared him. Yet despite the many scorners, his was a voice for decency, a visionary, impossible decency perhaps, but decency nonetheless.

The movement's dubious capacity for attaining the goals it set for itself should not blind us to its accomplishments. If it disdained literature, it encouraged some of the finest poets of the century: Eluard, Aragon, Prévert, Desnos, René Char, Tzara—poets whose influence will be felt long after surrealism has joined the other isms of literary history. Though it had higher praise for the cinema than for the theater, through the theories of Artaud and the practice of Vitrac it laid the foundations for the so-called Theater of Cruelty and the better-known Theater of the Absurd—two attempts at spotlighting the collective forces of evil and stupidity which surround us.[82] Its influence on the cinema, which lends itself more easily than any other medium to fusing the twin realms of dream and reality, has been so deeply felt that it would be impossible to write a history of that art form without a major chapter on surrealism.[83] In prose it brought forth the rambling autobiography of the exposed nerve (Aragon and Crevel), confessions of unaccustomed frankness (Michel Leiris), grating visions of dark humor (Péret), modern versions of the Gothic tale as dreamed by a neo-Freudian (Gracq, Pieyre de Mandiargues, Joyce Mansour), and everywhere in the avant-garde the soaring buoyancy associated with new-found freedom. Both Beckett and the City Lights Bookshop are indebted to it. The worst that can be said against the surrealists is that they were often naive, more naive than mischievous. One cannot base human policy on hypothetical cables received from an Unconscious whose bias is unknown. A suggestive literature may come to us in that way, but little else. At best only sporadic guidance can come from the depths, rarely a dynamic conception of personal or collective interests. *That* is a superstructure about whose conscious origins there can be little doubt.

In the Middle Ages, we are told, life was seen as a chess game which God played, while man watched and learned. Everyone knew God wanted white to win, but He had given the pieces free will. While every move was His, He was sometimes forced to concede a piece to black. The surrealists were in no position to enjoy this homey picture, for they were long since cut off from any possibility of divine benevolence. Sartre saw existence as a gratuitous gift, the raw material of life, the first version of the product essence. If the individual did not work the material honestly, regardless of the condition of the initial gift or the quality of the tools at hand, he would become a second-class citizen in a meaningless universe. The surrealists, for their part, more volatile than stoic, saw little merit in replacing love with drudgery, or poetry with some narrow good faith. The realization of the absurd, which may well have driven Aragon and others to political commitment, was less likely to overwhelm a practicing surrealist, who always had his revelation-full Unconscious to protect him. The preying feeling that it all has been done before—the same streets, the same ocean, the same words, gestures, loves—is presumably avoided by the surrealist whose bag of tricks is always full. The utter futility of it all does not touch him either, for he knows where he is going, as the folksong has it.

In an age of literary pretence Breton has in some ways been

the Great Pretender: his words have regularly been grander than his deeds, his claims grander than his accomplishments. Yet with it all, he has been one of this century's exemplary figures, and the movement he founded a model literary one (though not exclusively that). Despite numerous protestations to the contrary, surrealism has effectively passed most of the milestones that separate shock from custom—as was inevitable. Its morally fearsome leader became a Historical Personage and, as such, respected for his slightly odd qualities. Disciples have arisen speaking the same words, as disciples will, but the sound is not quite the same, and the situation significantly different:

> [Surrealism's] denunciation of the contemporary world [wrote Philippe Audoin in late 1965] can take no heed of any nostalgia for the past: each breech opened in the wall of would-be facts must afford a liberating glimpse of a Revelation which only 'the accomodation of desires' can effect, and which has nothing to do with escape, for both breech and vision tend to become real. Any revolution which does not leave room for some escape toward—or at least stretching in the direction of— the confines of the possible, which refuses to bring the flames of the inner reality to the attention of all, can be considered a failure, betrayed, even though it flatter itself at being in accord with historical necessity.[84]

There is, as ever, an enormous faith in surrealism, faith in man and in the possibility of bettering his lot; one can only hope there is balm in Gilead:

> They all go into the dark,
> The vacant interstellar spaces, the vacant into the vacant,
> The captains, merchant bankers, eminent men of letters,
> The generous patrons of art, the statesmen and the rulers,
> Distinguished civil servants, chairmen of many committees,
> Industrial lords and petty contractors, all go into the dark,
>
> . . . . . . . . . . . . . . . . . . . . . . . . .
>
> And we all go with them, into the silent funeral. . . .[85]

Where T. S. Eliot suffered from the vision of unhappy hollow men plunged into ultimate nothingness, the surrealists fix their eyes resolutely on the present. They would not say with Eliot:

To arrive where you are, to get from where you are not,
You must go by a way wherein there is no ecstacy.
In order to arrive at what you do not know
You must go by a way which is the way of ignorance.[86]

The serenity and calm assurance of resignation was never a surrealist virtue. The surrealists were and are still the Quixotes of the modern world, and the windmills they tilted at are still there. But if we must play, and we must, perhaps the game *is* worth the candle, death and the absurdity of it all notwithstanding. The absurd can be overcome through commitment, "And death shall have no dominion."[87]

# Appendix I

# A Selected Chronology of Surrealism

## From Its Origins in Dada to the Recent Past 1916-68

**1916.** Albert-Birot's *Sic* begins publication (Jan. 1916-Dec. 1919; 41 separate issues in 54 numbers). Hugo Ball composes his prelettristic *Verse ohne Worte*. Zurich newspapers announce on Feb. 2 the forthcoming opening of the Cabaret Voltaire (Feb. 5), whose principal animators were to be Hugo Ball, his wife Emmy Hennings, Arp, Tzara, Marcel Janco, and Richard Huelsenbeck—the latter arriving in Zurich on Feb. 16. (The Cabaret Voltaire, where Dada was born, was at 1 Spiegelgasse, just opposite the house where Lenin lived from Feb. 21, 1916, to Apr. 2, 1917.) The battle of Verdun begins Feb. 21 and ends in Nov. The Spartakus movement is founded in Germany, Mar. 24. Blaise Cendrars, in the employ of the couturier Jacques Doucet (100 francs per month), composes for him the presurrealistic *L'Eubage, aux antipodes de l'unité*. Sole number of the *Cabaret Voltaire* (June), with introduction by Hugo Ball (dated May 15): in this ephemeral magazine Dada is first mentioned in print. Shortly after the Cabaret Voltaire closed, there took place the first of several Dada soirées (July 14): poems, paintings, costumes, manifestos by Tzara ("Manifeste de M. Antipyrine"),

Huelsenbeck, et al. Tzara publishes his *Première aventure céleste de M. Antipyrine* (Zurich, July); Huelsenbeck, *Phantastische Gebete*, poems with 7 woodcuts by Arp (Zurich, Sept.), and the following month *Schalaben Schalabai Schalamezomai*, also illustrated by Arp. In the latter part of the year Breton, an army medical assistant, is transferred from Nantes, where he had known Vaché, to the psychiatric center at Saint Dizier.

**1917.** Huelsenbeck returns to Germany (Jan.). First number of Picabia's *391* (Barcelona, Jan. 25). Eluard marries Elena Dimitrovnie Drakonova, better known as Gala, on Feb. 21. First number of Reverdy's *Nord-Sud* (Mar. 15). Hugo Ball and Tzara found a Galerie Dada in Zurich, at whose opening (Grande Soirée Dada, Mar. 23) are exhibited works by Klee, Kandinsky, et al. The soirée ends in a wild dance by some 400 visitors and guests. Duchamp sends his "Fontaine" (a urinal), signed "R. Mutt," to the Independents Exhibition in New York (Grand Central Gallery, Mar.), where it is rejected. He subsequently brings out 2 issues of *The Blind Man* (N.Y., Apr. 1 and May 1), and the sole number of *Rongwrong* (May). In a letter to Breton dated Apr. 29, Vaché defines "umour" as "une sensation—j'allais presque dire un SENS—aussi—de l'inutilité théâtrale (et sans joie) de tout." Lenin arrives in Russia (Apr. 16: Zurich to Germany to the Finland Station). Subsequent soirées at the Galerie Dada feature Jarry, Apollinaire, Marinetti, Cendrars, Max Ernst, Feininger, Arp, Chirico, Janco, Richter, Modigliani, children's drawings and African sculpture (Zurich, Apr.-May). The first mention of Tzara in *391* appears in a letter by Max Jacob (no. 5, June), in which the name is spelled "Tsara." The Galerie Dada closes its doors on June 1. The following month *Dada 1*, "recueil d'art et de littérature," appears with contributions by Arp, Janco, Tzara, Savinio, Meriano, and Moscardelli. A single performance of Apollinaire's *Mamelles de Tirésias, drame surréaliste*, sponsored by Albert-Birot and the group around *Sic*, is presented in Paris, June 24. Shortly thereafter, at one of Apollinaire's *mardis* held at the Café de Flore, Breton makes the acquaintance of Soupault. (He had previously met Aragon at Adrienne Monnier's bookshop, the Maison des Amis des Livres, rue de l'Odéon.) Between July and November, Eluard, Picabia, and Soupault all publish their first collections of poetry; Man Ray, in New York, tries his hand at photographs made without a lens ("rayogrammes"), and Aragon is composing the poems later to be included in *Feu de joie*. The October Revolution breaks out (Nov. 6). Apollinaire delivers his lecture on "L'Esprit nouveau et les poètes" at the Théâtre du Vieux-Colombier (Nov. 26). *Dada 2* (Dec.) presents items by Arp, Delaunay, Kandinsky, Albert-Birot, and Gino Cantarelli.

**1918.** Picabia goes to Lausanne for psychiatric care (Feb.). While there he completes five brief collections of poetry, one of which (*Poèmes et dessins de la fille née sans mère*, April) is highly praised by Tzara in neighboring Zurich. Reverdy proposes his definition of the effective image (the more unexpected the better, in *Nord-Sud*, Mar.), later popularized by Breton in his *Manifeste du surréalisme*. Through the intermediary of Jean Paulhan, Breton enters into correspondence with Eluard (after Apr.), and the nucleus of the future surrealist group in Paris is formed: Breton, Soupault, Aragon, and Eluard. Tzara reads his "Manifeste Dada 1918" at a Zurich manifestation, later published in *Dada 3* (Dec.) and in *Littérature* (May 1920). Apollinaire, who died on Nov. 9, is buried on Armistice Day—one month before his lecture on "L'Esprit nouveau et les poètes" appeared in *Le Mercure de France*. Desnos at this time frequents the remnants of the anarchist *bande à Bonnot*, where he mets Henri Jeanson. He is also seen at the gatherings presided over by Louis de Gonzague-Frick, along with André Malraux. Still another acquaintance of this period is Benjamin Péret. By the end of the year Tzara and Picabia are in regular correspondence with one another. All that is now needed is to bring together in one place these disparate elements from Zurich, New York, and Paris.

**1919.** Vaché commits suicide (Jan.). Tzara and Picabia jointly prepare a special Zurich number of *391* (no. 8, Feb.) and an *Anthologie Dada* (*Dada*, no. 4-5, May), with contributions by Aragon, Breton, Soupault, Cocteau, Albert-Birot, Ribemont-Dessaignes, Giacometti, Huelsenbeck, et al. Breton reads Valéry's *Le Rameur* to a gathering at Adrienne Monnier's bookshop (Feb. 20). The first seven numbers of *Littérature* (Mar.-Sept.; Aragon, Breton, Soupault, eds.) will be distributed through her Maison des Amis des Livres; with the Oct. issue, following a quarrel over the merits of Claudel, the distribution is moved to René Hilsum's Au Sans Pareil (rue du Cherche-Midi).

In New York Man Ray publishes one issue of *TNT*, including

a poem by Soupault and art work by Duchamp (Mar.). Extracts of Lautréamont's *Poésies* appear in *Littérature*, no. 2 (Apr.). Breton's *Mont de piété* appears (June 10). Breton and Soupault publish parts of *Les Champs magnétiques* in *Littérature*, nos. 8-10 (Oct.-Dec.).

**1920.** Tzara arrives in Paris in mid-January, at Picabia's invitation, and immediately sets up headquarters in the apartment of Germaine Everling, Picabia's mistress. Here will be planned the first series of demonstrations to bring Dada to the attention of the Paris public (Jan.-May). The Spartakus revolt spreads to the Ruhr. In Cologne, Max Ernst and Johannes Baargeld bring out *Die Schammade* (Feb.), including contributions by Aragon, Breton, Eluard, Soupault, et al. That same month Tzara edits the first number of *Dada* to be published in Paris (no. 6). On Feb. 25 the Section d'Or (the Cubist dissidents of prewar days, reconstituted in 1919) excludes the Dada group (Picabia, et al.)—the first sign that the avant-garde felt menaced by these new insurgents. The flurry of Dada-oriented periodicals in Paris during this period include: *Dada, Littérature, 391, Cannibale, Proverbe, Z,* and *Action.* Péret is introduced to Picabia by his fellow Breton author, Max Jacob, and rapidly becomes an integral member of the Dada group (Mar.; his first appearance in *Littérature* comes with the July/Aug. number). *Les Champs magnétiques* published May 30. Breton reviews the new edition of Lautréamont's *Les Chants de Maldoror* for *NRF* (June). Jacques Rivière and Breton exchange views on Dada in *NRF* (Aug.). It is in Breton's article that he first uses the term "surréaliste" (with reference to Apollinaire). Tzara reads two new Dada manifestos in the course of an exhibition of Picabia's paintings (Dec. 12, 19). The *Congrès de Tours* gives birth to the French Communist Party (Dec. 15).

**1921.** First translations into French of Freud's works (publ. by Payot): *Introduction à la psychanalyse; La Psychanalyse.* Among the surrealist works which appear this year are Eluard's *Les Nécessités de la vie et les conséquences des rêves,* Aragon's *Anicet* and Péret's *Le Passager du transatlantique.* Breton is working on *Poisson soluble.*

The collective manifesto, *Dada soulève tout,* reiterates Dada's radical nonconformity (Jan. 12). *L'Oeuf dur,* a Dada derivative, begins publication (Mar. 1921-Summer 1924). The sole issue of *New*

*York Dada,* ed. by Duchamp and Man Ray, appears (Apr.). Breton makes his first overt attempt to wrest control of the movement from Tzara by leading the Dadaists on a mock visit to the church of Saint Julien-le-Pauvre (Apr. 14). Opening of the first Max Ernst exhibition in Paris, at the Sans Pareil bookshop, 37 avenue Kléber (May 2). The trial of Barrès (May 13), organized by Breton, leads Picabia to break with the movement. The refusal of Breton, Duchamp, and Picabia to take part in the Tzara-sponsored *Salon Dada* (June 6) further confirms the fractioning of the group. Among those who did join Tzara were Aragon, Eluard, Soupault, Th. Fraenkel, and Ribemont-Dessaignes. Man Ray arrives in Paris accompanied by Duchamp (July 14) and is introduced to the Parisian Dadaists. Picabia's *Pilhaou Thibaou* (no. 15 of *391,* July) attacks Tzara and Breton: his new collaborators include Jean Crotti, Ezra Pound, Céline Arnauld, Clément Pansaers, Pierre de Massot, and Paul Dermée. The last number of *Littérature* is devoted to the *procès Barrès* (no. 20, Aug.). Tzara's answer to *Pilhaou Thibaou* is *Dada au grand air* (in which he has the aid of Arp and Ernst), composed in Sept., in the Tyrol, and published in Paris the following month. Breton, on his honeymoon with his first wife, goes to Vienna to meet Freud (Oct.). From there the Bretons and Eluards go to Cologne to make the acquaintance of Max Ernst (Nov.). The first number of the Dada-related periodical *Aventure* begins publication (3 nos., Nov. 1921-Jan. 1922). The "mouvement Dada" organizes Man Ray's first Paris exhibition at the Librairie Six (Dec. 3). In the latter part of the year Desnos makes his first appearance among the Dadaists, either through the good offices of Péret or those of Matthew Josephson.

**1922.** Aragon informs Matthew Josephson that he intends to abandon his medical studies (Jan.). The *Congrès de Paris,* first proposed by Breton as a means of uniting the artistic and intellectual forces of the capital on some guidelines, is reluctantly abandoned when a number of the principals refuse to participate (Jan. 3-Apr. 5). One of the results of the collapse of the Congress was the break in relations between Breton and Tzara. The first number of the new series of *Littérature* appears (Mar.), with Breton and Soupault as joint editors. The second number (Apr.) contains Breton's "Lâchez tout," an attack on Dada and its founder. Ernst arrives in Paris (Aug.). No. 4 of *Littérature* appears with Breton as sole editor (Sept.), presaging the eventual exclusion of Soupault and others whose interests tended toward the "literary." Crevel joins the group and introduces a new game, the self-imposed hypnotic trance, whose practice will usher in the so-called *époque des sommeils* (Sept.). Mussolini marches on Rome and is asked to form the first Fascist ministry (Oct. 30). Eluard publishes two brief collections of poetry illustrated by Max Ernst, *Répétitions* and *Les Malheurs des immortels*. At the invitation of Picabia, Breton accompanies him to Barcelona and delivers a lecture on the avant-garde at the Ateneo (Nov. 17). In December, Ernst paints his "Rendez-vous des amis," which shows the following "amis": Crevel, Soupault, Arp, Ernst, Max Morise, Th. Fraenkel, Eluard, Jean Paulhan, Péret, Aragon, Breton, J Baargeld, Giorgio de Chirico, Gala Eluard, Desnos, Dostoevski, and Rafaele Sanzio. Among those who, while members of the group, since March at least, were either not available for the portrait or were not part of the inner circle are: Roger Vitrac, Jacques Baron, Man Ray, Duchamp, and Picabia. The only major surrealist not accounted for is Antonin Artaud, who makes his entry in 1924.

**1923.** France occupies the Ruhr (Jan.-Aug.). Kurt Schwitters, in Hanover, begins publishing the periodical *Merz*, a personal version of Dada highlighting the prelettristic type of "phonetic" poem previously practiced by Christian Morgenstern, Hugo Ball, and Richard Huelsenbeck (24 nos., 1923-32). Aragon, Breton, Crevel, Desnos, and others contribute texts to *Paris-Journal* (44 nos. in folio, 1923-25). Tzara's final attempt at a Dada resurrection, the Soirée du Coeur à barbe, takes place on July 6. The Hitler putsch in Munich is put down in Nov. Aragon publishes (anonymously) his *Plaisirs de la capitale;* Péret, *Au 125 du boulevard Saint-Germain;* Breton, *Clair de terre* (poems).

**1924.** Lenin dies (Jan.). Tzara's "Conférence sur Dada" appears in *Merz* (no. 7, Jan.). Publication of Breton's *Les Pas perdus*, Feb. 5; of Aragon's *Le Libertinage*, March 31. Tzara publishes his *Sept manifestes Dada*, with illustrations by Picabia; Péret, *Immortelle maladie;* Eluard, *Mourir de ne pas mourir;* Desnos, *Deuil pour deuil;* Crevel, *Détours;* Pierre Naville, a newcomer to the movement, *Les Reines de la main gauche;* Artaud, another newcomer, *L'Ombilic des limbes;* and Soupault his second novel, *Les Frères Duran-*

*deau*, which is runner-up for the *prix Goncourt*. (His first novel, *Le Bon apôtre*, appeared the year before.)

Eluard takes a six-month trip around the world on money "borrowed" from his father (Mar.-Oct.). The luxurious literary periodical *Commerce* is founded that summer. Its Fall number includes Aragon's "Une Vague de rêves," its Winter number Breton's "Introduction au Discours sur le peu de réalité." October sees a flurry of activity: Yvan Goll brings out the only number of *Surréalisme*, with texts by Albert-Birot, Crevel, Reverdy, Apollinaire, and others, but his attempt to take over this valuable trademark fails; the Bureau de Recherches Surréalistes opens 15, rue de Grenelle (Oct. 11); Breton publishes his *Manifeste du surréalisme* (Oct. 15); the collective pamphlet *Un Cadavre*, directed at Anatole France, leads Doucet to dismiss his two advisers, Aragon and Breton; the final issue of Picabia's *391* appears and, in deliberate opposition to Breton's movement, proposes a new one to be called *L'Instantanéisme*—a proposal that was still-born. *Clarté* reprimands Aragon for his political naiveté in having referred to "Moscou la gâteuse" (Nov. 15). Appearance of the new periodical *La Révolution surréaliste* (Dec. 1), ed. by Naville and Péret.

**1925.** Trotsky is relieved of his duties as People's Commissar. The anarchistic *Déclaration du 27 janvier* reveals a number of new adherents to surrealism, among others Francis Gérard, Michel Leiris, Georges Limbour, André Masson, and Raymond Queneau. On Jan. 30, the Bureau de Recherches Surréalists closes its doors to the public, but vows to continue its work in private. Artaud, the new director of the Bureau, prepares the third number of *La Révolution surréaliste*, with its wildly libertarian "Adresse au Pape," "Adresse au Dalai-Lama," "Lettre aux médecins-chefs des asiles de fous," etc. (Apr. 15). Later that month Abd-el-Krim invades French Morocco. Péret prefaces the catalogue for a Joan Miró exhibition (June). Riot at the Closerie des Lilas banquet given in honor of the symbolist poet Saint-Pol-Roux (July). Breton takes over the reins of *La Révolution surréaliste* and becomes its sole editor (with no. 4, July 15). By mid-July the group is slowly moving toward a political commitment, which leads Drieu La Rochelle to speak of their "véritable erreur" (in *NRF*, Aug.). The Oct. 15 issue of *La Révolution surréaliste* introduces a new surrealist in the person of the Abbé Ernest Gengenbach and also publishes (1) Breton's "Lettre aux voyantes," (2) his review of Trotsky's biography of Lenin, and (3) the recently signed collective manifesto, *La Révolution d'abord et toujours!* This last item is the first overt pact between the surrealist and the political avant-garde. Among other items published this year are: Péret and Eluard, *152 Proverbes mis au goût du jour;* Péret, *Il était une boulangère;* and Crevel, *Mon corps et moi.*

**1926.** Aragon collects his poems of 1920-24 under the title of *Le Mouvement perpétuel.* His *Paysan de Paris,* published serially in *La Revue européenne* (June 1924-June 1925) also appears this year, as does "Le Cahier noir," the only fragments now available of his novel *La Défense de l'infini* (in *La Revue européenne,* no. 36, Feb., and no. 37, Mar.). The Galerie Surréaliste opens in March (16, rue Jacques Callot). That same month Pierre Unik makes his first appearance in a surrealist publication (*La Révolution surréaliste.,* no. 6). The following month the Russo-German pact is renewed at Rapallo. Ernst and Miró have their wrists slapped for debasing the surrealist ideal by working for a member of the Establishment, Diaghilev, who had asked that they do the décors for a ballet (*Roméo et Juliette,* performed May 18; Aragon-Breton, "Protestation," in *La Révolution surréaliste,* June 15). First number of the new series of *Clarté:* its contents reflect the recent entente with the surrealists (16 nos., June 15, 1926 to Dec. 1927/Jan. 1928.) Eluard's *Capitale de la douleur,* a collection of previously published poetry with some new additions, appears in early Sept., shortly before the first printing of Breton's *Légitime défense.* This latter item, later reprinted in *La Révolution surréaliste* (no. 8, Dec.), was in reply to Naville's attack on the surrealists for their political ineptitude (*La Révolution et les intellectuels,* Sept.). Artaud and Soupault are expelled from the movement for engaging in "la stupide aventure littéraire" (end of Nov.); Vitrac, who had earlier joined Artaud in founding the "Théâtre Alfred Jarry," was the first to be so ostracized. (Extracts from the first manifesto of the "Théâtre Alfred Jarry" appeared in the *Nouvelle Revue française of* Nov. 1). Crevel's third novel in three years, *La Mort difficile,* is published at the end of the year (Nov. 6).

**1927.** In early Jan., Aragon, Breton, Eluard, Péret, and Pierre Unik join the Communist Party. (Many years later Péret claimed that he had been a member of the C.P. since 1925, which may be true, but there is no evidence that he was very active prior to his friends' joining.) This was followed by their collective series of letters—to Naville, the Belgian surrealists, and others—defending this unexpected move (*Au grand jour,* May). The Théâtre Alfred Jarry puts on its first performance (Jan. 15). Breton introduces the defrocked Abbé Gengenbach to a Paris audience at the Salle Adyar (Apr. 3). The best known of the avant-garde English-language periodicals in Paris, Eugène Jolas' *Transition,* begins publication (Apr. 1927- May 1938). Yves Tanguy's official entry among the surrealists is indicated by Breton's preface to the catalogue for the Tanguy exhibition at the Galerie Surréaliste (May 27-June 15). Execution of Sacco and Vanzetti: demonstrations in Paris (Aug. 23). Naville's uncertainty about the extent and the quality of surrealist political commitment is reiterated in "Mieux et moins bien" (*La Révolution surréaliste,* no. 9-10, Oct.). Trotsky and Zinoviev are expelled from the Russian Communist Party (Nov. 12). Within days Breton and his fellow surrealists leave the French Communist Party. Jacques Prévert, while never formally a member of the surrealist group, is a close friend of Tanguy, Queneau, and Desnos, and as such is often found in surrealist company. Crevel, continuing the pace of the previous years, brings out two new works, the novel *Babylone* and the shorter essay, *L'Esprit contre la raison* (autographed copies of which were sent to Gertrude Stein). *Clarté* folds with the Dec. 1927/ Jan. 1928 issue.

**1928.** Trotsky is exiled to Siberia (Jan. 16). *La Lutte des classes* replaces the now defunct *Clarté* (Feb.). The theme of *la sexualité* occupies the surrealists in the latter part of Jan; their discussions are reported in detail in *La Révolution surréaliste* (no. 11, Mar.), the sole number published that year. Artaud's presentation of a Strindberg play receives a typical surrealist hazing (June 7). Aragon destroys his novel *La Défense de l'infini* and attempts suicide in Venice (Sept.). Two months later he is introduced to Elsa Triolet (Nov. 6). Publications of note include: Breton, *Le Surréalisme et la peinture* (Feb. 11) and *Nadja* (May 25); Aragon, *Traité du style* (composed 1926-27); Eluard, *Défense de savoir* (Feb. 12); Péret, *Et les seins mouraient* and *Le Grand jeu.*

**1929.** Péret, who in 1927 had married a Brazilian singer, Elsie Houston, accompanies her to Brazil (1929-31). The U.S.S.R. decides to expel Trotsky (Jan. 18), and he is given temporary asylum in Turkey (Feb. 12). Breton organizes a protest meeting which is characterized by acrimonious debate having little to do with Trotsky and which is, moreover, without issue. Subsequent to this affair, Queneau ceases to be active in the surrealist movement. The dossier of the meeting is published in the Brussels periodical *Variétés* (June). In June, also, there appears a reprinting of Breton's first *Manifeste du surréalisme,* augmented by a preface and his "Lettre aux voyantes." *Un Chien andalou,* a film by Buñuel and Dali (neither known to the surrealists), is shown at the cinema Studio 28, rue Tholozé, and is rapidly hailed by the surrealists as a masterpiece (Oct. 1-Dec. 23). The stock market crash in New York marks the beginning of a world-wide economic crisis (Oct. 24). Jacques Rigaut, a sometime Dadaist-surrealist, commits suicide in New York (Nov. 5). Breton prepares the preface to the catalogue for the Dali exhibition at the Galerie Goemans, 49, rue de Seine (Nov. 20-Dec. 5). The final number of *La Révolution surréaliste,* in publishing extracts from Tzara's "L'Homme approximatif," makes public the recent rapprochement between Breton and the founder of Dada (no. 12, Dec. 15). Also included in this issue are: a first version of Breton's *Second manifeste du surréalisme* containing, among other things, a number of personal attacks on those who have drifted away from the surrealist party line; the scenario of *Un Chien andalou;* and a Breton-Eluard collaboration on a surrealist ars poetica, "Notes sur la poésie." Among the more significant new publications are: Eluard, *L'Amour la poésie;* Crevel, *Etes-vous fous?* (both appearing in late March); Aragon, *La Grande gaîté,* (April-May); and Max Ernst's comic-strip novel, *La Femme 100 têtes* (Dec.).

**1930.** Twelve victims of Breton's latest purge (see his *Second manifeste*) unite to publish *Un Cadavre,* a four-page vitriolic attack on the person and intentions of the surrealist leader (Jan.). The authors are Jacques Baron, Georges Bataille, J. A. Boiffard, Alejo Carpentier, Robert Desnos, Michel Leiris, Georges Limbour, Max Morise, Jacques Prévert, Raymond Queneau, Georges Ribemont-Dessaignes, and Roger Vitrac. Breton's partial reply is the "Avant, Après" insert to the published edition of the *Second manifeste du surréalisme* (June 25). The surrealist group at this time is composed of Maxime Alexandre, Aragon, Joë Bousquet, Luis Buñuel, René Char, Crevel, Dali, Eluard, Ernst, Marcel Fourrier, Camille Goemans, Paul Nougé, Péret, Francis Ponge, Marco Ristitch, Georges Sadoul, Tanguy, André Thirion, Tzara, and Albert Valentin. Several others, notably Pierre Unik, Man Ray, and Duchamp, will shortly join them. The Russian poet and friend of Aragon, Mayakovsky, commits suicide (Apr. 14). Sadoul is given a three-month prison term for a letter which he and Jean Caupenne had written in which they made a number of insulting comments on the flag and the army (June). *Le Surréalisme au service de la révolution* makes its first appearance (July). Aragon and Elsa Triolet leave for the Soviet Union (Oct. 20), followed shortly by Sadoul, who was then in the process of appealing his prison sentence. The two Frenchmen are invited to sit in on the Second International Congress of Revolutionary Writers, in Kharkov (Nov. 6–): on at least two occasions Aragon takes the floor to explain and defend the surrealist position (Nov. 9, 12). However, just prior to leaving the Soviet Union, Aragon and Sadoul sign a letter dated "Moscou, le 1er décembre 1930," in which they condemn Trotsky, Freud, and Breton's *Second manifeste* "to the extent it goes counter to the teachings of dialectical materialism." On their return to France, the two men publish a partial retraction, *Aux intellectuels révolutionnaires* (Dec.). One of the effects of this retraction is the temporary refusal of the newly founded Association des Artistes et Ecrivains Révolutionnaires to admit the surrealists to membership. (It should be added that the Association was more of a hope than a reality for more than a year after its inception. Its first public gesture, under a slightly changed name, came in Mar. 1932. See the collective surrealist tract *Paillasse!* [1932].) Breton and Eluard publish *L'Immaculée Conception* (Nov. 24), "qu'on a fait retirer des étalages" (Aragon, in *Le Surréalisme au service de la révolution*, no. 3, Dec. 1931). On Dec. 3 the cinema Studio 28, which was showing the second Dali-Buñuel film, *L'Age d'or*, was sacked by a group of extreme right nationalists (the Camelots du Roy and others), and the film was banned by the police (*première*, Nov. 28).

1931. Aragon, who had requested readmission to the Communist Party prior to his departure for Kharkov, has his request granted. Tzara publishes *L'Homme approximatif* (Mar. 30). The Spanish Republic is declared immediately after the departure of Alfonso XIII (Apr. 14). The surrealists, esp. Aragon and Eluard, attack the Exposition Coloniale held in Vincennes (May-June). Breton brings out a bibliophile edition of his poem *L'Union libre* (June 10). Ribemont-Dessaignes's "Histoire de Dada" (in *NRF*, June and July) is taken to task by Tzara, Giuseppe Ungaretti, Eluard, and Aragon— the latter concluding his statement with "salutations communistes" (*NRF*, Aug.). It should be mentioned, in Ribemont-Dessaignes's defense, that the text published was an unauthorized abridgment and that, as a consequence, Jean Paulhan must be held responsible for some of its errors and distortions. The second number of *Littérature de la révolution mondiale* containing Aragon's poem "Front rouge" is seized by the police (Nov.). Curiously enough, there was apparently no attempt made to ban his *Persécuté persécuteur* which opens with the same poem (achevé d'imprimer Oct. 25, but probably not distributed until some time later). The Dec. issues of *Le Surréalisme au service de la révolution,* which include Aragon's "Le Surréalisme et le devenir révolutionnaire" (no. 3) and Tzara's "Essai sur la situation de la poésie" (no. 4), make no mention of the seizure of *La Littérature de la révolution mondiale,* nor does Aragon, writing in Nov., mention the appearance of *Persécuté persécuteur.* (He refers to his most recent books as the *Traité du style* and *La Grande gaîté.*)

**1932.** Because of the sentiments expressed in "Front rouge," Aragon is indicted and charged with "demoralisation de l'armée et de la nation" (Jan. 16)—a charge which could have sent him to prison for up to five years. There follows the so-called *affaire Aragon,* whose last major document is the collective surrealist pamphlet, *Paillasse! Fin de "l'Affaire Aragon"* (March). When the affair draws to a close, Aragon has definitely left the surrealist camp. Two paradoxical phenomena closely related to his departure need to be mentioned: (1) the newly formed and Communist controlled Association des Ecrivains et Artistes Révolutionnaires felt obliged to admit the surrealists to membership not long after the fireworks had subsided; (2) Sadoul, Pierre Unik, and Tzara, who followed Aragon into the Communist Party, managed to maintain some semblance of surrealist affiliation until 1935.

Péret, imprisoned in Brazil for political activity, is expelled and returns to France, probably shortly *after* the *affaire Aragon*—this in spite of the fact that most commentators fix the date of his return some time in 1931. Aragon mentions that he is still in Brazil in Nov.: "Faut-il oublier Péret que quelques sous manquant retiennent stupidement au Brésil?" (in *Le Surréalisme au service de la révolution,* Dec. 1931, p.3). Péret's name is not among those who signed the petition condemning Aragon's indictment (circulated in early Feb. 1932 and published in Breton's *Misère de la poésie,* early Mar.), though it does appear on other, less "legal" documents published in 1931 and 1932. One can therefore assume that while Breton had Péret's authorization to use his name, he hesitated to do so on a petition that might have to be shown in court.

Surrealist works of note are: Crevel, *Le Clavecin de Diderot*, an essay which attempts to place surrealism "dans le cadre vivant du matérialisme dialectique" (p. 59; achevé d'imprimer April 30); the poems and prose of Breton, *Le Revolver à cheveux blancs* (June 25); his long essay on dream and reality, *Les Vases communicants* (Nov. 26); Eluard's poems from 1929-32, *La Vie immédiate*, and Tzara's *Où boivent les loups*. This same year Breton is asked to be the guest editor of a surrealist number of *This Quarter* (Sept.), an English-language periodical in Paris. This is perhaps the most significant indication of the movement's influence since the inclusion of Tzara's "Memoirs of Dadaism" in Edmund Wilson's *Axel's Castle* (1931). Georges Hugnet begins publication of "L'Esprit dada dans la peinture" (*Cahiers d'art*, nos. 1-2, 6-7, 8-10; completed in 1934). Four periodicals sympathetic to the avant-garde cease publication, due essentially to the worsening economic situation: *Commerce* (1924-32), *De Stijl* (Leyden, 1917-32), *Merz*, Hanover, (1923-32), and *Der Sturm* (Berlin, 1910-32). Henri Pastoureau joins the surrealists in late May. Artaud's manifesto on "Le Théâtre de la cruauté" appears in *La Nouvelle revue française* (Oct.).

**1933.** Hitler becomes chancellor of Germany (Jan. 30). Crevel's *prière d'insérer* for Tzara's *L'Antitête* (Jan. 20) notes: "Il n'y a que deux genres, le poème et le pamphlet, constate Monsieur Aa. Inspiration, colère." Tzara's *Monsieur Aa l'antiphilosophe* appears that same year, as does Crevel's novel *Les Pieds dans le plat* and Eluard's despondent poem *Comme deux gouttes d'eau*. (This is also the year of I. Silone's *Fontamara* and Malraux's *La Condition humaine*—obviously a bad time for bubbling whimsy.)

Breton, a member in good standing of L'Association des Ecrivains et Artistes Révolutionnaires, attacks the author-critic Ilya Ehrenburg and the editorial policies of *L'Humanité* (Feb.). Several months later, refusing to disavow a letter critical of a Russian film which he had printed in *Le Surréalisme au service de la révolution* (no. 5, May 15), Breton is excluded from the A. E. A. R. (late 1933). Bookburning day in Germany (May 10). Ten days after the simultaneous appearance of the final numbers (5 and 6) of *Le Surréalisme au service de la révolution, Minotaure* brings out its first two sumptuous numbers (both dated June): continuity of a sort, for *Minotaure* was not surrealist-controlled, could thus be maintained. A surrealist exhibition held at the Galerie Pierre Colle included among its participants: Arp, Breton, Dali, Duchamp, Eluard, Ernst, Giacometti, Maurice Henry, Marcel Jean, René Magritte, Miró, Picasso, Man Ray, and Tanguy (June 7-18); artistically the movement's strength has not at all diminished. Breton prepares a long "Introduction" for the French translation of Achim von Arnim's *Contes bizarres* (achevé d'imprimer June 19). The A. E. A. R. founds *Commune*, a "revue littéraire pour la défense de la culture" (July). Its editorial board is composed of Barbusse, Gide, Romain Rolland, and Paul Vaillant-Couturier; its *secrétaire de rédaction* is Aragon. Raymond Roussel, the millionaire whose "meaningless" works the surrealists so admired, commits suicide (July 14). Germany leaves the League of Nations (Oct. 19). Breton, Char, Eluard, and others collaborate on *Violette Nozières*, a volume of poetry in honor of a convicted murderess (Dec.). A warrant is issued for the arrest of Stavisky (Dec. 30).

**1934.** Tzara and Crevel join the Maison de la Culture, which Aragon had founded the previous year. The rightist putsch in Paris almost succeeds in toppling the Third Republic (Feb. 6-9). The surrealists and others sign an *Appel à la lutte,* calling for unity in face of the Fascist menace (Feb. 10). For some two months they are an integral part of the "democratic" front; but with their collective manifesto protesting the expulsion of Trotsky from France, *La Planète sans visa,* the surface harmony is shattered and they again are fellow travelers rather than partners (Apr. 24). *Documents 34,* a periodical published in Brussels and directed by the Belgian surrealists Jean Stéphane and E. L. T. Mesens, brings out a special number devoted to the *Intervention surréaliste* (June). Dali, whose Nazi sympathies had led to his provisional exclusion (in Jan.), is still enough a part of the group to be included in the surrealist exhibition at the Galerie Bonjean (June 20-July 15). Assassination of the Brownshirt (S.A.) leader Roehm in Hitler's first major blood purge (June 30). Breton lectures in Brussels early that summer on *Qu'est-ce que le surréalisme?* (pub. July 15). Breton, who had divorced his first wife (Simone Kahn, married Sept. 1921), takes a second (Jacqueline Lamba, Aug. 14). Speaking at the first All-Union Congress of Soviet Writers, Zdanov proposes the doctrine of socialist realism (Aug. 17). Breton writes the introduction to the catalogue for an exhibition by Victor Brauner (Nov. 28). Dali goes to the U.S. to open a show at the Julien Levy Gallery (late 1934). It is his version of surrealism, a blend of extravagance and foolishness, that catches

the public imagination as the distant and untranslated pronouncements of Breton never had.

Among the significant publications are: Breton's collection of
articles *Point du jour* (July), Eluard's poems *La Rose publique*
(Dec.), Ernst's collages *Une Semaine de bonté,* Péret's poems *De
derrière les fagots,* and Georges Hugnet's *Petite anthologie poétique
du surréalisme.* The year is marked by several new additions to the
group: the artists Oscar Dominguez and Kurt Seligmann, the young
poet Gisèle Prassinos (less a member than a prodigy the group
sponsored), Pierre Mabille and Henri Parisot. There are also two
notable departures by the year's end: the poet René Char and the
sociologist-critic Roger Caillois (Dec. 27 for the latter, who was a
member for a year and a half).

**1935.** This is a year of high hopes and of a great disappointment.
Breton and Eluard are invited to Prague to inaugurate an International Exhibition of Surrealism (late Mar.-early Apr.). Shortly thereafter, Breton, Péret, and others of the Paris group are invited to
Tenerife, in the Canary Islands, for still another surrealist exhibition (May 11-21; the invitation here was due to Oscar Dominguez).
Between these two trips, to the surprise of both Communists and
surrealists, a Franco-Russian Mutual Aid treaty was signed (May 2).
On June 25 Breton was to address, in Paris, a Congrès des Ecrivains
pour la Défense de la Culture, a Communist-sponsored but widely
supported attempt to form a common front against Fascism. Several
days prior to the opening of this Congress, Breton was informed he
would not be permitted to address the assembly. René Crevel, un-
successful in his attempt to have this ruling changed—and perhaps
for personal reasons as well—committed suicide (June 22); Eluard
was subsequently permitted to read Breton's speech, but only late at
night, after many of the delegates had left. The surrealist reaction
to this series of principled errors is vigorously expressed in the collective pamphlet *Du temps que les surréalists avaient raison* (Aug.),
signed by Breton, Dali, Dominguez, Eluard, Ernst, Marcel Fourrier,
Maurice Heine, Maurice Henry, Georges Hugnet, Sylvain Itkine,
Marcel Jean, Dora Maar, Magritte, Léo Malet, Marie-Louise and
Jehan Mayoux, E.L.T. Mesens, Paul Nougé, Méret Oppenheim,
Henri Parisot, Péret, Man Ray, Maurice Singer, André Souris, Tanguy, and Robert Valançay. Of these, several play no substantial role
in the movement (Jtkine, Maar, Malet, Marie-Louise Mayoux,
Parisot, Singer, Souris, Valançay), others are not normally resident

in Paris (Mesens and Nougé are Belgian, Oppenheim Swiss), and Dali, no longer an intimate of the group, will shortly be completely persona non grata. The absence of Tzara's name indicates quite as clearly as any formal exclusion could that, obliged to choose between the Communist Party and Breton, he has opted for the former. On Oct. 3 Italy invades Ethiopia in an unequal war that will be over in a little more than half a year. The two significant publications of the year are Breton's collection of speeches and manifestos, *Position politique du surréalisme* (Nov.) and Tzara's earlier "rêve expérimental," *Grains et issues* (Feb. 20).

**1936.** Germany reoccupies the Rhineland (Mar. 7). Ethiopia capitulates (Apr.). Victory of the Popular Front in the French elections (Apr.-May), followed by a wave of strikes (late May-early June) culminating in the Blum ministry (June 4). Breton prepares the Introduction for an Exposition Surréaliste d'Objets, to be held at the Galerie Charles Ratton (May 22-29). An International Exhibition of Surrealism is held in London (June 11-July 4), to which Breton, Eluard, Péret, et al are invited. The surrealists have now made direct contact with the avant-garde in Belgium, Czechoslovakia, Spain, and Great Britain, while related groups are in existence from Yugoslavia to Japan. Civil War in Spain (July 18); Péret is in Barcelona by early Aug., from there he moves to the Aragon front, with the Durruti Division. Opening of the first Soviet purge trials (Aug. 19; Kamenev condemned to death Aug. 23, then Zinoviev and others). The major publications of this year are related to the London exhibition: Péret, *Remove Your Hat* (tr. by Humphrey Jennings, David Gascoyne, and others); Eluard's lecture "L'Evidence poétique" and Breton's later "Limites non frontières du surréalisme" —both included in H. Read (ed.), *Surrealism.*

In addition: Péret's poetry, *Je ne mange pas de ce pain-là* (Jan. 3) and *Je sublime* (June); Eluard, *Les Yeux fertiles*; a special number of the *Cahiers d'art* devoted to the *objet surréaliste;* Breton's defense of revelation, "Le Merveilleux contre le mystère" (in *Minotaure,* Oct.); and Pastoureau's poems *Le Corps trop grand pour un cercueil,* with a preface by Breton. In New York, the Museum of Modern Art holds an exhibition devoted to "Fantastic Art" (Dec.), and Méret Oppenheim's fur-lined teacup, spoon, and saucer create a furor comparable to that of Duchamp's "Nude Descending a Stairway" at the Armory Show of Feb.-March 1913.

**1937.** Breton openly defends Trotsky and condemns the second Moscow purge trials (Jan. 26). Publication of his *L'Amour fou*. Jean-Richard Bloch and Aragon are coeditors of a new Paris daily, *Ce Soir*—ultimately banned by the police (Mar. 1, 1937-Aug. 25, 1939). Destruction of Guernica by German dive-bombers (Apr. 26). Fall of the Blum ministry (June 21). Eluard speaks on the "Avenir de la poésie" at the Comédie des Champs-Elysées (Oct. 2); a week later Breton speaks there on "L'Humour noir" (Oct. 9). In serious financial straits, Breton accepts the offer to run an art gallery (Gradiva, rue de Seine). That winter, Tériade, who had been the titular editor of *Minotaure*, is formally replaced by a committee composed of Breton, Duchamp, Eluard, Maurice Heine, and Pierre Mabille (no. 10, Winter [Dec.] 1937). After several years of peregrinations Trotsky arrives in Mexico. Eluard publishes two brief collections of poetry, *Les Mains libres* and the more significant *Quelques-uns des mots qui, jusqu'ici, m'étaient mystérieusement interdits*.

**1938.** The first International Surrealist Exhibition to be held in Paris opens at the Galerie des Beaux-Arts (Jan. 17). Special number of the *Cahiers GLM* edited by Breton and devoted to *Le Rêve* (no. 7, Mar.; the contributors include Albert Béguin and the painter Wolfgang Paalen). German troops enter Austria (Mar. 12). Breton leaves for Mexico on a government-sponsored mission to deliver a series of lectures (Apr.). E.L.T. Mesens, newly named director of the London Gallery, edits the *London Gallery Bulletin* (20 nos., Apr. 1938-June 1940; all issues subsequent to the first bear the title *London Bulletin*). The last number of *Transition* appears in May (no. 27). Breton and Trotsky sign the manifesto *Pour un art révolutionnaire indépendant* (July 25) shortly before Breton's return to France. While in Mexico Breton learned that Eluard had contributed several poems to the Communist-sponsored periodical *Commune*, alleging (later) that this collaboration did not imply any new political orientation. The rupture between the two men comes with Breton's return to the French capital (mid-Aug.), for it is inconceivable to Breton that a surrealist should overtly collaborate with a Communist or Fascist publication—both of which Eluard admitted having done. The tract *Ni de votre guerre, ni de votre paix!*—signed "Le groupe surréaliste"—condemned both sides in the crisis then threatening (Sept 27). On Sept. 30, the Munich Pact is signed.

Three works published this year merit attention: Breton, *Trajectoire de rêve* (Mar. 30); Eluard's last volume of "surrealist" poetry, *Cours naturel,* with a *prière d'insérer* by Breton (achevé d'imprimer March 10, but apparently not released for well over a month—after Breton's departure); Tzara's *La Deuxième aventure céleste de M. Antipyrine* (Nov. 15); and the novel by Julien Gracq, *Au chateau d'Argol,* whose imitation Gothic will win Breton's acclaim.

**1939.** The recently formed Fédération Internationale de l'Art Révolutionnaire Indépendant (see the Breton-Trotsky manifesto of July 1938) succeeds in publishing two issues of its bulletin *Clé* (Jan., Feb.). Barcelona falls Jan. 26, Madrid Mar. 28, and the Civil War is over. Eluard brings out two volumes, the recent poetry of *Chanson complète* (May 6), and the collection of prose and poetry, old and new, *Donner à voir* (June 3). On Aug. 24 the Russo-German nonaggression pact is made public. On Sept. 1 Germany invades Poland and general mobilization is declared in France. Breton, Péret, Tanguy, Eluard, Aragon, and others are called up; Ernst is interned as an enemy alien. Freud dies in London (Sept. 23). On Dec. 14 the League of Nations, in one of its last futile gestures, expelled the Soviet Union for having invaded Finland (Nov. 30).

**1940.** Wolfgang Paalen organizes an international surrealist exhibition in Mexico (Feb.). German invasion of Denmark and Norway (Apr. 9); major offensive against France, Belgium, and Holland (May 10); Paris falls (June 14) and an armistice is signed with the new Pétain government (June 22). Péret, after three months in prison for political reasons, obtains his release by bribing a German guard (July 22). Man Ray returns to the U.S. (Aug.). Battle of Britain (Aug.-Oct.). Trotsky is assassinated (Aug. 20). With the demobilization of French troops after the armistice, the surrealists, knowing what their fate would be in Occupied France, head for the Free Zone. Among those who spent the winter in Marseilles, awaiting passage out of the country, are: Hans Bellmer, Victor Brauner, Breton, Char, Oscar Dominguez, Ernst, Jacques Hérold, Sylvain Itkine, Wifredo Lam, André Masson, and Péret. The majority would eventually find themselves in New York, where Tanguy, declared unfit for military service, had preceded them in Dec. 1939. (Péret would join Paalen in Mexico; Char would remain in France and enter the Resistance.) Two works by Breton were completed in 1940, but distribution was held up by the censor: *L'Anthologie de l'humour noir* (achevé d'imprimer June 10) and his poem *Fata Mor-*

*gana* (Dec.). A number of former surrealists chose to remain and join the Resistance, including Aragon, Desnos, Eluard, and Tzara.

**1941.** Breton arrives in Fort-de-France, Martinique (April). That same month Aimé Césaire brings out the first number of *Tropiques* (Fort-de-France). Péret seeks refuge in Mexico, where he will remain until late 1947. Germany invades the Soviet Union (June 22). Breton arrives in New York (Aug.). The first official recognition of the surrealist presence in the U.S.A. comes with the special number devoted to them by *View*, edited by Charles Henri Ford (no. 7, Oct.-Nov.). The U.S.A. enters the war with the attack on Pearl Harbor (Dec. 7). Breton accepts a position as announcer for the Voice of America, a position he will hold until the end of the war. The Resistance in France begins to take shape (see, for example, the publications of Aragon and Eluard). From 1941 to 1946-47 Queneau is *secrétaire-général* of the Gallimard publishing house.

**1942.** Eluard joins the Communist Party. The surrealist-oriented *Leitmotiv* is founded by the Chilean Braulio Arenas, in Santiago (Chile). Paalen, in Mexico, begins publishing *Dyn* (6 nos., 1942-44). In an interview published in *Arson, An Ardent Review* (London), Breton names the following as surrealists: (writers) Péret, Pierre Mabille, Nicolas Calas (whose *Confound the Wise* appears this year), Gracq, E.L.T. Mesens, Char (who had not been active in the group for a number of years), Alice Paalen, Valentine Penrose, Aimé Césaire, René Ménil, J.-B. Brunius, Maurice Blanchard; (painters) Ernst, Masson, Tanguy, Magritte, W. Paalen, Kurt Seligmann, Victor Brauner, Leonora Carrington, Kay Sage, S. W. Hayter, Wifredo Lam, Matta Echaurren, Gordon Onslow-Ford, Esteban Frances, Joseph Cornell, and David Hare (Mar.) A special number of *View* is devoted to Max Ernst (N.Y., April). The first number of *VVV* appears, including Breton's "Prolégomènes à un troisième manifeste du surréalisme ou non" (June, edited by David Hare, with an advisory board composed of Breton, Duchamp, and Ernst). The Battle of Stalingrad begins (Sept.). An International Surrealist Exhibition, organized by Breton and Duchamp, opens in New York (Oct. 14-Nov. 7): the 48-page catalogue is published by the Coordinating Council of French Relief Societies. On Nov. 11 Germany occupies the so-called *Zone libre*. Breton is invited to address the students at Yale University; his subject: "Situation du surréalisme entre les deux guerres" (Dec. 10; first published in *VVV*, no. 2-3, Mar. 1943).

**1943.** Péret's *La Parole est à Péret* is published in N. Y.; the preface by Breton also bears the signatures of Duchamp, Ernst, Matta, Tanguy, and Charles Duit. The Battle of Stalingrad ends in a German defeat (Feb.). The only issue of *VVV* to be published this year appears (no. 2-3, Mar.). In Paris a clandestine group with the Rimbaldian name of "Editions de la Main à Plume" brings out one issue of *Le Surréalisme encore et toujours* (Aug.).

**1944.** The final number of *VVV* appears with Breton's poem "Les Etats généraux" and Péret's article, "La Pensée est UNE et indivisible" (no. 4, Feb.; the poem is dated Oct. 1943). Picasso gives the first public reading of his play, *Le Désir attrapé par la queue,* at his home in Paris; among those present are Hugnet, Leiris, Queneau, Simone de Beauvoir, Camus, and Sartre (Mar. 19). Hans Richter's film, *Dreams That Money Can Buy,* made with the aid of Man Ray, Duchamp, Ernst, and others, is a popular (and financial) success in New York. The Normandy landings take place on June 6; Paris is liberated in Aug. In Oct. Picasso joins the Communist Party. Breton's *Arcane 17* is brought out by Brentano's (Dec. 30). Both Kandinsky and Piet Mondrian die this year.

**1945.** In Mexico Péret publishes the tract *Le Déshonneur des poètes.* In New York, *View* brings out a special number devoted to Duchamp (Mar.). The following month an augmented edition of Breton's *Le Surréalisme et la peinture* appears. Pierre Unik, a Communist since 1932, and a prisoner of war after the French defeat, dies shortly before the German capitulation. The war ends in Europe on May 8. Desnos, arrested in Feb. 1944 for his work in the Resistance, dies in Czechoslovakia on June 8, 1945, unable to recover from the typhus, dysentery, and general mistreatment of the previous fifteen months. That summer Breton divorces his second wife in Reno and marries a young lady he had met two years before, Elisa Bindhoff. After the bombing of Hiroshima and Nagasaki in early August, Japan surrenders unconditionally (Sept. 2). At the invitation of Pierre Mabille, newly named cultural attaché in Port-au-Prince, Breton and his wife leave for Haiti where he is to deliver a number of lectures. In France Pierre Seghers begins a new series, Poètes d'aujourd'hui, with each volume devoted to a single poet, and including a long critical essay, bibliography, extracts from his previous work, and when possible some unpublished material. The first two volumes are given over to Eluard and Aragon. Maurice Nadeau publishes the first volume of his *Histoire du surréalisme*, which will have considerable influence in popularizing the surrealist contribution to French culture. In the new series L'Age d'or, of which he is the director, Henri Parisot publishes *Thalassa dans le désert*, a collection of very beautiful and highly atypical verse by Picabia.

**1946.** Breton's lectures in Port-au-Prince—on liberty, among other subjects—help bring down the dictatorship of Elie Lescot (Jan. 10). On his return to New York he has an opportunity to meet and speak with both Camus and Sartre. By spring Breton is back in France after an absence of five years. His first public appearance was at a meeting held to honor Artaud, recently released from the asylum at Rodez (June 7). Others present at this meeting organized by Gide and Paulhan are: Maria Casarès, J.-L. Barrault, Madeleine Renaud, Adamov, Dullin, Jouvet, and Vialar—hardly a surrealist gathering, but indicative of the role Artaud's theories would shortly play in the development of the theater. At the year's end the negotiations between Ho Chi Minh and the French government having collapsed, an armed revolt ensues (Dec. 1946-July 1954).

Henri Parisot devotes a special number of *Les Quatre vents* to *L'Evidence surréaliste*, with texts by Breton, Péret, Artaud, Gracq, Henri Michaux, Paulhan, Pansaers, Prévert, Queneau, and others (no. 4, Feb.). Two anthologies are indicative of the new interest in surrealism: the first collection of Breton's Manifestos, all three, appear under the title *Les Manifestes du surréalisme* (April), and eight of Péret's stories are gathered together in *Main forte,* published by Henri Parisot in the series L'Age d'or.

**1947.** Breton announces a forthcoming International Exhibition of Surrealism and invites contributions (circular letter dated Jan. 12). Breton's long poem, *Ode à Charles Fourier,* is published the following month in Parisot's series L'Age d'or. The surrealist group brings out its first major postwar tract, *Liberté est un mot vietnamien,* condemning the position of the French government (Apr.). Tzara lectures at the Sorbonne on *Le Surréalisme et l'après-guerre* (Apr. 11). The Communist Party withdraws from the French cabinet (May). Breton prepares the preface to the catalogue for an exhibition of Toyen's paintings, at the Galerie Denise René (June). That same month a new edition of Breton's *Arcane 17 enté d'ajours* appears (June 5), and the group publishes a declaration of political independence aimed primarily at the Communist Party, *Rupture inau-*

*gurale* (June 21, written in great part by Pastoureau). The Marshall Plan is proposed and accepted (June 5-Sept. 22), in spite of the vigorous opposition of the Soviet Union. The first International Exhibition of Surrealism to be held in Paris in almost ten years, organized by Breton and Duchamp and devoted to the elaboration of a "mythe nouveau," is a popular if not a critical success (July 7-Oct., at the Galerie Maeght). The arrangement of the various rooms was the work of Frédérick Kiesler, who handled the contributions of over eighty participants from twenty-four countries. Among those represented in the catalogue, *Le Surréalisme en 1947* (achevé d' imprimer June 27), are: Breton, Péret, Brauner, Henry Miller, Gracq, Maurice Nadeau, Jules Monnerot, Georges Bataille, Yves Bonnefoy, Arp, Robert Lebel, Aimé Césaire, Henri Pastoureau, Jacques Hérold, Pierre Mabille, Joë Bousquet, Nicolas Calas, Hans Bellmer, Marcel Jean, Arpad Mezei, J.-B. Brunius, Ferdinand Alquié, Ernst, Miró, Tanguy, and Alexander Calder. Péret, who had been in Mexico as recently as late March, is not listed among the participants in the July Exhibition. In the latter part of that month there took place in Paris a little discussed surrealist exhibition of works donated by Picasso, Miró, Ernst, Tanguy, Dominguez, and manuscripts by Breton and others, designed to raise sufficient funds to enable Péret to return to France (Galerie Rive Gauche, 44 rue Fleurus; see *Arts,* July 11, 1947, p.4). By late 1947 Péret has rejoined his friends and issues a volume of poetry, both old and new, *Feu central,* illustrated by Tanguy (Nov. 25). *Les Quatre vents* devotes a special number to *Le Langage surréaliste* (no. 8).

**1948.** The bookshop La Hune publishes the first number of the short-lived avant-garde periodical *Néon* (Jan.; its first four issues include texts by Breton, Péret, Pastoureau, Gracq, et al.). The intensification of the cold war is highlighted by the Communist takeover in Czechoslovakia (Feb. 25). Jindrich Heisler, who played a major role in *Néon,* was a Czech national, as was the painter Toyen—both of whom requested and received asylum in France. Artaud dies on Mar. 4, and a special number of *K,* also published by La Hune, is devoted to his work (no. 1-2, June). *Le Surréalisme révolutionnaire,* a diversionary periodical issued by an ad hoc "Bureau International du Surréalisme Révolutionnaire" (no. 1, Mar.-Apr., with contributions by Tzara, J. Doucet, et al.), meets with little success. Breton addresses the first public meeting of Front humain, the French version of the World Federalists (Apr. 30). The collective text *A la niche, les* *glapisseurs de dieu!*—written almost entirely by Pastoureau, and directed at those who would assimilate surrealism to some mildly heretical form of Christianity—is signed by over fifty sometime surrealists, including a number, like Jean Schuster and J.-L. Bédouin, whose role in the movement will progressively become more significant (June 14). In a declaration signed by Breton, Nora Mitrani, Jean Schuster, and others, Victor Brauner and Matta Echaurren are expelled from the movement along with their supporters: Sarane Alexandrian, Alain Jouffroy, Claude Tarnaud, Stanislas Rodanski, and Francis Bouvet (Oct.-Nov.); they will be reinstated Dec. 1959. A *Compagnie de l'art brut* is formed by Breton, Jean Dubuffet, Paulhan, Charles Ratton, Henri Pierre Roché, and Michel Tapié, whose purpose is to locate new works revealing qualities of invention and creation (Oct.). With this end in mind, a "centre de coordination" —a new version of the Bureau de Recherches Surréalistes—is opened to serve as clearing house for the manuscripts, etc., which might arrive (Autumn, rue de l'Université). The first anthology of Breton's poetry, *Poèmes, 1919-1948,* is published by Gallimard (Nov. 20). On Nov. 28 Garry Davis, who had previously renounced his U.S. citizenship to become a self-styled citizen of the world (May 25), interrupts the deliberations of the United Nations General Assembly at the Palais de Chaillot to call for the establishment of a world government. The surrealists and others (Sartre, Camus, et al.) support this "inspired" attempt to eliminate the red tape of national interests. Among the items published this year are: Breton, *La Lampe dans l'horloge* (Oct. 15); Nadeau, *Documents surréalistes,* vol. 2 of his *Histoire du surréalisme* (vol. 1 was reprinted in 1947); Julien Gracq's play, *Le Roi pêcheur;* his encomium, *André Breton, quelques aspects de l'écrivain;* and Malcolm de Chazal's *Sens plastique,* "un recueil de pensées, ou mieux de métaphores, ou plus exactement de correspondances" (from J. Paulhan's preface).

**1949.** Jean-Pierre Duprey, poet, painter, and sculptor, joins the surrealists in time to sign a collective open letter to Garry Davis, in which they proclaim their support of Davis' Citizens of the World movement (Feb.). Ernst returns to France from the U.S., where he had been living. A Picabia retrospective opens at the Galerie René Drouin (Mar. 4); the catalogue, *491,* includes contributions by Breton ("Jumelles pour les yeux bandés,") and others. The treaty establishing a Western defensive alliance (N.A.T.O.) is signed Apr. 4. The following month *La Chasse spirituelle,* falsely attributed to

Rimbaud, is published by the Mercure de France (May 17), and the celebrated "affaire" of *La Chasse spirituelle* is on. This affair ends, for the surrealists at least, with the publication of Breton's *Flagrant délit: Rimbaud devant la conjuration de l'imposture et du truquage* (July 6), whose title adequately reflects its contents and tone. Despite certain ambiguities in his presentation, this text probably did more to elicit critical respect for a surrealist-type intuitive analysis than the sum total of surrealist proclamations from 1924 on, and in the most reticent circles. Eluard prepares five programs for the Chaîne Nationale of the Radiodiffusion Française, which mirror his surrealist formation more clearly than most of his work of the post-war period (*Les Sentiers et les routes de la poésie*, Oct. 13-Nov. 11). Toward the end of the year Breton breaks with the Citizens of the World movement because he feels that Garry Davis, overly sympathetic toward things religious, has become a tool in the hands of the reaction (Oct. 21). Péret's tale, *La Brebis galante*, dated "Automne 1924" and illustrated by Max Ernst, is published for the first time this year. In Switzerland, Marc Eigeldinger edits the excellent *André Breton, essais et témoignages* (Dec. 15).

**1950.** Surrealism, which had entered the Sorbonne in the person of Tzara (1947), and had shown itself to be more perspicacious than one of the nation's most respected publishing houses (the Mercure de France, in the affair of *La Chasse spirituelle*, 1949), was now the dean of the avant-garde literary currents in France. In recognition of this new status, Breton is considered for the *prix de la ville de Paris* for his previous literary accomplishments—an award which he informs one and all he will refuse. (Gracq had just recently published *La Littérature à l'estomac* [Feb.], in which he condemned the vogue of literary prizes.) Aragon, who for eighteen years had served non-surrealist principles, is named deputy member of the Central Committee of the French Communist Party. Volume 18 of the Poètes d'aujourd'hui series is devoted to Breton, with an introductory essay by Jean-Louis Bédouin. Michel Carrouges commends himself to the surrealist leader with his very perceptive and very flattering *André Breton et les données fondamentales du surréalisme* (Feb.). Breton and Péret edit an essentially retrospective *Almanach surréaliste du demi-siècle* (Mar.). Among "new" names are: the Mexican poet Octavio Paz, Robert Lebel, Georges Schéhadé, Michel Carrouges, Jean-Pierre Duprey, André Pieyre de Mandiargues, Malcolm de Chazal, and Adrien Dax. Some two months later Breton's *Anthol-*

*ogie de l'humour noir* appears in expanded form (May 25). Thanks to Breton, Jean-Pierre Duprey's *Derrière son double* finds a publisher. Far from being moribund, the movement is carrying its years very lightly. By early 1950 the government of Chiang Kai-shek, which had already lost the mainland of China in the Communist offensive of 1949, retreats to the island of Formosa. On June 25 the North Korean forces cross the 38th parallel and the relations between East and West become still more tense.

**1951.** Julien Gracq is awarded the Prix Goncourt for his novel *Le Rivage des Syrtes,* which he immediately refuses. (As the award carries an extremely small monetary prize—it is the attendant publicity that makes it a financial plum—his rejection is not quite as audacious as might at first appear.) Robert Motherwell publishes his excellent anthology of *Dada Painters and Poets,* with two separate "inserts" by Huelsenbeck (1949) and Tzara (1951), which make clear both their continuing divergence of views and the permanence of the Dada spirit. The *affaire* Pastoureau (or Carrouges), in which Breton and Péret are seen in the unlikely role of moderates defending the religiously oriented Carrouges against the attacks of an anticlerical left wing, leads to the departure of a number of surrealists: Carrouges, Pastoureau, and several of the latter's allies, Marcel Jean, Patrick Waldberg, Adolphe Acker, Robert Lebel, and Maurice Henry (Feb.-Mar.). The tract *Haute fréquence* (May 24) lists those supporting Breton in this crisis. Of the more than thirty names, including Henri Parisot, Pieyre de Mandiargues, Octavio Paz, Man Ray, and Jean Schuster, there are a number of recent additions to the movement—among them Robert Benayoun, Georges Goldfayn, Adonis Kyrou, Gérard Legrand, François Valorbe, and Michel Zimbacca. Jean Dubuffet dissolves the *compagnie de l'art brut* through the simple expedient of transferring the various materials gathered to the U.S. (Sept.). Breton denounces Camus' sharp criticism of Lautréamont (in *Arts,* Oct. 12; Camus' article, originally published in *Les Cahiers du sud* later appeared in his *L'Homme révolté*) and finds his brilliant contemporary both unpoetic and humorless (*Arts,* Nov. 16). Lacking any publication of their own, the surrealists agree to contribute a weekly "billet surréaliste" to *Le Libertaire,* the organ of the Fédération Anarchiste (Oct. 12). Some forty of these "letters" appear before their collaboration ceases (Jan. 1953). Wolfgang Paalen returns to Paris from Mexico, where he had resided since 1939. Pieyre de Mandiargues publishes two items: *Les Masques de*

*Léonor Fini* and *Soleil des loups*. Volume 22 of the Poètes d'aujourd' hui series is devoted to René Char.

**1952.** Volume 32 of the Poètes d'aujourd'hui series is devoted to Tzara. Péret publishes a series of articles on "La Révolution et les syndicats" in *Le Libertaire* (June-Aug.). Breton's radio interviews with André Parinaud (March-June) appear in book form (*Entretiens,* July 31). Roger Vitrac dies. Eluard dies (Nov.). *Médium: informations surréalistes,* edited by Jean Schuster, begins publication (Nov.). A new surrealist art gallery opens under the name of L'Etoile Scellée (Dec. 5; 11, rue du Pré-aux-Clercs). Pierre Mabille dies.

**1953.** The surrealist collaboration with *Le Libertaire* ceases in Jan. Stalin dies (Mar. 5). Nadeau brings out the first issue of *Les Lettres nouvelles* (Mar.) which, while not a surrealist publication, is widely open to writers who influenced the movement (like Reverdy and Albert-Birot), paralleled it (like Henri Michaux), or profited from it (like Artaud and Queneau). Péret's *Mort aux vaches et au champ d'honneur,* which dates from 1922-23, is published in book form (May 28). *Médium: informations surréalistes* ceases publication in June. The Korean armistice is signed (July 27). Breton's collection of essays *La Clé des champs,* similar in format to his earlier *Les Pas perdus* (1924) and *Point du jour* (1934), appears (Aug.). The first number of *Medium: communication surréaliste,* a more substantial version of the other *Médium,* appears in Nov. (ed. Jean Schuster). One of its early collaborators, who will become increasingly more active in the movement, is José Pierre. *Adieu ne plaise* is the title of Breton's funeral oration, delivered at the Montmartre Cemetery, in honor of his long-time mentor, rival, and friend, Francis Picabia (Dec. 4; pub. Jan. 22, 1954, by P.A. Benoît). Pieyre de Mandiargues publishes his "récit" *Marbre.*

**1954.** Two numbers of *Médium: communication surréaliste* appear in the first part of the year (no. 2, Feb; no. 3, May), introducing a distinguished alchemist and recent convert to surréalism, René Alleau. *Médium,* no. 1 (Nov 1953) had been illustrated by the Hungarian artist Simon Hantaï, no. 2 (Feb.) was illustrated by the Viennese W. Paalen, no. 3 (May)—carrying on the international tradition—by the Swede Max Walter Svanberg. The 27th Venice Art Biennial, devoted to "fantastic art," awards the first prize in painting to Ernst, in sculpture to Arp, in engraving to Miró (June-July). Ernst is immediately expelled, accused not only of accepting the award, but of having actively sought it. Mendès-France, prime minister as of June 18, signs the Geneva Convention ending the war in Indo-China (July). On the occasion of the Rimbaud centenary, the surrealists join forces with the Internationale Lettriste (5 names) to denounce an unworthy edition of *Le Bateau ivre* (Oct., *Ça commence bien!*). On Nov. 1, the Algerian war of independence officially begins. At the end of the year Joyce Mansour's volume of poetry *Cris* appears, and she is invited to join the group. She will rapidly become one of its principal literary pillars, along with Breton and the far less committed Pieyre de Mandiargues.

**1955.** The final number of *Médium* (no. 4, Jan.) contains "A son gré," the collective declaration excluding Ernst from the movement, signed by Bédouin, Benayoun, Breton, Adrien Dax, Charles Flamand (whose first appearance among the surrealists was in *Médium*, no. 3, May 1954), Goldfayn, the artist E. F. Granell, Simon Hantaï, Gérard Legrand, Péret, José Pierre, Jean Schuster, and Toyen. Yves Tanguy dies in the U. S. (Jan. 15). Two items of special interest appear this year: a surrealistically designed edition of Breton's *Manifestes du surréalisme*, and Péret's edition of the Mexican *Livre de Chilam Balam de Chumayel*—one of the earliest overt indications of his interest in folk myths and legends.

**1956.** The surrealists publish a collective manifesto, *Au tour des livrées sanglantes!* (Apr. 12), demanding that the revelations of the XX[th] Congress of the Communist Party concerning Stalin's crimes be considered a first step in correcting the errors of the party. Needless to say this suggestion, in all its tactless splendor, is ignored. Aragon, a long-time supporter of the hierarchy, is elected to full membership in the Central Committee of the French Communist Party (July). The Hungarian revolt (Oct.) is saluted by the surrealists in a collective declaration, *Hongrie, soleil levant,* in which the Russians are called Fascists and the Hungarian defeat (Nov.) is termed a loss for the "prolétariat mondial." Among the signatories who make their first appearance here and who will be heard from again are Louis Janover (more Trotskyite than surrealist), Jean-Jacques Lebel (soon to be better known as a creator of Happenings), and Jean-Claude Silbermann. At about the time the Hungarian revolt was beginning, there appeared the first number of *Le Surréalisme, même* (Oct.).

This sumptuous periodical, subsidized by the publishing house of Jean-Jacques Pauvert, had Breton as "directeur" and Jean-Schuster as "rédacteur en chef." From one of its "notes" we learn that the surrealists, who had admired Ionesco's early plays (*Les Chaises, La Cantatrice chauve,* and *La Leçon*), now reproach him for putting on the unworthy *L'Impromptu de l'Alma.* Toward the end of this month Péret brings out his *Anthologie de l'amour sublime* (Oct. 31). The surrealist art gallery, L'Etoile Scellée, which had opened in Dec. 1952, is obliged to close its doors. Pieyre de Mandiargues, an aristocratic neo-surrealist, whose most recent appearance in a surrealist periodical had been in *Le Surréalisme, même,* no. 1 (Oct.), publishes *Le Lis de mer.*

**1957.** Two luxuriously designed and illustrated numbers of *Le Surréalisme, même* (no. 2, Spring; no. 3, Autumn) are conclusive evidence that the movement is still very much alive. Among the names that reappear are: Gérard Legrand, Joyce Mansour, José Pierre, Jean-Louis Bédouin, Nora Mitrani, Adrien Dax, Jehan Mayoux, Robert Lebel, Charles Estienne, Jean-Claude Silbermann, and Robert Benayoun. A new addition is Alain Joubert (no. 3, Autumn). Simon Hantaï is expelled from the group because of his clerical sympathies (Mar.). Breton and Gérard Legrand bring out the excellent volume devoted to *L'Art magique* (May 25). A collection of Péret's major stories appears under the title *Le gigot, sa vie et son oeuvre,* published by Le Terrain Vague, a publishing house that will progressively become more closely identified with the movement—what Au Sans Pareil was for Dada and the Editions du Sagittaire for the early years of surrealism. Pieyre de Mandiargues is responsible for three titles: *Les Monstres de Bomarzo, Astyanax,* and a new edition of *Le Musée noir, soleil des loups.* On Dec. 31 Oscar Dominquez commits suicide. Volume 58 of the Poètes d'aujourd'hui series is devoted to Soupault.

**1958.** Only one issue of *Le Surréalisme, même* appears this year (no. 4, Spring), but it serves to introduce to the surrealist public two persons who will subsequently become quite important to the group: Vincent Bounoure and the author-editor J.-F. Revel, who, however, will regularly maintain a certain distance. Joyce Mansour publishes *Les Gisants satisfaits;* Pieyre de Mandiargues, *Le Cadran lunaire* and *Le Belvédère.* Toward the end of the year Le Terrain Vague undertakes to publish a second surrealist periodical, *Bief,* *jonction surréaliste* (12 thin numbers, Nov. 15, 1958-Apr. 15, 1960), this one edited by Gérard Legrand, with Jean-Claude Silberman as *secrétaire de rédaction.* For the first time the group has two publications at its entire disposition: *Le surréalisme, même* will carry the substantial messages, *Bief,* originally conceived as a four-page illustrated newsletter, will take the place of the earlier surrealist tracts and "papillons." The contributors to the first two numbers (Nov. 15, Dec. 15) include J.-L. Bédouin, Robert Benayoun, Vincent Bounoure, Breton, Adrien Dax, Charles Flamand, Jean-Jacques Lebel, Gérard Legrand, Joyce Mansour, Péret, José Pierre, and Jean Schuster. Gracq brings out a volume of prose poems under the title *Liberté grande.*

**1959.** Volume 66 of the Poètes d'aujourd'hui series is devoted to Artaud (Feb.). The final number of *Le Surréalisme, même* appears in the Spring (no. 5). Seven numbers of *Bief* are scattered from Jan. to Dec. (nos. 3-9). Radovan Ivsic makes his public appearance with the group in *Bief,* no. 3 (Jan. 15), Mimi Parent in no. 8 (July 15). Pieyre de Mandiargues brings out *Feu de braise.* A surrealist festival is held in Milan, in part to celebrate the appearance of Péret's excellent *La Poesia surrealista francese* (French and Italian on facing pages; Apr. 27-May 2). Breton prepares a series of twenty-two prose passages to parallel a series of twenty-two plates made by Miró between 1940 and 1941: this collaboration is published under the title *Constellations.* Wolfgang Paalen commits suicide in Mexico (Sept.). That same month Péret dies in Paris (Sept. 18). Barely two weeks later Jean-Pierre Duprey takes his life (Oct. 2). Marcel Jean's superb *Histoire de la peinture surréaliste,* prepared in collaboration with Arpad Mezei, is published at the end of the year (Nov. 10). Matta Echaurren and Victor Brauner are reinstated in the good graces of the movement (Dec. 4; they had been expelled in Oct. 1948). On Dec. 15 the 8th International Exhibition of Surrealism, devoted to the theme of eroticism, opens at the Galerie Cordier, 8 rue de Miromesnil, Paris. (The "8th" comes from the catalogue to the Exhibition, *Boite alerte,* prepared by Breton and Duchamp, and is presumably based on what they consider to be *authentic* exhibitions.) The participants include Breton, Duchamp, José Pierre, G. Legrand, J. Schuster, R. Benayoun, Méret Oppenheim, Hans Bellmer, Man Ray, Arp, Svanberg, Vincent Bounoure, Octavio Paz, Nora Mitrani, Joyce Mansour, Pieyre de Mandiargues, Robert Lebel, J.-L. Bédouin, Jean-Claude Silbermann, Guy

Cabanel, and a number of recent additions: notably Jean Benoît, who on Dec. 2, at the home of Joyce Mansour and before a large gathering, had acted out the mummery of Sade's last will and testament. As might be expected, most of the critics were unhappy at what they saw, but the Exhibition was a popular success and ran until Feb. 29 of the following year.

**1960.** Péret's posthumous *Anthologie des mythes, légendes et contes popularies d'Amérique* (achevé d'imprimer Dec. 20, 1959) appears in early Jan. Camus dies Jan. 4. J.-L. Bédouin's history of recent surrealism appears first in an Italian translation, *Storia del surrealismo dal 1945 ai nostri giorni* (Feb.). The young poet Jean-Claude Barbé makes his surrealist début in the final number of *Bief*, the same issue in which we learn that Jean-Jacques Lebel has been expelled from the movement, accused of using his surrealist affiliations to advance his personal interests (no. 12, Apr. 15). The Breton-supported *Déclaration sur le droit à l'insoumission dans la guerre d'Algérie,* commonly known as the *Déclaration des 121,* is released in late Sept. A handsome anthology of Breton's writings, edited by his right-hand man Gérard Legrand, is put out by Le Club du meilleur livre (Nov. 20). Pieyre de Mandiargues publishes two brief items: *Sugaï* and *Cartolines et dédicaces.* Volume 72 of the series Poètes d'aujourd'hui is devoted to Queneau. Breton organizes a surrealist exhibition for the D'Arcy Galleries in New York (Nov. 1960-Jan. 1961), with an extensive catalogue entitled *Surrealist Intrusion in the Enchanters' Domain.*

**1961.** One firm indication that Breton has become a classic in his own lifetime is the appearance of a critical edition of one of his poems, the *Ode à Charles Fourier,* by a university professor, Jean Gaulmier (Mar.). Breton organizes still another surrealist exhibition, this time for the Galleria Schwarz in Milan (May). A new surrealist periodical, published by Le Terrain Vague, appears in Oct.: *La Brèche: action surréaliste,* edited by Breton with the help of a committee composed of Robert Benayoun, Gérard Legrand, José Pierre, and Jean Schuster. Among the newer surrealists who will reappear with some regularity are Radovan Ivsic and the poet Jean-Claude Barbé. The revised, "original" version of J.-L. Bédouin's *Storia del surrealismo* (1960) is published under the title *Vingt ans de surréalisme: 1939-1959* (Nov. 10). Pieyre de Mandiargues publishes *L'Age de craie suivi de Hedera* and *La Nuit l'amour.* Volume 78 of the series

Poètes d'aujourd'hui is devoted to Péret. J. Gracq publishes a volume of essays, *Préférences*.

**1962.** Cease-fire in Algeria (Mar. 19). Two numbers of *La Brèche* appear (no. 2, May; no. 3, Sept.), the latter containing Breton's recollections of Pierre Mabille, "Pont-levis." Pieyre de Mandiargues publishes two new items: *Deuxième Belvédère* and *La Marée*. Breton introduces the anthology *Les Inspirés et leurs demeures*, containing the photos of Gilles Ehrmann and texts by several authors (Nov. 19).

**1963.** *La Brèche* brings out two new issues (no. 4, Feb.; no. 5, Oct.). Vincent Bounoure joins the "comité de rédaction" with no. 4. The collective publication *De la part de Péret* assembles various *hommages* to the deceased surrealist and announces the formation of an Association des Amis de Benjamin Péret. The prolific Pieyre de Mandiargues publishes *La Motocyclette*, almost immediately a critical success. The *bête noire* of the surrealists, Jean Cocteau, dies in Oct.

**1964.** Jean-Louis Bédouin brings out an "official" anthology of surrealist poetry, *La Poésie surréaliste* (Apr. 2), containing some fifty-four names, from Aragon to Michel Zimbacca. Patrick Waldberg organizes the largest and most comprehensive exhibition of surrealist art at the chic Galerie Charpentier, 76 rue du Faubourg Saint-Honoré (Apr. 15-Sept. 30). Even before the exhibition opens, the group questions his moral qualifications (read, his *surrealist* moral qualifications) for the task in a well-publicized declaration, *Face aux liquidateurs* (Apr. 13). Among the signatories are: Philippe Audoin, J.-L. Bédouin, Robert Benayoun, Jean Benoît, Raymond Borde, Vincent Bounoure, Breton, Guy Cabanel, Adrien Dax, Radovan Ivsic, Alain Joubert, Gérard Legrand, Joyce Mansour, Jehan Mayoux, Mimi Parent, José Pierre, Jean Schuster, Jean-Claude Silbermann, and Toyen. When the initial flare-up between the partisans of surrealism-as-art and surrealism-as-activity had somewhat died down—the two attitudes are clearly not mutually exclusive—José Pierre edited a pamphlet in which are collected the principal texts relating to the Waldberg exhibition and the problems it raised: *Cramponnez-vous à la table* (*Petite suite surréaliste à l'affaire du Bazar Charpentier*). Pieyre de Mandiargues brings out *Le Point où j'en suis* and a new edition of *Astyanax*. Two numbers of *La Brèche* are published (no. 6, June; no. 7, Dec.). A new edition of J.-P. Duprey's *Derrière son double* appears, including the previously unpublished *Spectreuses* (Oct. 25).

**1965.** A new edition of Breton's *Le Surréalisme et la peinture*, revised and much expanded, is brought out by Gallimard (Oct. 15). No. 8 of *La Brèche* appears in November with the announcement that the long-awaited rejoinder to the Waldberg exhibition would open on the sixteenth of that month. (Revel, at one point, had announced it for Oct. 1964. See *L'Express*, Apr. 29, 1964, p. 33.) What with various last minute delays, the XI⁰ Exposition Surréaliste finally opened on Dec. 8 at the Galerie L'Oeil—run by Georges Bernier. The catalogue, *L'Ecart absolu*, was published in the art periodical *L'Oeil*, edited by the same Bernier—one of whose principal collaborators was J.-F. Revel (no. 131, Nov.). The exhibition itself was organized by Breton, Revel, and Philippe Audoin—the last best known for his "pages magistrales" (Breton's phrase) on surrealist games in René Alleau's *Dictionnaire des jeux* (1964). Pieyre de Mandiargues brings out two more items: the short stories of *Porte dévergondée* and a text I have not as yet seen, *Beylamour*. Joyce Mansour publishes her most striking prose, *Carré blanc*, dedicated to André Breton. Alain Jouffroy prepares the preface to J.-P. Duprey's *La Fin et la manière*.

**1966.** Breton dies Sept. 28.

**1967.** *La Nouvelle revue française* (April) devotes an entire number (more than 350 pp.) to Breton and surrealism. Jean Schuster edits 2 numbers of *L'Archibras* (Apr., Oct..), the latest of the surrealist periodicals. Among the contributors are Schuster, Audoin, G. Legrand, José Pierre, Joyce Mansour, Vincent Bounoure, J.-C. Silbermann, Jehan Mayoux, and Guy Cabanel. The movement, it would appear, is still very much alive. Sadoul dies (Oct.).

**1968.** *Archibras*, no. 3, appears in March; no. 4 (*hors série*) on June 18, shortly after the worst of the student demonstrations were over. Sir Herbert Read dies (June). Marcel Duchamp dies (Oct. 1).

# Appendix II

# A Schematic View of the Foundations of Surrealism

| Thesis | Antithesis | Synthesis |
|---|---|---|
| 1. *Love,* as exemplified by the individual and fleeting bolt from the blue. | *Marriage,* as a social phenomenon. | *L'Amour fou,* the momentary bolt from the blue made eternal. |
| 2. *Individual Liberty.* | *Social Responsibilities.* | *The Independent Reformer (le révolté).* |
| 3. *Freedom, Free Will.* | *Determinism.* | *Le Hasard objectif.* |
| 4. *Poetry,* as an inspired phenomenon. | *Prose,* as a conscious reconstruction of reality. | *The Prose-Poem* (sometimes *récit de rêve*), founded in the Unconscious, but arranged. |
| 5. *Dreams-Desires* (internal reality). | *The World of Things* (external reality). | Breton's *Les Vases communicants,* where the internal and the external meet and fuse. |

| 6. *Disorder* (chaos). | *Order* (fixed Beauty). | *La Beauté convulsive* (underlying order in apparent disorder). |
|---|---|---|
| 7. *Action* (chance surprise, novelty). | *Thought* (pre-determined style). | *Disciplined Spontaneity,* aiming at *le merveilleux.* |
| 8. *Life.* | *Art.* | *Life-as-a-work-of-art,* as a serious game. |
| 9. Romanticism (?) | Classicism (?) | Surrealism. |

# Notes

*Unless otherwise indicated the place of publication for works in French is Paris, for works in English New York.*

CHAPTER I

1. The distinction between *le merveilleux* and *le mystère* is discussed in André Breton, "Le Merveilleux contre le mystère," *Minotaure*, no. 9 (Oct. 1936), pp. 25-31. Reprinted in Breton, *La Clé des champs* (Ed. du Sagittaire, 1953). The term aesthetic is used here, incidentally, in spite of Breton's numerous disclaimers of interest in literature or art. The interest, nevertheless, is manifestly there. What he rejected were the *traditional criteria* of evaluation and, more importantly, the *function* of art and literature in society, their role as either a pleasurable commodity, a moral guide (rather old fashioned), or a financial investment.

2. See T. S. Eliot, "Introduction to Baudelaire's *Intimate Journals*" (1930), *Selected Prose* (London: Faber & Faber, 1953), pp. 193-94. This theme recurs regularly in *Les Fleurs du mal;* see, e.g., "La Vie antérieure," "Obsession," "Le Rêve parisien," or "Le Voyage."

3. From Baudelaire's "L'Invitation au voyage," *Les Fleurs du mal*. The second quotation is from "Le Voyage" in the same work.

4. From the poem "Correspondances," *Les Fleurs du mal*.

5. Strongly influenced by Baudelaire, Rimbaud first proposed his *"dérèglement de tous les sens"* in the so-called *lettre du voyant* of May 15, 1871. In Rimbaud, *Oeuvres complètes* (Gallimard [Bibl. de la Pléiade], 1951), p. 254.

6. See André Breton, *Poisson soluble*, appended to the first edition of his 1924 Manifesto, and the comment in that Manifesto, "n'est-ce pas moi le poisson soluble, je suis né sous le signe des Poissons et l'homme est soluble dans sa pensée!" In *Manifestes du surréalisme* (J.-J. Pauvert, 1962), p. 56. This type of hermeticism has a long tradition in French literature going

back to Mallarmé and ultimately to the sixteenth-century poet Maurice Scève.

7. See the *Second Manifeste du surréalisme* (1930), in *Manifestes du surréalisme* (1962), p. 184. The concept of revelation, incidentally, is undoubtedly derived in part from Apollinaire's relatively uncomplicated search for *surprise* and *adventure*. See, for example, his article on "L' Esprit nouveau et les poètes," *Mercure de France*, CXXX, no. 491 (Dec. 1, 1918), pp. 384-96, and the poem "La Jolie rousse," in *Calligrammes* (1918), esp. the lines "Soyez indulgents quand vous nous comparez / A ceux qui furent la perfection de l'ordre / Nous qui quêtons partout l'aventure."

8. *Les Champs magnétiques* by André Breton and Philippe Soupault were the first texts to demonstrate this technique. Originally published in *Littérature*, Oct., Nov., and Dec. 1919, they were subsequently brought out in book form by the Surrealist-affiliated press Au Sans Pareil in 1920.

9. Valéry refers to the Priestess in his poem "La Pythie" (1919) as a "mime de noirs enthousiasmes." In *Charmes* (Gallimard, 1922).

10. The initial cause of this turning toward the spirit world was René Crevel. See André Breton, "L'Entrée des médiums," *Littérature*, n.s., no. 6 (Nov. 1922); reprinted in Breton, *Les Pas perdus* (NRF, 1924). Breton was ultimately obliged to put an end to these habit-forming seances in order to keep the group this side of madness and uninhibited violence.

11. Breton blew hot and cold with regard to the success of automatic writing. Interspersed with lavish praise we find comments such as, "L'histoire de l'écriture automatique dans le surréalisme serait, je ne crains pas de le dire, celle d'une infortune continue." In "Le Message automatique," *Minotaure*, no. 3-4 (Dec. 15, 1933), p. 57; reprinted in Breton, *Point du jour* (NRF, 1934), p. 226. His pessimism, however, appears directed primarily at its limited results in effecting a literary revolution. "J'ai compté sur le débit torrentiel pour le nettoyage définitif de l'écurie littéraire" (*ibid.*, in *Point du jour*, pp. 226-27). And in that, of course, he failed. Nonetheless, the technique remains the best formal approach for eliciting literary "revelations."

12. See, for example, André Breton, *L'Amour fou* (NRF, 1937), and Benjamin Péret, ed., *Anthologie de l'amour sublime* (Albin Michel, 1956). There is only a chronological difference between Péret's *amour sublime*, Breton's earlier *amour fou*, and the now classic Stendhalian concept of *amour passion*: each stresses a slightly different aspect—indicated by the terms themselves—of the same phenomenon.

13. Breton speaks of "la période d'attente que nous vivons" in his *Légitime défense* (Editions Surréalistes, 1926), p. 10; also printed under the same title in *La Révolution surréaliste*, no. 8 (Dec. 1926).

14. While a comparison in depth between neo-Platonists and surrealists is beyond the scope of this study, the interested reader can consult R.P. Festugière, *La Révélation d'Hermès Trismégiste* (Librairie Lecoffre, 1949-54), 4 vols.; I. *L'Astrologie et les sciences occultes* (1949), II. *Le Dieu cosmique* (1949), III. *Les Doctrines de l'âme* (1953), IV. *Le Dieu inconnu et la gnose* (1954); D.P. Walker, *Spiritual and Demonic Magic from Ficino to Campanella* (London: The Warburg Institute, University of London, 1958); Alexandre Koyré, *Mystiques, spirituels, alchimistes du XVIᵉ siecle allemand* (Lib. Armand Colin, 1955); Ernst Cassirer, *The Individual and the Cosmos in Renaissance Philosophy* (1927), tr. with an Introduction by Mario Domandi (Harper and Row, 1963); Eugenio Garin, *Dal medioevo al rinascimento* (Firenze: Sansoni, 1950); Charles G. Nauert, Jr., *Agrippa and the Crisis of Renaissance Thought* (Urbana, Ill.: University of Illinois Press, 1966).

15. The surrealists became interested in communism shortly after the publication of Breton's first *Manifeste du surréalisme* (1924). Their last attempt to join forces with the Communist Party came at the time of the Congrès International pour la Défense de la Culture (June 1935). See Breton's review of Trotsky's study on Lenin, "Léon Trotsky: Lénine," *La Révolution surréaliste* no. 5 (Oct. 15, 1925), p. 29; Breton, *Entretiens avec André Parinaud* (Gallimard, 1952), pp. 118-19; and for the most detailed surrealist version of the break with the Communist leadership Breton, *Position politique du surréalisme* (1935), partly reprinted in *Manifestes du surréalisme* (Pauvert, 1962), pp. 237-333. See also, Robert S. Short, "The Politics of Surrealism, 1920-1936," in W. Laqueur and G.L. Mosse, eds., "The Left-Wing Intellectuals Between the Wars 1919-1939," *The Journal of Contemporary History*, no. 2 (1966), pp. 3-25.

16. "Le Merveilleux contre le mystère," *Minotaure*, no. 9 (Oct. 1936), pp. 25-31, reprinted in *La Clé des champs* (Editions du Sagittaire, 1953); and *L'Amour fou* (NRF, 1937). (R)

17. Breton, "Entrée des médiums," *Littérature* n.s., no. 6 (Nov. 1922), reprinted in his *Les Pas perdus*, pp. 147-58; and Breton, "Introduction au Discours sur le peu de réalité," *Commerce*, III (Hiver 1924), pp. 27-57, reprinted in Breton, *Point du jour*, where it is dated Sept. 1924. We might mention in this context Aragon's equally important "Une Vague de rêves," which appeared in *Commerce*, II (Automne 1924), pp. 89-122, and has never been reprinted.

18. Benjamin Péret in the Introduction to his *Anthologie des mythes, légendes et contes populaires d'Amérique* (Albin Michel, 1960), p. 31. Shortly before this statement Péret had noted that poetry and science have a common origin (in man's desire to know) and a common goal (to augment man's knowledge and by so doing free him from the un-

known). *Ibid.*, pp. 30-31. The quotation originally appeared in the same author's *La Parole est à Péret* (Mexico, 1943).

19. It is worth noting that the conservative motto of the Vichy regime, found among other places on the coins minted during World War II, was *travail, famille, patrie*.

20. Péret, ed., *Anthologie de l'amour sublime* (Albin Michel, 1956), pp. 19-20.

21. Péret, *Anthologie de l'amour sublime*, p. 21. Breton had previously discussed certain of the social and moral implications of this phenomenon in his *L'Amour fou*, pp. 135-37.

22. Rimbaud and Marx, respectively. These two sides of the surrealist coin, regularly referred to in almost all their writings from 1924 on, have the effect of talismans. They not only effectively summarize the fundamental aspirations of the group but also have the added virtue of placing them under the protection of the Promethean Rimbaud and the revolutionary Marx. See, for example, Breton, "Discours au Congrès des écrivains" (June 1935), in *Manifestes. . .* (1962), p. 285.

23. See "Avis aux exposants," in the catalogue *Boîte alerte* (Galerie Daniel Cordier, 1959), where Breton stresses that "L'exposition internationale du Surréalisme, qui se tiendra à la Galerie Daniel Cordier du 15 décembre 1959 à la fin de février 1960 prendra pour thème l'érotisme" (p. 5). Gore Vidal, in one of the more rewarding recent essays on the subject, discusses and defines pornography (which he does not however, distinguish from eroticism) in his review of the *Olympia Reader*, Maurice Girodias, ed., (Grove Press, 1966), in the *New York Review of Books*, VI, 5 (Mar. 31, 1966), pp. 4-16.

24. This revitalization of an almost medieval concept of love was not their only attempt at myth-making. Most of these, however, were short lived for want of what Péret would probably have termed an orientation toward "la poursuite de la toujours provocante chimère de la perfection à jamais inaccessible" (*Anthologie des mythes, légendes et contes populaires d'Amérique*, p. 28). Perhaps the longest lived of these other myths is that of the unrecognized writer, *le poète maudit*. Verlaine had applied the term in 1883 (in *Lutèce*) to those whom society had insufficiently recognized, prophets who had gone unheard. From a statement of fact concerning a bare half-dozen poets, the surrealists went on to elaborate the myth of the subversive revolutionary writer who, singlehanded (except for the surrealists themselves who regularly act in unison), attacks the society—or that part of it—which limits man's freedom, which prevents the full flowering of his imaginative and creative potential. Hence the rehabilitation of Sade, who had alone and at the risk of his life launched his dream-siege against the moral code. (See, for example, *Le*

*Surréalisme au service de la révolution,* from its second number [Oct. 1930] on.) Lautréamont and Rimbaud, both for the subversive nature of their writings—themes of murder with no subsequent punishment or remorse, senseless violence, the prodigal son who does *not* return, and so on—their abandonment of literature, and the mystery of their lives are fit companions for Sade in the surrealist pantheon.

25. In *L'Amour fou,* p. 26. Earlier, in *Nadja* (Gallimard, 1928, p. 215), Breton had offered a somewhat less detailed definition: "La beauté sera CONVULSIVE ou ne sera pas." As *Nadja* was recently reissued in an "édition entièrement revue par l'auteur" (Livre de Poche, 1964) without that sentence, the last in the book, having been modified in any way, we can only assume that his views had not changed appreciably.

26. Two recent analyses of this poem are to be found in (1) Baudelaire, *Les Fleurs du mal,* édition critique établie par Jacques Crépet et Georges Blin (Corti, 1942), pp. 39, 359-60, and (2) Robert-Benoît Chérix, *Commentaires des "Fleurs du mal"* (Genève: Pierre Cailler, 1949), pp. 145-47. The first studies primarily the literary sources of the poem, one of only four regular sonnets in *Les Fleurs du mal;* the second examines its autobiographical content. An indication of the favorable surrealist reaction to this sonnet is its inclusion in Péret's *Anthologie de l'amour sublime,* p. 281.

27. A form which Rimbaud termed, with specific reference to Baudelaire, as "mesquine." See his *lettre du voyant* (to Paul Demeny) of May 15, 1871, in Rimbaud, *Oeuvres complètes* (Gallimard [Bibl. de la Pléiade], 1951), p. 257. Presumably, Rimbaud felt that the opulence and grandeur of Baudelaire's poetry would have been more in evidence had the form been less classical, less disciplined. As there is no question in Rimbaud's time of poetry being tied to any so-called "noble" subjects, and as he specifically rejects the form, we can only assume that true poetry resides in the man and can be brought to the surface by a thorough *"dérèglement de tous les sens"* (same letter).

28. *Manifeste du surréalisme* (1924), in *Manifestes . . .* (1962), p. 41.

29. "Rimbaud est surréaliste dans la pratique de la vie et ailleurs." *Ibid.*

30. The title and general theme of the bewitched lover have their immediate literary origins in the Epilogue to Cazotte's *Le Diable amoureux.* The exclamation in line 14, for example, *"O mon cher Belzébuth, je t'adore,"* is to be found in that work in the form "Mon cher Belzébuth, je t'adore." (End of chap. 17 of *Le Diable amoureux;* see the Crépet-Blin edition of *Les Fleurs du mal* (pp. 359-60) referred to in footnote 26.)

31. From "El Desdichado," first published in Dec. 1853.

32. This sonnet's rhythm is at least as erotic as Diderot's, for example, which Leo Spitzer studied so thoroughly in "The Style of Diderot," *Linguistics and Literary History* (Princeton, N.J.: Princeton University Press, 1948), pp. 135-91.

33. A variant dating from 1958 gives "*O Soleil* de mon *âme.*" The final version presents a far more striking contrast: not the sun, but the moon, the star of the lovesick, is the celestial body dear to Venus.

34. The prologue to *Les Fleurs du mal*, "Au lecteur," reflects the typical Baudelairian view of *Ennui*: of all our monstrous vices, "Il en est un plus laid, plus méchant, plus immonde! / . . . / C'est l'Ennui!" Even in the prologue it has an active, anguished component uncommon to his predecessors and contemporaries.

35. Albert-Marie Schmidt, ed., *L'Amour noir, poèmes baroques* (Monaco: Editions du Rocher, 1959). The page references in the text refer to this edition. More recently Jean Rousset has edited an extensive two-volume *Anthologie de la poésie baroque française* (Armand Colin, 1961) from which additional examples could easily be culled.

36. In *L'Amour fou*, pp. 12, 21.

37. Frederick Brown, "The Inhuman Condition: An Essay Around Surrealism," *The Texas Quarterly*, V, 3 (Autumn 1962), p. 161. It was this article, originally delivered at a conference of scholars at the 1962 annual convention of the Modern Language Association of America, that helped crystalize the present author's understanding of surrealism and also suggested the translation of *revelation* for *le merveilleux*.

38. See, for example, the "Enquête sur l'amour" in the final number of *La Révolution surréaliste*, no. 12 (Dec. 15, 1929), which reflects this curious dialogue between neo-Platonism and eroticism, and which was subsequently to be "codified" in Breton's *L'Amour fou* (1937).

39. Johan Huizinga, *Homo Ludens* (Boston: Beacon Press [1950] 1955), p. 7. Subsequent references to this work will be given in the body of the text.

40. Freud had earlier come to a similar conclusion when he wrote, "The opposite of play is not serious occupation but—reality." In "The Relation of the Poet to Daydreaming," *Delusion and Dream* (Boston: Beacon Press, 1958), p. 123; first published in the *Neue Revue*, I (1908). For further discussion of the opposition between reality and ideal constructs, see Paul Valéry, "Introduction à la méthode de Léonard de Vinci" (1895) and the annexed "Note et digression" (1919), in vol. I of his *Oeuvres* (Bibliothèque de la Pléiade, 1957), pp. 1153-1233. Valéry rejected all formal systems of philosophy, and this would apply equally well to the formal

systems of games, as being works of art irrelevant to the world of flesh and blood, the world of reality: "Il faut . . . avoir quelque défiance à l'égard des livres et des expositions trop pures" (p. 1158), for there is always something *inhuman* about them. When one realizes that until 1919 Breton revered Valéry as one of his two literary mentors (the other being Apollinaire), the origin of this dichotomy, pure vs real, becomes somewhat clearer.

41. See the excellent summary of surrealist games by Philippe Audoin in René Alleau, ed., *Dictionnaire des jeux* (Claude Tchou, 1964), pp. 478-87. Breton himself referred to Audoin's article as "pages magistrales consacrées aux 'jeux surréalistes,'" in *Arts*, no. 959 (Apr. 22, 1964), p. 3. Perhaps the best known of these games is the *cadavre exquis*, normally played with five participants. Each player writes, say, a noun on a sheet of paper, folds the paper so as to hide the word and passes it to his neighbor on the right who proceeds to jot down an adjective (without seeing the noun), folds it again and passes it on to the third player who, in like fashion, adds a verb; to the fourth player who adds another noun; to the fifth who completes the sentence with a final adjective. The paper is then unfolded and the words made to agree grammatically. The first such sentence formed was *le cadavre exquis boira le vin nouveau*, the exquisite corpse will drink the new wine.

42. Breton, in *Manifestes. . .* (1962), pp. 16, 17. This sets the stage for the subsequent nominalist attack on reality.

43. Coleridge originally defined the creative imagination, which he termed "secondary Imagination," as that which "dissolves, diffuses, dissipates, in order to recreate." In *Biographia Litteraria* (1817), chap. xiii; see *The Selected Poetry and Prose of Samuel Taylor Coleridge*, D.A. Stauffer, ed. (Random House, 1951), p. 263. The idea, if not the term, is omnipresent in the theoretical writings of the surrealists. Perhaps the closest Breton ever came to paraphrasing Coleridge's definition occurs in the first Manifesto: "Je crois à la résolution future de ces deux états, en apparence si contradictoires, que sont le rêve et la réalité, en une sorte de réalité absolue, de surréalité, si l'on peut ainsi dire" (*Manifestes . . ,* 1962, p. 27). The term *imagination créatrice* made its first appearance in French in a letter by Delacroix to Balzac (end of 1832). *Correspondance de Delacroix*, I, 342-45, mentioned in Margaret Gilman's study of *Baudelaire the Critic* (Columbia University Press, 1943), p. 125.

44. See Franz Kafka, "A Hunger Artist," in *Selected Short Stories*, tr. by Willa and Edwin Muir (Random House, 1952). It is worth noting that the hunger artist lived in a circus. . . and ultimately starved to death ignored by those unable to comprehend the sublimity of the task he had set for himself.

45. In "Introduction au Discours sur le peu de réalité," *Commerce,* III (Hiver 1924), p. 57.

46. *Manifeste du surréalisme* (1924), in *Manifestes. . .* (1962), p. 26.

47. *Ibid.,* p. 27.

48. This dualism is a major theme of Norman O. Brown's excellent study, *Life Against Death: The Psychoanalytical Meaning of History* (Random House, 1959). Without ever alluding to the surrealists, he manages to describe the world as they would see it. The most recent indication of their favorable reaction to this work (translated as *Erôs et Thanatos*) can be found in a lecture delivered by Gérard Legrand, Mar. 26, 1963, on "Quelques aspects de l'ambition surréaliste," *La Brèche,* no. 5 (Oct. 1963), p. 76.

49. See David Riesman, *The Lonely Crowd* (New Haven: Yale University Press, 1950). It will be recalled that Riesman sees three major orientations in the modern world: (1) that of the *tradition-directed* person who has internalized the patterns and folkways of the past to such an extent that they become an integral and unquestioned part of his daily behavior—his *creencias,* to use a term proposed by Ortega y Gasset (see vol. V of his *Obras completas,* Madrid: Revista de Occidente, 1947, pp. 375 sq.); (2) that of the *inner-directed* person for whom the rigid (and unconscious) patterns of the past have turned into more flexible goals and principles; he *knows* where he is going, *wants* to go there, and does not care who goes with him—roughly, Ortega's *ideas* (same essay); (3) that of the *other-directed* person who has replaced the gyroscope of goals with a radar system. He will move when his radar tells him others want him to; he will think and feel what others would have him think, and so on. Principles, to the surrealist, are more important than people.

50. Breton, for example, in an overly quoted passage, suggests that a typical surrealist act would be to shoot at random into a crowd. *Second Manifeste du surréalisme* (1930), in *Manifestes. . .* (1962), p. 155. Earlier we see Péret insulting a passing priest . . . carefully photographed for posterity in *La Révolution surréaliste,* no. 8 (Dec. 1, 1926), p. 13. As for political activity, their most recent major sortie was in Sept. 1960, when Breton joined forces with 120 others in the *Manifeste des 121,* which asserted the right of the individual to refuse to take part in the Algerian war. Among the other signatories were Sartre, Simone de Beauvoir, Vercors, Robbe-Grillet, N. Sarraute, Marguerite Duras, and the sometime surrealists, Th. Fraenkel, Michel Leiris, and André Masson. See "La Déclaration des 121, *Sédition* et les surréalistes," *La Brèche,* no. 2 (May 1962), pp. 61-70, for a résumé of their position as of early 1962.

51. In "Joë Bousquet le rêveur" (1953), *Pour un nouveau roman* (Gallimard, Coll. Idées, 1963), p. 116. Robbe-Grillet had previously praised

the surrealists for their ability to "rendre, par une recherche systématique, aux 'miracles apparents qui jettent un doute si vif sur la vision commune du réel' toute leur valeur et leur poids: ceux de 'gages évidents d'un ordre inconnu'" (*ibid.*, p. 115).

52. *Manifeste du surréalisme* (1924), in *Manifestes . . .* (1962), p. 28 note 1.

53. Sartre discusses this point at some length in "Qu'est-ce que la littérature," *Situations II* (Gallimard, 1948), esp. the section "Pour qui écrit-on?"

54. Paul Eluard, *Donner à voir* (Gallimard, 1939), p. 164; quoted by Ph. Audoin in René Alleau, ed., *Dictionnaire des jeux*, 1964, p. 480. It should be stressed that if there is any special virtue to these surrealist games, it is their open-endedness. It would be impossible, for example, to foresee what sentences would be produced by recourse to the technique of the *cadavre exquis.*

55. Given the situation in which man is free and everything else on earth is determined, Breton sees *le hasard objectif* as "*le problème des problèmes*," "l'élucidation des rapports qui existent entre la 'nécessité naturelle' et la 'nécessité humaine,' corrélativement entre la nécessité et la liberté." In *Entretiens 1913-1952 avec André Parinaud* (Gallimard, 1952), p. 136. Objective chance thus refers to "le lieu géométrique de ces coïncidences" (*ibid.*). Understood in this way, surrealism becomes the study of the interaction of free man and determined universe, esp. on the thin line where these two meet.

56. Breton refers to this "volonté d'émancipation *totale* de l'homme" in "Le Merveilleux contre le mystère," *Minotaure*, no. 9 (Oct. 1936), p. 25. Not long afterward he reiterated his belief in "l'*apparition* miraculeuse" and "la *coïncidence* bouleversante," which recalls both his earlier definition of beauty and his later description of objective chance. In "Limites non-frontières du surréalisme" (1937), *La Clé des champs*, 1953, p. 23; first publ. in *NRF*, no. 281 (Feb. 1937), pp. 200-215. That Breton believed *literally* in these surrealist "miracles" appears undeniable. See, for example, the list of "prophecies" he offers to the sceptical as proof of surrealist power: in his introduction to the 1947 International Exhibition of Surrealism, "Devant le rideau," *Le Surréalisme en 1947* (Maeght éditeur, 1947), p. 14 note 1; reprinted in *La Clé des champs*, pp. 87-95.

57. Philip Rieff, *Freud: The Mind of the Moralist* (Doubleday Anchor Book [1959], 1961), p. xix.

CHAPTER II

1. Perhaps the best brief introduction, in English, to surrealist painting is J. H. Matthews, "The Case for Surrealist Painting," *Journal of Aesthetics and Art Criticism*, XXI, 2 (Winter 1962), pp. 139-47.

2. These two exhibitions were reviewed by Pierre Schneider in "L'Objet du litige," *L'Express*, no. 756 (Dec. 13, 1965), p. 81, and by Otto Hahn, "Le Surréalisme face à la machine à laver," *ibid.*, pp. 80-81. The latter exhibition is the most recent attempt by the surrealists to demonstrate that they are still active and that they are not what others think they are—whatever that may be. As most of the items displayed date from before 1935, and quite a few from the Dada period, their effort to be *different* does not seem to be overly successful.

    The only formal attempt by the surrealists to analyze surrealistic novelty (or revelations) occurred during the brief life of the Bureau des Recherches Surréalistes, from Oct. 11, 1924 to Jan. 30, 1925, at which time its doors were closed to the public. The original director of the Bureau, Francis Gérard (pseud. for Gérard Rosenthal), was then replaced by Antonin Artaud, who presumably was to continue the "research" away from the maddening crowd. (The original Bureau had been plagued by large numbers of curiosity seekers.) As no progress report has ever appeared, unless the third number of *La Révolution surréaliste* (Apr. 15, 1925), edited by Artaud, can be so considered, it is difficult to know what conclusions, if any, were arrived at.

3. Breton is here quoting Dali, in *Entretiens 1913-1952* (Gallimard, 1952), p. 155. Eroticism, as used by the surrealists, refers to the physical (material) manifestation of *l'amour fou*, which is its subjective mainspring. See chap. I on surrealist aesthetics.

4. In Breton, *Adieu ne plaise*, discours prononcé à l'occasion de l'enterrement de Picabia, le 4 déc. 1953, au cimetière Montmartre (Alès: P. A. B[enoît], 1954), s.p. Elsewhere in the same oration, he refers to Picabia's work as "fondée sur la souveraineté du caprice, sur le refus de *suivre*, toute entière axée sur la liberté, même de déplaire."

5. See the several references to this in the index to Robert Motherwell, ed., *Dada Painters and Poets* (Wittenborn, Schultz, Inc., 1951), esp. pp. 207-18. The Mona Lisa with moustaches was first painted in 1919, but was not displayed publicly until 1920. See cover of *391*, no. 12 (Mar. 1920).

6. *Manifeste du surréalisme* (1924), in *Manifestes du surréalisme* (Pauvert, 1962), p. 35 note. See also Breton *Le Surréalisme et la peinture* (Gallimard, 1928), and Louis Aragon, *La Peinture au défi* (Galerie Goemans, 1930) for two specific treatments of painting by the two major theoreticians of the day. (A new, revised, and much enlarged edition of

Breton's *Le Surréalisme et la peinture, 1928-1965* [Gallimard, 1965] has recently been brought out. As my research was completed before this volume appeared, it is only exceptionally referred to in this study.) With the arrival of Dali in late 1929 the importance of the nonverbal arts increased appreciably, as bear witness the pages of *Le Surréalisme au service de la révolution* (6 nos., July 1930-May 1933) and *Minotaure* (13 nos. in 11 issues, June 1933-39).

7. The contradiction between life-as-a-work-of-art, which is its own justification, and the call of social justice is more apparent than real. To the surrealists, especially after 1925, there could be no full life without the Revolution, for one implied the other. What the surrealists lacked was a term to describe this attitude. Years later Sartre coined it: *engagement*, art and freedom placed at the service of some social goal. (But Sartre never satisfactorily explained what became of freedom *after* it was committed.)

8. Both Duchamp and Picabia, years before Dada, had already demonstrated a firm grasp of the then dominant impressionist and cubist techniques and were well on their way to becoming "famous" painters. See, for example, Marcel Jean, *Histoire de la peinture surréaliste* (Editions du Seuil, 1959), pp. 29-37 and passim; Michel Sanouillet (ed.), *Marchand du sel, écrits de Marcel Duchamp* (Le Terrain Vague, 1958), illus.; Robert Lebel, *Sur Marcel Duchamp* (Trianon Press, 1959), including, in addition to Breton's excellent essay, "Phare de la mariée," over 170 plates, 7 in color; Michel Sanouillet, *Picabia* (Editions du Temps, 1964), illus.

9. See Guillaume Apollinaire, *Chroniques d'art, 1902-1920*, L. C. Breunig, ed. (Gallimard, 1960).

10. See the several works by Michel Sanouillet and Robert Lebel mentioned in note 8 of this chapter. The best single book-length study of surrealist painting, with numerous illustrations and an index, is that of Marcel Jean.

11. Dali entered the surrealist group in 1929, at the age of twenty-three. In January 1934 he was officially denounced for his Nazi and Fascist sympathies, but his collaboration in exhibitions and periodicals was still solicited, perhaps because of the surrealist quality of his work, perhaps because of his public appeal. (He was one of Breton's "conseillers spéciaux" in planning the Exposition Internationale du Surréalisme, held in Paris, Jan.-Feb. 1938. Yet, in spite of this, Breton later remarked that "vers 1935" Dali ceased being a member of the surrealist group. In *Entretiens*, p. 282.) His first Paris exhibition was at the Galerie Goemans in Sept. 1929. From Oct. to Dec. of that same year Paris had the opportunity of seeing the results of the first Luis Buñuel-S. Dali collaboration, *Le Chien andalou*. Their second film, *L'Age d'or*, which led to riots by offended

rightist groups, appeared the following year. Dali's earliest contribution to the discussion on the object was "Objets surréalistes," *Le Surréalisme au service de la révolution*, no. 3 (Dec. 1931), pp. 16-17. For Dali on the edible quality of art—great art must be assimilable—see his "De la beauté terrienne et comestible de l'architecture modern'style," *Minotaure*, no. 3-4 (Oct. 15, 1933), pp. 69-76. In mid-1935 the Editions Surréalistes in Paris brought out his brief *La Conquête de l'irrationnel*, published in this country under the title *Conquest of the Irrational* (Julian Levy, 1935), 24 pp., 38 pls., tr. by D. Gascoyne. The major summary of his views on art can be found in his *Les Cocus du vieil art moderne* (Fasquelle, 1956), translated the following year into English as *Dali on Modern Art* (Dial Press, 1957). The most lavish single work on the man and his work is that of Robert Descharnes, *The World of Salvador Dali* (Harper & Row, 1962), first printed by Edita in Lausanne.

12. Breton wrote the preface for Picabia's Nov. 1922 Barcelona exhibition (reprinted in Breton, *Les Pas perdus*, 1924), and years later a preface to an anthology of his poetry (*Choix de poèmes de Picabia*, 1947) and to a retrospective of his art work at the Galerie Artiste et Artisan (1951). In November 1927 he introduced the Exposition Arp at the Galerie Surréaliste. Ernst, Chirico, Miró, Braque, Picasso, Man Ray, Masson, and Tanguy are all spoken of favorably in *Le Surréalisme et la peinture* (NRF, 1928). Picasso merited a special comment in "Picasso dans son élément," *Minotaure*, no. 1 (June 1933), pp. 9-37, reproduced in *Point du jour* (1934). Ernst, the long-time artistic mainstay of the group, was honored with a preface to his first Paris exhibition (May 1921) and again with an "Avis au lecteur" to his book of collages, *La Femme 100 têtes* (Editions du Carrefour, 1929), the latter "Avis" reprinted in *Point du jour* (1934). Breton's "Première Exposition Dali," introducing Dali's first one-man Paris show, is also included in the same collection of essays, *Point du jour*. In 1936, Dali's art theories served as the basis for "Le 'Cas' Dali," incorporated in the American edition of *Le Surréalisme et la peinture, suivi de Genèse et perspective artistiques du surréalisme et de fragments inédits* (Brentano's, 1945). On Nov. 28, 1934, Breton presented Victor Brauner to the Paris public (in Maurice Nadeau, *Histoire du surréalisme, suivie de Documents surréalistes*, Editions du Seuil, 1964, pp. 396-97). Arshile Gorky's death came as a sharp blow, whose echo is heard in "L'Adieu à Arshile Gorky" (1947), in *Néon*, no. 4 (1948). Gorky, whom he had known during the war years in New York, had previously been examined in 1945 (see the 1945 edition of *Le Surréalisme et la peinture*, pp. 196-99). For the Exposition Baya in Paris, Breton drafted one of his typically allusive texts, "Derrière le miroir" (Galeries Maeght, Nov. 1947). The exhibition of the works of the Brazilian Maria at the J. Levy Gallery in New York, 1947, was welcomed by Breton and M. Tapié in *Les Statues magiques de Maria* (Paris: R. Drouin, 1948). Toyen,

a Czech painter, received her major accolade in the 104-page work au-
thored by Breton, Jindrich Heisler, and Benjamin Péret (*Toyen*, Paris,
Sokolova, 1953). And at different times, artists as dissimilar as Wifredo
Lam (1942), Matta Echaurren (1944)—both in *Le Surréalisme et la
peinture*—and Yves Laloy (1958) have all profited from his pen.

13. A. Breton and Marcel Duchamp, *First Papers of Surrealism* (Coordinating Council of French Relief Societies, Inc., 1942), a 48-page (unnumbered) brochure commemorating the International Surrealist Exhibition organized by the two men, Oct. 14-Nov. 7, 1942. A. Breton and
Marcel Duchamp, eds., *Le Surréalisme en 1947* (Maeght, 1947) introduces the International Surrealist Exhibition held in Paris, July 1947,
this too organized by Breton and Duchamp. In 1959, the two men combined forces to direct still another International Surrealist Exhibition,
this one at the Galerie Cordier (Dec. 15, 1959-Feb. 29, 1960), the catalogue bearing the title *Boîte alerte* (Cordier, 1959). Daniel Cordier, incidentally, the gallery owner, was one of the major resistance leaders of
World War II. Also in 1959 Breton and Miró collaborated on twenty-two
"parallels," prose and painting, published as *Constellations* (N.Y.: Pierre
Matisse, 1959), reproduced in Breton, *Poésie et autre*, textes choisis et
présentés. . . par Gérard Legrand (Club du Meilleur Livre, 1960).

14. See, for example, A. Breton and Gérard Legrand, *L'Art magique*
(Club Français de l'Art, 1957). In addition to 231 pages of heavily illustrated text, the work contains some 80 full-page plates, all illustrating
aspects of magic surrealist art from Paolo Uccello to the present.

15. *Ibid.*, p. 229. Earlier Breton, in his "Avis au lecteur" to Ernst's *La
Femme 100 têtes* (Editions du Carrefour, 1929), had been even more
precise with regard to what he found objectionable in traditional painting
and praiseworthy in his disciple: "Max Ernst est le seul, de nos jours, à
avoir réprimé durement en lui tout ce qu'il y a . . . de préoccupations de
'forme' subalternes, à l'égard desquelles toute complaisance mène à enton-
ner le cantique idiot des 'trois pommes' commises en fin de compte . . .
par Cézanne et Renoir." And indeed Ernst's comic-strip novel brings to
mind less Cézanne than Rimbaud, to the extent that it might almost be a
pictorialization of "les peintures idiotes, dessus de portes, décors, toiles de
saltimbanques, enseignes, enluminures populaires; la littérature démodée,
latin d'église, livres érotiques sans orthographe, romans de nos aïeules,
contes de fées, petits livres de l'enfance, opéras vieux, refrains niais,
rythmes naïfs" (Rimbaud, "Alchimie du verbe," *Une Saison en Enfer*).

16. *L'Art magique*, pp. 230-31: "son mot d'ordre fondamental: *liberation
sans conditions de l'esprit* dans le sens du mieux . . ." And in a note to
that phrase, there is Breton's earlier statement, "Nous savons à présent
que la poésie doit mener quelque part," which effectively eliminates any

possibility of assimilating surrealism to a form of art-for-art's sake. This last phrase was originally *"On sait maintenant* que la poésie doit mener quelque part" (emphasis ours), in Breton's review of *Les Chants de Maldoror* of Lautréamont, in *NRF*, no. 81 (June 1920), p. 918.

17. S. Dali, *Journal d'un génie* (La Table Ronde, 1964), pp. 23-24.

18. Duchamp and Man Ray had earlier edited the sole number of *New York Dada*, Apr. 1921, reproduced in Robert Motherwell, ed., *The Dada Painters and Poets* (Wittenborn, Schultz, Inc., 1951), pp. 214-18. By June of that year Duchamp had introduced his American protégé to his Paris friends. It is interesting to note that the catalogue for Man Ray's first one-man Paris show (Dec. 1921), presented "sous la présidence du mouvement Dada" at the art gallery-bookshop, La Librairie Six (which was run by Soupault's wife), contains texts by Max Ernst, Jean Arp, Philippe Soupault, Tristan Tzara, Paul Eluard, and Georges Ribemont-Dessaignes—but nothing by Breton or Aragon.

19. See Claude Lévi-Strauss' letter to Breton in the latter's *L'Art magique*, p. 56.

20. In Breton, *Le Surréalisme et la peinture*, quoted by J. H. Matthews, *An Introduction to Surrealism* (University Park, Penn.: Penn. State Univ. Press, 1965), p. 61.

21. The poster for this May 3-June 3, 1921 exhibition, containing the phrase "au-delà de la peinture," is reproduced in Max Ernst, *Beyond Painting* (Wittenborn, Schultz, Inc., 1948), p. 12, where, however, it is incorrectly dated 1920. This same error is found in Motherwell, ed., *Dada Painters and Poets*, pp. 144, 176, 184, where the editor was undoubtedly led astray by Ernst's oversight. This exhibition, correctly dated, is described in some detail by Michel Sanouillet, *Dada à Paris* (Pauvert, 1965), pp. 248-53. Sanouillet's reference to contemporary newspaper reviews leaves little doubt that 1921 is the proper date. See also, Breton, *Entretiens* (Gallimard, 1952), p. 69; Marcel Jean, *Histoire de la peinture surréaliste* (Editions du Seuil, 1959), p. 62; Hans Richter, *Dada-Kunst und Antikunst* (Cologne: Verlag M. DuMont Schauberg, 1964), p. 169; and G. Ribemont-Dessaignes, *Déjà jadis* (Julliard, 1958), p. 97, all of whom give 1921.

22. This thesis is developed by Marcel Brion in his *Art fantastique* (Albin Michel, 1961).

23. Breton, "D'une décalcomanie sans objet préconçu" (1936), *Le Surréalisme et la peinture* (1945), p. 135. The above reference to Da Vinci's recommendation is borrowed from Breton's earlier "Le Message automatique," *Minotaure*, no. 3-4 (Dec. 15, 1933), reprinted in *Point du jour*, pp. 220-21: "On répète volontiers que Léonard de Vinci recommandait à

ses élèves, en quête d'un sujet original qui leur convînt, de regarder longtemps un vieux mur décrépi: 'Vous ne tarderez pas, leur disait-il, à
remarquer peu à peu des formes, des scènes qui se préciseront de plus en
plus . . . . Dès lors vous n'aurez plus qu'à copier ce que vous voyez, et à
compléter au besoin.' "

24. "Prestige d'André Masson" (1939), in *Le Surréalisme et la peinture*,
pp. 156-57.

25. *Le Surréalisme et la peinture*, p. 20. He subsequently extended his
condemnation to include "la vue," to the extent that we see only *surface*
reality. The true painter seeks to express a state of soul, an "état d'âme."
In "Genèse et perspective artistiques du surréalisme (1941), in *Le
Surréalisme et la peinture*, p. 84. It might be added in this context that
as a painting is seen as a whole immediately, its effect is instantaneous,
a *revelation* of sorts, while music, on the other hand, obliged to operate
in time, can never have as *immediate* an effect. One ignores time, the
other cannot.

26. In *Le Surréalisme et la peinture*, p. 92.

27. *Ibid.*, p. 94.

28. See J.-P. Sartre, "Qu'est-ce que la littérature," *Situations* II (Gallimard, 1948), subsequently reprinted as a separate volume in the collection Idées, 1964.

29. Pierre Naville, "Beaux arts," *La Révolution surréaliste*, no. 3, (Apr.
15, 1925), p. 27.

30. "Genèse et perspective artistiques du surréalisme," *Le Surréalisme et
la peinture*, p. 94.

31. Breton, "Crise de l'objet" (1936), *Le Surréalisme et la peinture*, pp.
125-32. This article was originally published in *Les Cahiers d'art*, 11ᵉ
année (1936), pp. 21-26, as part of a special number devoted to the *objet
surréaliste*. From May 22-29 of that year, there had been an Exposition
Surréaliste d'Objets at the Charles Ratton Gallery in Paris, for which
Breton had drafted the introduction. The first reference to what would
be termed the *objet surréaliste à fonctionnement symbolique* can be found
in A. Breton, "Introduction au Discours sur le peu de réalité," *Commerce*,
III (Hiver 1924), p. 51. The first "poème-objet" was produced by Breton
in 1929. See *Le Surréalisme et la peinture* (1945), p. 178. The variation,
*le poème-objet*, was defined by Breton as "une composition qui tend à
combiner les ressources de la poésie et de la plastique en spéculant sur
leur pouvoir d'exaltation réciproque" (Breton, *Entretiens*, p. 162).

32. A. Breton, "Crise de l'objet" (1936), *Le Surréalisme et la peinture*,
p. 128.

33. "Du poème objet" (1942), *Le Surréalisme et la peinture,* pp. 178-80, and the photograph of the object in question facing p. 177.

34. From "Des tendances les plus récentes de la peinture surréaliste" (1939), *Le Surréalisme et la peinture,* pp. 149-50. This inevitably recalls Tzara's description of how to write a Dadaist poem:

> Prenez un journal.
> Prenez des ciseaux.
> Choissisez dans ce journal un article ayant la longueur
> que vous comptez donner à votre poème.
> Découpez l'article.
> Découpez ensuite avec soin chacun des mots qui forment
> cet article et mettez-les dans un sac.
> Agitez doucement.
> Sortez ensuite chaque coupure l'une après l'autre.
> Copiez consciencieusement
> dans l'ordre où elles ont quitté le sac.
> Le poème vous ressemblera.
> Et vous voilà un écrivain infiniment original et d'une
> sensibilité charmante, encore qu'incomprise du vulgaire.

From Tzara, "Manifeste sur l'amour faible et l'amour amer," first read at the Povolozky Gallery, Dec. 12, 1920, at a soirée celebrating a Picabia exhibition then under way (Dec. 10-25). The extract cited above originally appeared in *Littérature,* no. 15, (July-Aug. 1920) p. 18. The complete manifesto can be found in Tristan Tzara, *Sept manifestes Dada . . .* (Pauvert, 1963). The specific passage quoted above is on p. 64.

35. In "Arshile Gorky" (1945), *Le Surréalisme et la peinture,* p. 198.

36. Breton, "Comme dans un bois," *La Clé des champs* (Editions du Sagittaire, 1953), p. 241. First published in *L'Age du cinéma,* special surrealist issue, nos. 4-5 (Aug.-Nov. 1951).

37. Max Ernst's *La Femme 100 têtes* (Editions du Carrefour, 1929) is a tale told in black and white collages, a printed version of the movie serials of the day.

38. "Les analogies découvertes entre les images," according to J.-L. Bédouin, "ont commandé entièrement le montage et l'articulation même des séquences" of the film *L'Invention du monde* (1952). Private communication to J. H. Matthews in his "Du cinéma comme langage surréaliste," *Etudes cinématographiques,* nos. 38-39 (Printemps 1965) p. 68.

39. See Breton, "Comme dans un bois," *La Clé des champs,* p. 242.

40. *Ibid.*, pp. 242-43. "Anywhere out of the world" is the title of a Baudelaire poem. See Baudelaire, *Oeuvres complètes* (Bibliothèque de la Pléiade, 1956), pp. 355-56.

41. Breton, "Comme dans un bois," *La Clé des champs*, p. 243.

42. As Soupault remarked: "nous [les surréalistes] considérions alors le film comme un merveilleux mode d'expression du rêve." In Jean-Marie Mabire, "Entretien avec Philippe Soupault," *Etudes cinématographiques*, nos. 38-39 (Printemps 1965), p. 29. The surrealist view of the role desire plays in the universe is a curious inversion of J.-J. Rousseau. For Rousseau, man's desires (which are wicked) were instilled in him by society; for the surrealists, man's desires (which are good, in that their satisfaction will presumably make him happy) are regularly thwarted by society.

43. According to Paul Eluard, "Le poète agit comme un phénomène contagieux. L'intelligence du poème ne vient qu'après." Cited by André Delattre in "Personal Notes on Paul Eluard," *Yale French Studies* (1948), and repeated by J. H. Matthews, "Du cinéma comme langage surréaliste," *Etudes cinématographiques*, nos. 38-39 (Printemps 1965), p. 74 note 17. What Eluard says for the poem is equally applicable to the cinema.

44. Quoted by Georges Sadoul, "Souvenirs d'un témoin," *Etudes cinématographiques*, nos. 38-39 (Printemps 1965), p. 13.

45. *Ibid.*, p. 14.

46. Sadoul describes the surrealists' meeting with Buñuel and Dali, *after* the initial projection of *Le Chien andalou* (Oct. 1929), in his "Souvenirs d'un témoin," *ibid.*, p. 19. Several pages further on (p. 24) he refers to a manifesto of the period which restricts the appellation surrealist to the two films of Buñuel (*Le Chien andalou* and *l'Age d'or* [1930]) and Eisenstein's *The Battleship Potemkin* (1926). It is ironic that among the signatories were Man Ray and Albert Valentin, who had both been active in the cinema. Man Ray's films include *Le Retour à la raison* (1923), *Emak Bakia* (1926), *L'Etoile de mer* (1928, based on Desnos' script), and *Le Mystère du château de dès* (1929)—none of which were apparently considered surrealist enough to mention in the manifesto. It would be interesting to know what Man Ray had done (or had not done) to merit this rather cavalier treatment.

47. "*L'Age d'or* n'était donc en rien un ciné-roman, mais sa négation: un ciné-poème." Sadoul, "Souvenirs d'un témoin," *Etudes cinématographiques*, nos. 38-39 (Printemps 1965), p. 26.

48. Man Ray ["Témoignages"] in *Etudes cinématographiques*, nos. 38-39 (Printemps 1965), p. 45. His own films, he tells us, were by preference short, based essentially on the inspiration of the moment, with no scenarios

or other frivolities (*ibid.*, pp. 43-46). Short subjects may not be the most promising means of obtaining an enduring masterpiece, but as Man Ray said, "Je crois que les films n'ont pas une valeur permanente" (*ibid.*, p. 44), to which one might add, "le surréalisme n'a jamais eu pour but la production des chefs-d'oeuvre." Georges Neveux, "De *Judex* à *L'Etoile de mer*," *Etudes cinématographiques*, nos. 38-39 (Printemps 1965), p. 47.

49. Man Ray refers to "le parti pris de Kyrou de voir du surréalisme dans tous les films" (*ibid.*, p. 44). Michel Beaujour is equally accurate, but less kind, when he calls Kyrou's study "un livre riche, mais dépourvu de rigueur." Michel Beaujour, "Surréalisme ou cinéma?" *Etudes cinématographiques*, nos. 38-39 (Printemps 1965), p. 61. See Ado Kyrou, *Le Surréalisme au cinéma* (Le Terrain Vague, 1963), first published by Arcanes, 1953.

50. André Pieyre de Mandiargues, ["Témoignages"] *Etudes cinématographiques*, nos. 38-39 (Printemps 1965), p. 48.

51. Eluard in *L'Evidence poétique* (GLM, 1937), "fragments d'une conférence prononcée à Londres le 24 juin 1936," first published in *Cahiers d'art*, 11ᵉ année, no. 6-7 (1936), pp. 185-88, and reprinted in *Donner à voir* (Gallimard, 1939), pp. 79-87. The citation is from this last volume, p. 81. This same phrase is also found in the unpaged *Avenir de la poésie*, conférence à la Comédie des Champs-Elysées, samedi le 2 octobre 1937 (GLM, 1937). In a similar vein, Valéry had noted that "Un poète . . . n'a pas pour fonction de ressentir l'état poétique: ceci est une affaire privée. Il a pour fonction de le créer chez les autres. On reconnaît le poète . . . à ce simple fait qu'il change le lecteur en 'inspiré.'" Paul Valéry, "Poésie et pensée abstraite," conférence à l'Université d'Oxford: *The Zaharoff Lecture for 1939* (Oxford: Clarendon Press, 1939), reprinted in *Oeuvres* (Bibliothèque de la Pléiade, 1957), vol. I, p. 1321.

52. Michel Beaujour, "Surréalisme ou cinéma?" *Etudes cinématographiques*, nos. 38-39 (Printemps 1965), p. 58. Dream recitals disappeared with *La Révolution surréaliste* (1924-29) as a major publishable surrealist pastime, except for an occasional fantasy of Dali—see, for example, his "Rêverie," *Le Surréalisme au service de la révolution*, no. 4 (Dec. 1931), pp. 31-36. What has happened, of course, is that the dream recital, the *spectacle* part of surrealism, has become an integral part of contemporary literature to such an extent that its early form now seems quite naive. Breton was correct: his *vases communicants* do communicate, and quite effectively, at least in the works of Joyce Mansour, Pieyre de Mandiargues, and others of the more recent contingent. It is this that explains the recent (literary) interest in Benjamin Péret, who more consistently than any other, with the possible exception of Breton, mingled in his work the two realities of dream and consciousness.

53. Sadoul, "Souvenirs d'un témoin," *Etudes cinématographiques,* nos. 38-39 (Printemps 1965), p. 22.

54. René Crevel and Paul Eluard, "Un Film commercial," *Le Surréalisme au service de la révolution,* no. 4 (Dec. 1931), p. 29.

55. Michel Beaujour, "Surréalisme ou cinéma?" *Etudes cinématographiques,* nos. 38-39 (Printemps 1965), p. 59.

56. See the section "Les Possessions," in Breton and Eluard, *L'Immaculée conception* (Editions Surréalistes, 1930), pp. 26-67.

57. The phrase *critique synthétique* was first used by Aragon in *SIC,* Oct. 1918, in the title of his review of Apollinaire's *Calligrammes.* (Cited by Marguerite Bonnet, "L'Aube du surréalisme et le cinéma: attente et rencontres," *Etudes cinématographiques,* nos. 38-39 [Printemps 1965], p. 99 note 6.) Soupault's review of the film *Charlot voyage* (*The Immigrant*) originally appeared in *Littérature,* no. 6 (Aug. 1919), p. 22, and is reproduced by Bonnet in the article just mentioned (p. 85).

58. In Marguerite Bonnet, "L'Aube du surréalisme . . . ," *Etudes cinématographiques,* nos. 38-39 (Printemps 1965). The Aragon citation originally appeared in his "Cinéma et Cie," *Littérature,* no. 4 (June 1919); Rigaut's in "Mae Murray," *Littérature,* n.s. no. 1 (Mar. 1922).

59. Breton refers to the "infortune continue" of automatic writing in "Le Message automatique" (Dec. 1933), in *Point du jour* (Gallimard, 1934), p. 226.

60. Breton, "Introduction, 1919," to *Lettres de guerre de Jacques Vaché,* précédées de quatre préfaces d'André Breton (K éditeur, 1949), s.p. [p. 3].

CHAPTER III

1. *Manifeste du surréalisme* (1924), in *Manifestes du surréalisme* (Pauvert, 1962), p. 40.

> SURREALISME, n.m. Automatisme psychique pur par lequel on se propose d'exprimer, soit verbalement, soit par écrit, soit de toute autre manière, le fonctionnement réel de la pensée. Dictée de la pensée, en l'absence de tout contrôle exercé par la raison, en dehors de toute préoccupation esthétique ou morale.
>
> ENCYCL. *Philos.* Le surréalisme repose sur la croyance à la réalité supérieure de certaines formes d'association négligées jusqu'à lui, à la toute puissance du rêve, au jeu désintéressé de la pensée. Il tend à ruiner définitivement tous les autres mécanismes psychiques

et à se substituer à eux dans la résolution des principaux problèmes de la vie. Ont fait acte de SURREALISME ABSOLU MM. Aragon, Baron, Boiffard, Breton, Carrive, Crevel, Delteil, Desnos, Eluard, Gérard, Limbour, Malkine, Morise, Naville, Noll, Péret, Picon, Soupault, Vitrac.

2. Robert Champigny, "Analyse d'une définition du surréalisme," *Publications of the Modern Language Assn.*, vol. 81, no. 1 (Mar. 1966), pp. 139-44.

3. Breton reproduced significant extracts from Freud's *La Question de l'analyse par les non-médecins* (NRF, 1927), in *La Révolution surréaliste*, no. 9-10 (Oct. 1, 1927), pp. 25-32.

4. *Manifestes*, p. 18. The two most rewarding studies of surrealist "philosophy" are (1) Ferdinand Alquié, *Philosophie du surréalisme* (Flammarion, 1955; tr. *The Philosophy of Surrealism*, Ann Arbor: The University of Michigan Press, 1965) and (2) Michel Carrouges, *André Breton et les données fondamentales du surréalisme* (Gallimard, 1950). An earthly paradise is the only one possible to a materialist, for salvation, such as it may be to him, must of necessity be immanent.

5. [Premier] *Manifeste,* in *Manifestes,* p. 63.

6. See chap. I on the surrealist aesthetic, esp. note 3. In "Délires I" of his *Saison en Enfer*, Rimbaud has his Vierge folle insist that "La vraie vie est absente. Nous ne sommes pas au monde." After which he attributes to the Epoux infernal the view that "L'amour est à réinventer." In Rimbaud, *Oeuvres*, S. Bernard, ed. (Garnier, 1960), p. 224. In "Délires II" Rimbaud speaks of "l'hallucination simple," "sophismes magiques" which he would explain by means of "l'hallucination des mots." And finally, as he says, "Je finis par trouver sacré le désordre de mon esprit" (*ibid.*, p. 230).

7. [Premier] *Manifeste,* in *Manifestes,* p. 60. See also Breton's *Misère de la poésie* (Editions Surréalistes, 1932).

8. *Manifestes,* p. 61.

9. "Lettre à A. Rolland de Renéville" (Feb. 1932), in Breton, *Point du jour*, pp. 124-25.

10. The last line of Verlaine's "Art poétique" (1874), in the collection *Jadis et naguère* (1884), is "Et tout le reste est littérature," where the context leaves no doubt that the final term has the sense of something worthless, trashy.

11. *Manifestes,* p. 44.

12. *Ibid.,* p. 27.

13. In *Arts,* no. 382 (Oct. 1952), p. 10.

14. Breton, *Entretiens* (Gallimard, 1952), p. 82.

15. From "Introduction au Discours sur le peu de réalité," *Commerce,* III (Hiver 1924), p. 49. Reprinted in *Point du jour,* pp. 26-27.

16. Breton, *Entretiens,* p. 56.

17. Soupault published the section "Hôtels" (*Les Champs magnétiques,* Au Sans Pareil, 1920, pp. 74-75) in *Littérature,* no. 12 (Feb. 1920), s.p. In this same issue can be found a poem by Valéry and one by Raymond Radiguet. Breton's "Lune de miel" and "Usine" (*Les Champs magnétiques,* pp. 78-80) were included in his *Poèmes,* pp. 27-28.

18. *Manifestes,* p. 60 note 1. There would appear to be two distinct techniques used in *Les Champs magnétiques*: (1) justaposition of texts composed independently, "simultaneously"; (2) passages on which each author collaborated, e.g., by writing one sentence each. See Michel Sanouillet, *Dada à Paris* (Pauvert, 1965), p. 125 note 1.

19. Breton had tried several years before, with only moderate success, to convert his close war-time friend, Jacques Vaché, to an appreciation of Rimbaud. See, e.g., Jacques Vaché, *Lettres de guerre* (K éditeur, 1949), esp. the letter dated "9-5-18" to André Breton. The two passages from *Les Champs magnétiques,* are from pages 23 and 31. Cf. Rimbaud, "Mauvais sang" and "Alchimie du verbe," both in his *Saison en Enfer.*

20. *Les Champs magnétiques,* p. 50. Cf. the section in Lautréamont's second *Chant* beginning "Il est minuit; on ne voit pas un seul omnibus" (Corti, 1946, pp. 49 sq.). Lautréamont's *Poésies,* previously unpublished, were first made available in *Littérature,* nos. 2 and 3 (Apr., May 1919), which would indicate that Breton and Soupault had some knowledge of his work prior to composing *Les Champs magnétiques.* Sanouillet has convincingly shown that *Les Champs magnétiques* was written in the late spring or very early summer of 1919, that is, shortly after Breton had laboriously transcribed the *Poésies* from the only known copy, in the Bibliothèque Nationale. (See Sanouillet, *Dada à Paris,* chap. 5, esp. p. 124, and Breton, *Entretiens,* p. 46.) Interestingly enough, the first twentieth-century edition of *Les Chants de Maldoror* was undertaken by Blaise Cendrars in 1920, while employed by the publishing house La Sirène.

21. Lautréamont's works, *Chants* and *Poésies* alike, are in prose. Breton and Soupault on occasion gave their prose creations a free-verse form, at least to the extent of starting each line with a capital letter. Meter, however, is irregular and rhyme is absent. Poetry would therefore seem to refer to the intention or the attitude of the author(s) more than to any stylistic traits or themes in the works themselves.

22. Rimbaud, "Délires II: Alchimie du verbe," *Saison en Enfer.* Breton-Soupault, *Les Champs magnétiques,* p. 31. Lautréamont, *Les Chants de Maldoror,* Chant II (Corti, 1946, p. 65). Breton-Soupault, *Les Champs magnétiques,* p. 44.

23. Breton and Soupault in the first section of *Les Champs magnétiques,* p. 12.

24. Aragon's *Anicet* was published by Gallimard in 1921. Breton's *Poisson soluble* appeared as an appendix to the first Manifesto (1924), presumably designed to illustrate and exemplify what is best, or at least typical, in surrealist writing.

25. The page references to Breton's *Poisson soluble* are to the 1962 reprinting in his *Manifestes.* The references to Rimbaud's *Illuminations* are to the Suzanne Bernard edition of Rimbaud's *Oeuvres* (Garnier, 1960).

26. Cf. "J'ai horreur de tous les métiers. [ . . . ] La main à plume vaut la main à charrue.—Quel siècle à mains!—Je n'aurai jamais ma main. Après, la domesticité mène trop loin." Rimbaud, "Mauvais sang," *Saison en Enfer,* in *Oeuvres,* S. Bernard, ed., p. 213. "L'amour est à réinventer," in "Délires I," *Saison en Enfer, Ibid.,* p. 224. "La musique savante manque à notre désir," from "Conte," *Illuminations, ibid.,* p. 260.

27. On the spur of the moment Eluard left Paris in Mar. 1924 for a trip around the world, via Tahiti, Singapore, and Saigon. He returned in Oct., just in time to learn of the publication of Breton's *Manifeste du surréalisme.* The most detailed account of this *fugue* is given by P. Waldberg in his study on *Max Ernst* (Pauvert, 1958), pp. 182-86. Eluard had absconded with his father's money, headed for Monte Carlo, where he played and won, and then on to Indochina. Once there, he telegraphed his wife, Gala, to come with Max Ernst (her lover) and join him in Saigon. Eventually, Eluard returned to France alone, joined shortly thereafter by Gala and Ernst. See also, *P. Eluard, oeuvres choisies,* first volume in the series Poètes d'aujourd'hui (Seghers, 1953, rev. ed.), pp. 35-37.

28. Breton's early writings are discussed by H. Pastoureau, "Des influences dans la poésie présurréaliste d'André Breton," *André Breton. Essais et témoignages,* Marc Eigeldinger, ed. (Neuchâtel: A la Baconnière, 1950), pp. 137-73. The curious tale of Rimbaud's *La Chasse spirituelle,* along with a brief description of previous Rimbaud forgeries, can be found in B. A. Morrissette's fascinating (and very scholarly) study, *The Great Rimbaud Forgery* (St. Louis: Washington Univ. Studies, 1956). Morrissette points out that Breton may well have been apprised of the document's disputed authenticity by one of the "insiders." (*The Great Rimbaud Forgery,* pp. 157-58)

29. Breton, *Entretiens,* p. 42.

30. From the collective broadside *Lautréamont envers et contre tout* (early 1927), reprinted in Nadeau, *Histoire du surréalisme* (Editions du Seuil, 1964), p. 245. The occasion for this restatement, signed by Aragon, Breton, and Eluard, was a new edition of *Les Chants de Maldoror*, with a preface by the recently expelled Soupault.

31. Among the more recent adherents of this approach are André Pieyre de Mandiargues and Joyce Mansour.

32. This is the beginning of the final section of Péret's *La Brebis galante*, dated "Automne 1924," but first published by Le Terrain Vague in 1959.

33. "La Fourmi" and "Les Hiboux" were first published in *Trente chantefables pour les enfants sages* (Gründ, 1944), and reprinted in the Desnos anthology *Domaine public* (Gallimard, 1953), p. 375. The Prévert selections, "La Cène" and "L'Amiral," are from his *Paroles* (Gallimard, [1946] 1949), pp. 192, 268. The final passage is from Péret's *La Brebis galante*, p. 49.

34. *La Brebis galante*, p. 41.

35. As early as 1916, Tzara had insisted that "Dada est notre intensité." In "Manifeste de Monsieur Antipyrine," *Sept manifestes Dada* (Pauvert, 1963), p. 15. The movement, as he explains, was born "d'un besoin d'indépendance" ("Manifeste Dada 1918," *ibid.*, p. 22). In a Dada work, "chaque page doit exploser" (*ibid.*, p. 26), which is not without recalling similar statements by Breton, esp. in *Nadja* and *L'Amour fou*. Tzara continues by affirming that "L'expérience est aussi un résultat du hasard. . ." and "L'art est une chose privée, l'artiste le fait pour lui" (*ibid.*, pp. 28-30). Thanks to M. Sanouillet, we now have conclusive evidence of Breton's enthusiasm on reading "Le Manifeste Dada 1918": "Je me suis réellement enthousiasmé pour votre manifeste," he writes on Jan. 22, 1919. If Vaché, "ce que j'aimais le plus au monde," is dead, Tzara, as if by miracle, has come to replace him: "il [Vaché] aurait reconnu votre esprit pour frère du sien . . . " (*Dada à Paris*, p. 440). Freud is no stranger to automatism, but what of the author of "La pensée se fait dans la bouche"? (Tzara, "Dada manifeste sur l'amour faible et l'amour amer" [Dec. 12, 1920], *Sept manifestes Dada*, p. 58).

36. Tzara, in a statement that prefigures Communist opposition to Freud, noted that "La psychanalyse est une maladie dangereuse, endort les penchants anti-réels de l'homme et systématise la bourgeoisie"—this just prior to a section devoted to "La Spontanéité dadaiste," in "Manifeste Dada 1918," *Sept manifestes Dada*, p. 28.

37. Breton, *Entretiens*, p. 68. Breton is here referring to Péret.

38. J. H. Matthews, Introduction to *Péret's Score*, an anthology with translations on facing pages (Minard, 1965), p. 7.

39. In the first Manifesto, which is the one most likely to express views that would have had a determining influence on Péret. (Breton, *Manifestes*, p. 48). The practice of surrealist speech would lead to a type of activity not significantly different from that suggested by Tzara's "La pensée se fait dans la bouche" (*Sept manifestes Dada*, p. 58). Breton regularly returned to this idea, e.g., "Il ne faut donc pas s'étonner de voir le surréalisme se situer tout d'abord *presque uniquement* (italics mine) sur le plan du langage. . ." (*Second manifeste*, 1929, in *Manifestes*, p. 183); and still later, in the opening sentence of "Du surréalisme en ses oeuvres vives" (1953), "Il est aujourd'hui de notoriété courante que le surréalisme, en tant que mouvement organisé, a pris naissance dans une opération de grande envergure portant sur le langage" (*ibid.*, p. 355).

40. In his first Manifesto Breton speaks of "L'intraitable manie qui consiste à ramener l'inconnu au connu" (*ibid.*, p. 21). The Péret quotation is the title of a brief statement in *VVV*, no. 4 (Feb. 1944), s.p.

41. In *Péret's Score* (J. H. Matthews, ed.), pp. 24 and 38.

42. *Ibid.*, pp. 9-10. The citation from Ristitch is found in "L'Humour, attitude morale," *Le Surréalisme au service de la révolution*, no 6 (May 15, 1933), p. 36.

43. Camus, *L'Homme révolté* (Gallimard, 1951), p. 328.

44. *Le Mythe de Sisyphe* (Gallimard, 1942), p. 166.

45. Breton, "Paratonnerre" (1939), Introduction to his *Anthologie de l'humour noir* (Sagittaire, 1950), p. 11. This anthology was first published in 1940 (achevé d'imprimer 10 juin 1940), enlarged in 1945 and again in 1950. According to certain letters from Mme Neumann, director of the Editions du Sagittaire, to Breton, the work was conceived as early as Oct. 1935. See the Catalogue, no. 10, of the Librairie Nicaise (145, Boulevard St-Germain), 1960, entry no. 324, pp. 82-83. The anecdote concerning the convict is from the same *Anthologie*, p. 14.

46. Surrealist humor, says Breton, following Freud, is "un mode de pensée tendant à l'épargne de la *dépense nécessitée par la douleur*." In "Paratonnerre," Introduction to *Anthologie de l'humour noir*, p. 14. Immediately thereafter he quotes Freud on the pleasure derived from this type of humor: "nous le ressentons [ce plaisir] comme particulièrement apte à nous libérer et à nous exalter" (*ibid.*).

47. Camus, "L'Homme absurde: La Comédie," *Le Mythe de Sisyphe*, p. 110. It is clear in context that Camus takes the actor to be one type of "absurd" man, eminently conscious of the transitory nature of his activities.

48. In "La Création absurde: Philosophie et roman," *Le Mythe de Sisyphe*, p. 130. Allusions to this quantitative ethic recur with some fre-

quency in Malraux, one of Camus' early guides. Garine, for example, in Malraux's *Les Conquérants*, affirms "J'ai appris aussi qu'une vie ne vaut rien, mais que rien ne vaut une vie." In the Livre de Poche edition (1955), p. 195.

49. Camus, "La Création absurde: Philosophie et roman," *Le Mythe de Sisyphe*, p. 138. As early as 1938, Camus, in his review of Sartre's *La Nausée*, remarked that "Constater l'absurdité de la vie ne peut être une fin, mais seulement un commencement." In *Alger républican*, Oct. 20, 1938; reprinted in Camus, *Essais* (Bibliothèque de la Pléiade, 1965), p. 1419. The various forms that *la révolte* can take— the next step implied by Camus—are amply illustrated in his works. As he said in *Le Mythe de Sisyphe* (p. 118), "Il vient toujours un temps où il faut choisir entre la contemplation et l'action. Cela s'appelle devenir un homme."

50. Claude Courtot, *Introduction à la lecture de Benjamin Péret* (Le Terrain Vague, 1965), p. 27.

51. *Le Canard enchaîné*, Sept. 23, 1959; reprinted in the collective *hommage*: *De la part de Péret*, s.l.n.d. [1963], p. 20. (Péret had died Sept. 18, 1959.) The poems published under the title "Je ne mange pas de ce pain-là" first appeared in *La Révolution surréaliste*, no. 12 (Dec. 15, 1929), pp. 51-52, and include in addition to the two items quoted, "La Stabilisation du franc," "Hymne aux anciens combattants patriotes," and "La Loi Paul Boncour." Aragon's "Front rouge," written in the USSR in Nov. 1930, and published in the second number of the Moscow review *Littérature de la révolution mondiale*, first appeared in France in his collection of poems *Persécuté persécuteur* (Ed. Surréalistes, 1931) and later was reprinted in Breton's *Misère de la poésie* (Ed. Surréalistes, 1932) and in Nadeau, *Histoire du surréalisme* (1964).

52. Confronting these two works written scarcely a year apart, similar in technique, content, and inspiration (and neither showing any signs of automatism), it seems indisputable that Péret's "Je ne mange pas de ce pain-là" *is* a surrealist work only because Péret said it was and Breton did not object; Aragon's "Front rouge" is *not* a surrealist work because Aragon had second thoughts about his surrealist affiliation, and so did Breton. With criteria of that sort, objective history (and criticism) would become even more perplexing than it normally is. And yet, dealing with the surrealist *period*, as we are, we have little choice in the matter. Were this a *topical* study, and this an analysis of surrealism as a web of themes running through French literature rather than one limited chronologically, the approach would, of course, be different, as might some of our conclusions.

53. See Matthew Josephson, *Life Among the Surrealists* (Holt, Rinehart and Winston, 1962), pp. 135-38, in which the author describes Breton's

wrath at what he saw in a Paris brothel, where he and his wife—with M. Josephson and his wife, Soupault and his, Ribemont-Dessaignes, Vitrac, Baron, and Péret—had gone, piped along by "the true soul of Dadaism in this band," Phillippe Soupault (Josephson, p. 121). According to a later member of the group, who at the time of writing had no reason to be anything but favorably inclined, Breton was marked by a "ton prophétique et une volonté de sérieux excluant tout badinage." Patrick Waldberg, *Max Ernst* (Pauvert, 1958), p. 171. And Breton himself, in answer to the question, "Pensez-vous que le libertinage chez l'homme enlève à cet homme toute possibilité d'aimer?" answered "Sans aucun doute." In *La Révolution surréaliste*, no. 11 (Mar. 1928), p. 40.

54. Breton, "Ode à Charles Fourier" (1947), *Poèmes* (Gallimard, 1948), p. 243. See the excellent critical edition of this ode by Jean Gaulmier (Librairie C. Klincksieck, 1961).

55. Breton, "L'Union libre" (1931), *Poèmes*, pp. 65-67.

56. The novelty of "L'Union libre" is somewhat less convincing when we compare it with the extracts of Tzara's "L'Homme approximatif," published shortly before in *La Révolution Surréaliste*, no. 12 (Dec. 15, 1929), pp. 18-20, immediately following Breton's Second Manifesto. Tzara's poem, almost twice as long as "L'Union libre," has as its main rhythmic device the repetition of *le* (*la, les*), *un* (*une*) and *et*. Breton, it would seem, borrowed the technique and refined it. (There are *only* four syntactic patterns in the Breton poem; Tzara uses three primarily, but not exclusively.) Tzara's relationship with surrealism is discussed at greater length later in this chapter.

57. André Gide, "L'Evolution du théâtre," lecture delivered in Brussels, 1904, quoted by Pierre Brodin, *Présences contemporaines* (Debresse, 1955), t. 2, p. 60.

58. Breton, "Ode à Charles Fourier," *Poèmes*, pp. 239-40.

59. "Les mots du reste ont fini de jouer. Les mots font l'amour," says Breton, concluding his article on "Les Mots sans rides," *Pas perdus*, p. 171.

60. "Ode à Charles Fourier," *Poèmes*, p. 253, 255-56.

61. Péret, "La Pensée est *UNE* et indivisible," *VVV*, no. 4 (Feb. 1944), s.p.

62. *Ibid.*

63. Or as Breton put it: "Bien que, par mesure de défense, parfois cette activité [le jeu] ait été dite par nous 'expérimentale,' nous y cherchions avant tout le divertissement." In "L'Un dans l'autre," *Médium*, no. 2 (Feb. 1954), p. 17.

64. Breton concludes his explanation of the change in administration by saying, "Dût l'ampleur du mouvement surréaliste en souffrir, il me paraît de rigueur de n'ouvrir les colonnes de cette revue qu'à des hommes qui ne soient pas à la recherche d'un alibi littéraire." From "Pourquoi je prends la direction de *La Révolution surréaliste*," *La Révolution surréaliste*, no. 4 (July 15, 1925), p. 3.

65. *Ibid.*, p. 3. Several months earlier Breton had commented, "Or je pense avec tous les hommes vraiment libres que la Révolution, jusque dans ses abus, demeure la plus haute, la plus émouvante expression qui se puisse donner de cet amour du Bien, réalisation de l'unité de la volonté universelle et des volontés individuelles." In "La Dernière Grève," *ibid.*, no. 2 (Jan. 15, 1925), p. 1. This identification of the French Revolution, including its abuses, with the idea of Good is developed by Desnos in the very next issue: "La Révolution, c'est-à-dire La Terreur," *ibid.*, no. 3 (Apr. 15, 1925), pp. 26-27. Lest there be any misunderstanding, Desnos, who opened his *mise au point* with "C'est l'instauration de celle-ci qui m'intéresse et son avènement seul aujourd'hui me fait encore espérer la disparition des canailles qui encombrent la vie," concludes with an injunction which might have been taken from Breton's article cited above: "QU'IL EST TEMPS ENFIN DE S'OCCUPER DE L'ETERNITE" (*ibid.*).

66. The text of "La Révolution d'abord et toujours!" is reproduced, along with any number of other significant surrealist pronouncements, in M. Nadeau, *Histoire du surréalisme suivie de Documents surréalistes* (Editions du Seuil, 1964). Previous editions of this work appeared in 1945, 1947-48 (2 vols.), and 1958.

67. From *Le Devoir et l'inquiétude* (1917) in *Choix de poèmes* (Gallimard, 1951), p. 14. Subsequent references to this edition will be given in the body of the text.

68. First published in 1911, with illustrations by Raoul Dufy.

69. Patrick Waldberg, *Max Ernst*, p. 172. This bittersweet quality, incidentally, may well have its origin in the unexpected liaison between Eluard's wife, Gala, and Max Ernst, established during their first meeting in Cologne in the fall of 1921. (See Waldberg, *Ernst*, pp. 172-73.) Gala eventually left her husband, in the late twenties, to live with Dali, whom she ultimately married.

70. Nusch, "la compagne inséparable de sa vie et de son oeuvre," who died Nov. 1946. See René Lacôte, "La Vie et l'oeuvre," *Europe*, no. 91-92 (July-Aug. 1953), p. 28. This special number of *Europe* was devoted to Eluard, who died Nov. 18, 1952.

71. With the obvious exception of those few "regular" poems, such as "Denise disait aux merveilles," *Mourir de ne pas mourir* (1924), in *Choix de poèmes,* p. 59.

72. The one "hermetic" line of the poem is "Comme une pierre sur le ciel." Grammatically, one might have expected "une pierre *dans* le ciel" which, while obscure, would at least present a comprehensible image. Hence the translation found above. "Une pierre *sur* le ciel" is meaningless; but given the previous line, and the proportion implied by *comme,* *pierre* must refer to *elle* and *ciel* to the poet. This image therefore reenforces the picture of the *amoureuse* so in love that she is a thing in the hands of her poet-creator. The literary language is, almost by definition, ungrammatical, and the above line is but an extreme case in point. The poem is from *Mourir de ne pas mourir* (1924), in *Choix de poèmes,* p. 58.

73. Breton speaks of the "choix de mots qui s'exerce d'ailleurs à travers lui et non, à proprement parler, qu'il exerce" in his *prière d'insérer* for *Capitale de la douleur* (1926). See the copy of this in the advertisement on the back cover of *La Révolution surréaliste,* no. 8 (Dec. 1, 1926), reprinted in Breton's *Point du jour* (1934), pp. 68-69.

74. See Francis Carmody's excellent "Eluard's Rupture with Surrealism," *Publications of the Modern Language Assn.,* LXXVI, no. 4, Pt. 1 (Sept. 1961), pp. 436-46, and English Showalter, Jr., "Biographical Aspects of Eluard's Poetry," *P.M.L.A.,* LXXVIII, no. 3 (June 1963), pp. 280-86. Eluard's Resistance poetry and postwar politically inspired verse are, regularly, too far removed from any surrealist inspiration to warrant discussion here. In that verse, according to Péret, he is no longer the "Inventeur pour qui la découverte n'est que le moyen d'atteindre une nouvelle découverte," but rather one among a horde, whose writing is on "le niveau lyrique de la publicité pharmaceutique" (B. Péret, *Le Déshonneur des poètes,* Mexico, 1945, s.p.).

75. There is, of course, a rhythmic unity in "L'Union libre" (1931) and a thematic unity in the "Ode à Charles Fourier" (1947), but these are exceptions. That Breton may have had difficulty in "letting himself go" and plunging to Unconscious bedrock is suggested by Breton himself in his "Entrée des médiums," when he mentions that "Eluard, Ernst, Morise et moi qui, en dépit de toute notre bonne volonté, ne nous sommes pas endormis" (*Pas perdus,* p. 158).

76. The untitled "Monde dans un baiser. . ." is from Breton's *L'Air de l'eau* (1934), in *Poèmes,* pp. 125-26. The translation is here, even more than elsewhere, an approximation, as there is only the vaguest of contexts to use as a guide. Such is the hallucinatory effect of a kiss. The poem is a series of verbal "points," one evoking the next, where phonetic association and dream imagery play hide-and-seek. *Coudrier* brings on *cousues*

(l.2); the series of sibilants conjures up *essaim* (l.3). The monkey-like lions may well be composites from paintings of Ernst or Dali, or *singes* may be taken in the sense of "ugly." The Mexican salamanders with blue shoes (l.6) is a bit of Nahuatl exoticism that attests to some dictionary hunting as much as it does to any observation of surrealist paintings. *Voie* (l.7), normally in the plural in the phrase *voies de fait*, recalls *la corniche* of l.4. From lines 7-10 the twin themes of beauty (love) and death alternate. The worlds of dream and reality continue their game of leapfrog in the lines immediately following: the frontiers of reality (*bornes mentales*, l.11), with stringy vine-like (recalling wine?) hair, are breeched, thus permitting the imprisoned tufted birds to regain their liberty. *Barreaux* leads to *fuseau*, and man's flight in the early morning is like that of the long-necked birds above (l.14-18). The gypsy lass with the flowered skirt is the one by whom we measure time (l.19-20). The bare-back rider, who might be expected to be juggling *orange balls* in some circus, is here seen galloping on a horse (a) turning gray, (b) dappled with small clouds: *pommelé* has the first meaning when referring to horses, the second when referring to the sky. The shape of the equestrian's undergarment presumably recalls an inverted tepee decorated by dream-worked Indians (l.23-26). Outside the wind blows through the trees and on the water. Mine are the shells, says the poet, but *écailles* (l.30) are also scales, such as those which cover the eye. *Hydrophile* (l.31) is normally used in the phrase *coton hydrophile*, and means absorbent cotton. It also, however, can refer to a certain type of water bug *Scolopendre* (l.34) too evokes two distinct items: a poisonous centipede and a type of fern—both of which are feminine in French, in spite of Breton's use of the masculine (probably a typographical error.) Did terms such as *axolotls*, *coéopsis*, and *scolopendre* come to Breton automatically, or the phrases *tu te diapre*, *fuseau d'air*, and *Les Indiens de l'oreiller*?

77. *La Rose publique* (1934), in *Choix de poèmes*. The selection "Comme deux gouttes d'eau" is from p. 137. It is interesting to note, in comparing this fragment with the previous selection from Breton, that the only verbal problem here is the sense of the last word, *loups*, which I have translated by the obvious *wolves*—implying that the poet is isolated from civilization, an outcast and an enemy. Neither of its two other meanings, however, *mask* or *error* (or even a type of fish), would significantly modify the sense of the poem.

78. Breton's "magic dictation" would have shocked—as it did—those committed to the then new doctrine of socialist realism. See Breton, "Entrée des médiums," *Pas perdus*, p. 150.

79. First published in *La Vie immédiate* (1932) and reprinted in *Poèmes pour tous par Paul Eluard. Choix de poèmes 1917-1952*, préface de Jean

Marcenac (Les Editeurs Français Réunis, 1952), p. 41. It is interesting that the much more extensive anthology published by Gallimard the preceding year, *Choix de poèmes*, does not include this poem, nor any number of other politically oriented items. The later anthology, on the other hand, very definitely stresses the political aspect of his work.

80. From Breton's first Manifesto, in *Manifestes*, pp. 43-44.

81. Quoted by Rosa Buchole, *L'Evolution poétique de Robert Desnos* (Bruxelles: Palais des Académies, 1956), p. 221.

82. According to Breton, "Le seul mot de liberté est tout ce qui m'exalte encore" (*Manifestes*, p. 17). For Eluard, "Il y a un mot qui m'exalte, un mot que je n'ai jamais entendu sans ressentir un grand frisson, un grand espoir, le plus grand, celui de vaincre les puissances de ruine et de mort qui accablent les hommes, ce mot c'est: fraternisation." In "L'Evidence poétique," first published in *Cahiers d'art, 11e année*, no. 6-7 (1936), reprinted separately by GLM in 1937 and incorporated in *Donner à voir* (Gallimard, 1939), pp. 85-86.

83. Prior to his discovery of surrealism, Desnos had written at least one alexandrine lament dealing with Marseilles whores and sailors chanting nostalgic refrains:

> Les putains de Marseille ont des soeurs océanes
> Dont les baisers malsains moisiront votre chair.
> Dans leur taverne basse un orchestre tzigane
> Fait valser les péris au bruit lourd de la mer.
>
> Navigateurs chantant des refrains nostalgiques,
> Partis sur la galère ou sur le noir vapeur,
> Espérez-vous d'un sistre ou d'un violon magique
> Charmer les matelots trop enclins à la peur?

From "Le Fard des Argonautes" (1919), in *Domaine public*, an anthology of Desnos' poetry introduced by René Bertelé (Gallimard, 1953), p. 23. The first reference to Desnos appears just after the break with Dada, in Breton's recapitulation "Clairement," *Littérature*, n.s., no. 4 (Sept. 1922), p. 2; reprinted in *Pas perdus*, p. 136. The first of Desnos' contributions signed "Rrose Sélavy" were published in *Littérature*, n.s., no. 5 (Oct. 1922). The genre, as far as the surrealists were concerned, was "invented" by Marcel Duchamp, then developed and extensively used by Desnos. There is a tip of the hat by Desnos in the direction of his predecessor when he says, "Rrose Sélavy connaît bien le marchand du sel" (Marcel Duchamp), in *Domaine public*, p. 40. The items in the text are all from *Domaine public*. Equally impressive in this spoonerism genre was Roger

Vitrac, now known principally for his theater. See, e.g., *Dés-Lyre,* poésies complètes de R. Vitrac présentées et annotées par Henri Béhar (Gallimard, 1964), esp. "Peau-Asie," first published in *Littérature,* n.s., no. 9 (Feb.-Mar. 1923), pp. 18-20. Can there be any doubt that this type of spoofing derives more from Dada than from principled surrealism?

84. The first two examples given are from the collection "L'Aumonyme," the third from "Langage cuit." Both collections date from 1923 and are included in *Domaine public,* to which the page references refer. It is not without interest that the parody on the Pater Noster, which originally appeared in the January 1923 issue of *Littérature,* and was dedicated to B. Péret, was later borrowed and modified by Jacques Prévert.

*Pater Noster*
Notre Père qui êtes aux cieux
Restez-y
Et nous nous resterons sur la terre
Qui est quelquefois si jolie
Avec ses mystères de New-York
Et puis ses mystères de Paris
Qui valent bien celui de la Trinité
Avec son petit canal de l'Ourcq
Sa grande muraille de Chine
Sa rivière de Morlaix
Ses bêtises de Cambrai
Avec son Océan Pacifique
Et ses deux bassins aux Tuileries
Avec ses bons enfants et ses mauvais sujets
Avec toutes les merveilles du monde
Qui sont là
Simplement sur la terre
Offertes à tout le monde
Éparpillées
Emerveillées elles-mêmes d'être de telles merveilles
Et qui n'osent se l'avouer
Comme une jolie fille nue qui n'ose se montrer
Avec les épouvantables malheurs du monde
Qui sont légion
Avec leurs légionnaires
Avec leurs tortionnaires
Avec les maîtres de ce monde
Les maîtres avec leurs prêtres leurs traîtres et leurs
reîtres
Avec les saisons
Avec les années

> Avec les jolies filles et avec les vieux cons
> Avec la paille de la misère pourissant dans l'acier des
> canons.

From *Paroles* (Gallimard, 1949), pp. 70-71. What is a source of word play to Desnos in 1923 becomes in Prévert's hands the point of departure for some astringent social commentary.

85. See André Breton, "Entrée des médiums" (1922), *Pas perdus*, pp. 147-58. In the first Manifesto Breton speaks of these fortunate few as "modestes *appareils enregistreurs*" (*Manifestes*, p. 42). It is worth repeating that Breton himself apparently never successfully experienced this hypnotic state. (See *Pas perdus*, p. 158.) The only techniques ever mentioned by Breton that would give him access to the Unconscious were dreams—and of these he wrote sparingly.

86. In *Blaise Cendrars vous parle*, interviews with Michel Manoll, recorded Apr. 14-25, 1950 (Denoël, 1952), p. 51.

87. See Breton, "Pourquoi je prends la direction de *La Révolution surréaliste*," *La Révolution surréaliste*, no. 4 (July 15, 1925), p. 3. His warning against the "poncif indiscutable à l'intérieur de ces textes [récits de rêves et autres textes surréalistes]" appears in the second Manifesto. In *Manifestes*, p. 189. Desnos' other errors—hesitancy in commiting himself on the political questions of the day, servile journalistic activities, pastiches of Rimbaud, use of the classical alexandrine line, calling a favorite Montparnasse night club *Maldoror*—are ticked off in that Manifesto (*Manifestes*, pp. 198-202). Along the same line is Jean Tortel's recent criticism: Desnos' poetry, he suggests, brings to mind Musset; it is sincere, musical, and not very substantial. See Jean Tortel, "Desnos aujourd'hui," *Critique*, no. 219-20 (Aug.-Sept. 1965), pp. 725-26. Tortel, unfortunately, never gets around to indicating whom he would consider substantial, so it is rather difficult to know exactly how to interpret his statement.

88. The lines cited are the first and last stanzas of "The Night of Loveless Nights" (1930), *Domaine public*, pp. 215-35.

89. Desnos' *La Liberté ou l'amour!* (Kra, 1927) was condemned and withdrawn from circulation by order of the "tribunal correctionnel de la Seine" (R. Buchole, *L'Evolution poétique de R. Desnos*, p. 223). It was reprinted along wtih *Deuil pour deuil* by Gallimard in 1962. His children's rhymes were published under the title *Chantefables et chantefleurs* (Librairie Gründ, 1944), extracts from which can be found in *Domaine public*: "La Fourmi," p. 375; "Le Pélican," p. 378.

90. R. Buchole, *L'Evolution poétique de R. Desnos*, p. 24.

91. That Desnos did not abandon his "popular" style when he left the movement can be seen in the opening lines to "Couplets de la rue Saint-Martin" (1942), *Domaine public*, p. 384:

> Je n'aime plus la rue Saint-Martin
> Depuis qu'André Platard l'a quittée.

In "Réflexions sur la poésie" (Jan. 1944), Desnos suggests that for poetry to endure it must be part fire, part glacier, "délirante et lucide" (*Domaine public*, p. 404). While this is clearly a recollection of Breton's *beauté convulsive* (see last page of *Nadja*), it could quite as easily hark back to Racine's heroines—Phèdre, for example.

92. In Rimbaud's *Lettre du voyant* (to Paul Demeny, May 15, 1871), he speaks of a "langue qui sera de l'âme pour l'âme, résumant tout . . . de la pensée accrochant la pensée et tirant" (*Oeuvres*, S. Bernard, ed., p. 347).

93. First published in Picabia's *Cannibale*, no. 1 (Apr. 25, 1920).

94. First published in *Le Mouvement perpétuel* (1926), a collection of verse written between 1920 and 1924. Quoted from Claude Roy's edition of Aragon in the series Poètes d'aujourd'hui (Seghers, 1945), p. 69. *Persiennes* are exterior venetian blinds.

95. Aragon, *La Grande gaîté*, 1927-1929 (Gallimard, 1929), p. 18.

96. M. Sanouillet, in his *Dada à Paris*, has effectively defended this filiation between Dada and surrealism. See esp. pp. 123-30.

97. Desnos' "Confession d'un enfant du siècle" first appeared in *La Révolution surréaliste*, no. 6 (Mar. 1, 1926), pp. 18-21; no. 8 (Dec. 1, 1926), pp. 21-22. "Le Veilleur du Pont au Change" was first published in *Honneur des poètes II: Europe* (1944), pp. 51-56, under the pseudonym "Valentin Guillois." In *Domaine public*, pp. 395-400. It is probably one of the three or four most moving poems to come out of World War II, along with sections of Eluard's *Au rendez-vous allemand* and Aragon's *Crève-coeur* and *Le Musée Grévin*.

98. Péret, on the last page of *Le Déshonneur des poètes* (Mexico, 1945, s.p.). He, however, is there referring to surrealist poetry, not the circumstantial verse of his former colleagues.

99. *Anicet* (Gallimard, 1921). There is an unpublished *Clé d'Anicet*, by Aragon, in the Fonds Doucet (Paris). Its essential elements are reproduced by R. Garaudy in his *L'Itinéraire d'Aragon* (Gallimard, 1961), pp. 106-9.

100. *Les Aventures de Télémaque* (Gallimard, 1922), p. 9.

101. In Aragon, "A quoi pensez-vous?" *Ecrits nouveaux*, VIII, no. 8-9 (Aug.-Sept. 1921) pp. 151-52. This is, incidentally, one of the earliest uses of the term surrealist by a member of the group-to-be, but here it would appear to have the restricted meaning of "Paris Dada." Apollinaire had, of course, previously given his play *Les Mamelles de Tirésias* (1917) the subtitle "drame surréaliste"—which was the first use of the term anywhere.

102. Aragon, in *La Revue européenne*, Aug. 1924, p. 106; quoted by Roger Garaudy, *L'Itinéraire d'Aragon*, p. 155. This antedates Breton's comment on the surrealist "poncif" by several years. (See Breton's Second Manifesto, in *Manifestes*, p. 189.) Soupault, at this time, was one of the editors of *La Revue européenne*.

103. "Lorsque tout est fini. . . ," *Ecrits nouveaux*, IX, no. 1 (Jan. 1922), pp. 32-42; "Barrès," *L'Information d'Extrême-Orient*, quotidien illustré, Jan. 28, 1924, p. 4. It is worth noting that the introduction to this last article speaks of Aragon as a "disciple de Barrès"—this less than three years after the *procès Barrès* at which Aragon and Soupault played the roles of defense attorneys eager to have their "client" condemned. The article in question, however, makes quite clear that Aragon felt he had been strongly influenced by Barrès. (For information on the procès Barrès, see *Littérature*, no. 20, Aug. 1921, and M. Sanouillet, *Dada à Paris*, pp. 254-66.)

104. The resemblance in subject matter and tone between Aragon's "Une Vague de rêves," *Commerce*, II (Automne 1924), and Breton's "Introduction au Discours sur le peu de réalité," *Commerce*, III (Hiver 1924)— both describing the surrealism of the day, with the nod going to Aragon's as the more *envoûtant*—is too patent to be stressed. There is a comparable resemblance in form and subject matter between Aragon's *Le Paysan de Paris* (Gallimard, 1926), a fascinating travelogue through a Paris then fast disappearing, where the *hasard objectif* and the *lieu sacré* sometimes appear to trip over one another's feet, and Breton's first excursion into the prose tale, *Nadja*. See P. E. Firchow, "*Nadja* and *Le Paysan de Paris* . . . ," *Wisconsin Studies in Contemporary Literature*, VI, 3 (Autumn 1965), pp. 293-307, for a summary treatment.

105. *Le Libertinage* (Gallimard, 1924), p. 7. The work, incidentally, is dedicated to Pierre Drieu La Rochelle, a close friend of Aragon's, and about whom we shall have more to say later. (See chap. IV on surrealism and politics.)

106. Both *Le Paysan de Paris* and *Le Traité du style* were published by Gallimard, the first in 1926, the second in 1928. M. Josephson, *Life Among the Surrealists* (Holt, Rinehart and Winston, 1962).

107. *Paysan de Paris*, pp. 125 sq. and passim.

108. *Certâ* was the name of one of the group's favorite cafés. See *Paysan*, pp. 90-99. Aragon is here following Desnos, "ce singulier sage moderne" (*ibid.*, p. 110).

109. Aragon in *Paysan*, pp. 80-81, 157-58.

110. Aragon, "Une Vague de rêves," *Commerce*, II (Automne 1924), p. 99. The state of utter exhaustion in which surrealist "games" often left the members of the group is described in some detail in *Paysan*, pp. 163 sq. Breton himself was not unaware of this danger. See, e.g., "Le surréalisme ne permet pas à ceux qui s'y adonnent de le délaisser quand il leur plaît. Tout porte à croire qu'il agit sur l'esprit à la manière des stupéfiants. [. . .] . . . le surréalisme se présente comme un *vice nouveau*, qui ne semble pas devoir être l'apanage de quelques hommes; il a comme le haschisch de quoi satisfaire les délicats . . ." From the first Manifesto in *Manifestes*, p. 51.

111. "Je vivais au hasard, à la poursuite du hasard, qui seul parmi les divinités avait su garder son prestige" (*Paysan*, p. 139), from the first page of the section entitled "Le Sentiment de la nature aux Buttes-Chaumont." "Ayant pris ces clartés en moi de la nature, des mythes, de leurs liens, j'éprouvais une sorte de fièvre à la recherche de ces mythes. Je les suscitais. Je me plaisais à m'en sentir cerné" (*ibid.*, p. 153). And the passage of *Paysan*, pp. 51-52, dealing with *la passante considérable* named Nana (the prototype for Breton's Nadja?)—for example, "Je suis, dit-elle, le goût même du jour, et par moi tout respire. Connais-tu les refrains à la mode? Ils sont si pleins de moi qu'on ne peut les chanter. . . " (p. 52).

112. "J'aimais cet enivrement dont j'avais la pratique, et non pas la méthode," notes Aragon speaking of surrealism and its "hallucinations déifiées . . . ce détour de la distraction qui me procurait l'enthousiasme" (*Paysan*, p. 140). Later in the same work he refers to "notre abattement" as being so great as to make even speaking difficult—and his solution at that time is to stop for a drink (*ibid.*, p. 164).

113. *Ibid.*, p. 165.

114. *Ibid.*, p. 218.

115. *Ibid.*, p. 251.

116. *Ibid.*, p. 240. Aragon here identifies Sisyphus with the constant failures of transcendental idealism, all, however, necessary in man's progress toward a better universe, a concrete paradise on earth. Camus, on the other hand, sees the rock falling, but Sisyphus' recognition of the absurdity of it all makes him superior to his fate, and happy: "Il faut imaginer Sisyphe heureux" (*Le Mythe de Sisyphe*, p. 168). Where Camus parts company with the surrealists is on the question of hope.

Without hope there can be no revelation, no *merveilleux quotidien*—only life, and there even the Outsider is inside. With hope come dreams for the future, and slavery in the present. See *Le Mythe de Sisyphe*, p. 21.

117. *Journals of Arnold Bennett 1921-1928*, ed. Newman Flower (London, 1933), p. 183. Quoted by Peter E. Firchow, "*Nadja* and *Le Paysan de Paris*: Two Surrealist 'Novels,'" *Wisconsin Studies in Contemporary Literature*, VI, no. 3 (Autumn 1965), p. 297.

118. *Le bonheur* is defined by Aragon as an "Illusion de dernier ordre qui subsiste" (*Traité du style*, Gallimard, 1928, p. 104). The diatribe against the word continues on the following page when he ironically questions, "N'êtes-vous pas honteux . . . d'aller toujours cacher votre nez dans les jupes d'un mot?"

119. *Ibid.*, pp. 108, 111.

120. *Ibid.*, p. 113 .

121. In a letter to Breton dated "Zurich, le 21 sept. [1919]," Tzara writes: "Je pense, mon cher Breton, que vous cherchez aussi des *hommes*. Si l'on écrit, ce n'est qu'un refuge: de tout 'point de vue.' Je n'écris pas par métier. Je serais devenu un aventurier à grande allure et aux gestes fins si j'avais eu la force physique et la résistance nerveuse pour réaliser ce seul exploit: ne pas m'ennuyer. On écrit parce qu'il n'y a pas assez d'hommes nouveaux, par habitude, on publie pour chercher des hommes et pour avoir une occupation. Et même cela est très bête." Is it surprising that Breton saw in Tzara a spirit kindred to Vaché? Breton's reply is dated "Mardi 7 octobre 1919": "Il n'y a sans doute, mon cher Tristan Tzara, que vos lettres pour me conduire au bout de mes réflexions et mûrir l'un après l'autre mes desseins, si ce mot n'est pas trop fort. Je viens d'être infiniment ému de l'aveu de votre faiblesse devant l'ennui.—De même que vous dites: je serais devenu un aventurier à grande allure et aux gestes fins si . . . , voilà qui je deviendrais, me dis-je à chaque instant en pensant à vous, si. . . . Possibilité qui me tente et m'éloigne tour à tour. Tous mes efforts sont dirigés momentanément dans ce sens: vaincre l'ennui." And further on: "C'est même ce qui m'a donné l'idée d'ouvrir prochainement dans Littérature l'enquête: 'Pourquoi écrivez-vous?' Cela vous amuse-t-il un peu?" In Sanouillet, *Dada à Paris*, pp. 449-51.

122. *Traité*, p. 112.

123. *Ibid.*, p. 115.

124. *Ibid.*, p. 116. "Aujourd'hui sans avoir à faire à ceux [les Dadaistes] pour qui un paradoxe est passé à l'état de principe je me heurte chaque jour à la bêtise, à ses thuriféraires inconscients, quand je ne peux ouvrir un livre, parler à un homme, sans être couvert littéralement de cette poussière épaisse et suffocante qui sort des cervelles et des paillassons.

Un assez singulier tic de ce temps, celui de quelques esprits spécialisés, qu'une longue habitude du vocabulaire philosophique engage à douter de la signification du mot intelligence dans le langage courant. Le mélange ainsi de deux codes, de deux patois, fait vivre bien des gens qui se sentent subtils" (*ibid.*, pp. 116-17). Can these last few lines refer to anyone other than Breton? And if they do refer to Breton, can Breton have been unaware of it? There would seem to be little doubt that by 1928, with the publication of *Traité du style*, Aragon's days among the surrealists were numbered and that everyone concerned was aware of it.

125. *Traité*, pp. 60-61. And only then are others mentioned: Jacques Vaché, *Transition, Pas perdus*, Charles Cros . . . all apparently examples of striking surrealist style (pp. 61-62). It is quite clear that Aragon's views on surrealism do not coincide with Breton's. The latter would never have accepted the eighteenth-century moralist Vauvenargues or the nonaffiliated English-language periodical *Transition*.

126. *Traité*, p. 67.

127. *Ibid.*, pp. 78 sq. for his description of 1927. The absence of any allusion to communism would suggest that his early affiliation with the Party had not made any strong impression. See "Au Grand Jour" (1927), a statement announcing the Communist sympathies and affiliation of the signers (Aragon, Breton, Eluard, Péret, and Pierre Unik), in Maurice Nadeau, *Histoire du surréalisme* (1964). Jean Larnac, in *La Littérature françiase d'aujourd'hui* (1948), assures his readers that in Nov. 1926 "Aragon, Breton, Eluard, Péret, Unik adhérèrent au Parti [Communiste]" p. 71. Nov. 1926 is also the date regularly given for the expulsion of Soupault and Artaud from the surrealist group, and one of the contributing factors was their lack of enthusiasm for political commitment, their preference for "la poursuite *isolée* de la stupide aventure littéraire" ("Au Grand Jour," in Nadeau, *Histoire du surréalisme*, p. 261). But how sincere was Aragon's affiliation? Given the subsequent *Traité du style* there is good reason to wonder.

128. "J'ai horreur des plaisanteries sur ce sujet-là [le suicide]," he says at one point, only to add, "De toutes les idées celle du suicide est celle qui dépayse le mieux son homme, après tout" (*Traité*, pp. 88-89).

129. *Ibid.*, p. 92.

130. "Partir, voyager, s'évader, se tuer, infinitifs pris sur le ton de l'évidence. [ . . . ] Dans un cas comme dans l'autre, il s'agit toujours de paradis" (*ibid.*, p. 92).

131. "Paradis artificiels. C'est un pléonasme. Il n'y a pas de paradis naturel" (*ibid.*, p. 93). According to Camus, "Je tire ainsi de l'absurde trois conséquences qui sont ma révolte, ma liberté et ma passion" (*Mythe de Sisyphe*, p. 89).

132. *Traité*, p. 106.

133. The nausea, without the term, is very evident in *Traité*, esp. pp. 108-16. As for Dada, "à quoi bon revenir sur ce qui m'a mis dans les rages il y a sept huit ans. . . " (*ibid.*, p. 116).

134. Aragon discusses humor in *Traité*, pp. 132 sq. On page 137 he notes, "L'humour est d'avis qu'où solution pas d'humour."

135. "La poésie est par essence orageuse, et chaque image doit produire un cataclysme" (*ibid.*, p. 140). He had previously suggested that "pour qu'il y ait poésie il faut que l'humour fasse d'abord abstraction de l'anti-poésie" (*ibid.*, p. 138).

136. "L'inspiration d'ailleurs est partout chez elle, comment ne circulerait-elle pas dans le style? (*ibid.*, p. 182). "J'exige que les rêves qu'on me fait lire soient écrits en bon français" (*Ibid.*, p. 183).

137. *Ibid.*, pp. 186-87. It may be of some interest to mention that the first eleven numbers of *La Révolution surréaliste* contain dreams by Giorgio de Chirico (no. 1), Breton (no. 1), Renée Gauthier (no. 1), Michel Leiris (no. 2, 4, 5, 7), Max Morise (no. 3, 4, 5, 11), Artaud (no. 3), Eluard (no. 3), Naville (no. 3, 9-10), Queneau (no. 3), J.-A. Boiffard (no. 3), Marcel Noll (no. 7), and Aragon (no. 9-10). Except for Michel Leiris and Max Morise there doesn't seem to have been much publishable dreaming going on between 1925 and 1929.

138. *Traité*, p. 187.

139. *Ibid.*, p. 189.

140. *Ibid.*, p. 189.

141. In Sir Lewis Namier, "Human Nature in Politics," *Personalities and Powers. Selected Essays* (Harper Torchbooks, 1965), p. 4.

142. The most recent study on Aragon summarizes his contribution to surrealism by suggesting that *Anicet* is a ground-clearing adventure story, an attempt both to wipe out the past and to set a revolutionary tone for the future. *Les Aventures de Télémaque*, a parody on the Dada crisis of 1921, and *Le Libertinage* become two works of transition. *Le Paysan de Paris* announces the discovery of "le merveilleux dans le réel." *Le Traité du style*, the last prose work studied, serves to indicate Aragon's forthcoming rupture with Breton. (From the *prière d'insérer* to Yvette Gindine, *Aragon, prosateur surréaliste*, Genève, Droz, 1966. This work was published too late to be used in the present study.) The great merit of Miss Gindine's book is its scope and organization. Her comments, however, are on occasion overly categoric. *Anicet* is by definition an early work and could scarcely avoid revealing a Futurist-Dada influence, given

the climate in which it was composed. The techniques and themes which she sees so clearly in *Le Paysan de Paris* are no less evident in his previous writings. As for the *Traité du style*, as I hope I have shown, if it is not as theory-oriented as Breton's prose, it nonetheless fits far more easily into a surrealist frame than into a Marx-Engels-Lenin triangle— deviant and oppositional though his views may be. Aragon's break with surrealism, in short, came for personal reasons, and after 1930.

143. Breton took over *Littérature* with its fourth issue of the new series (Sept. 1922). The first three numbers had been jointly edited by Breton and Soupault. See Breton's explanation of the change in his article "Clairement," *Littérature*, n.s., no. 4. (Sept. 1922), pp. 1-2. It is this issue which consecrates the rupture with Tzara: "Il ne sera pas dit que le dadaisme aura servi à autre chose qu'à nous maintenir dans cet état de disponibilité parfaite où nous sommes [shades of Gide!] et dont maintenant nous allons nous éloigner avec lucidité [and of Aragon!] vers ce qui nous réclame." Last sentence of Breton's "Clairement."

144. "Caractères de l'évolution moderne et ce qui en participe," Conférence à l'Ateneo de Barcelone, Nov. 17, 1922, in *Pas perdus*, p. 209.

145. Soupault, *Le Bon apôtre* (Le Sagittaire, 1923), pp. 217-18. Earlier in the novel, speaking of Paris and literature, the author remarks that "Le grand ennemi c'était le public." Dada faced outward and never lost sight of the public; Breton shifted the emphasis inward, and with rare exceptions it remained turned in that direction until the opening to the left in the late twenties.

146. See Soupault, "Que reste-t-il de nos amours?" *Réalités*, no. 166 (Nov. 1959), pp. 82-88, 120-21. His remarks on Breton's interest in politics must be taken with caution, as that interest is not apparent before the Oct. 15, 1925, issue of *La Révolution surréaliste*, in which he reviews Trotsky's biography of Lenin.

147. Soupault, "Que reste-t-il de nos amours?" *Réalités*, no. 166 (Nov. 1959), p. 121. Aragon's review appeared in *La Révolution surréaliste*, no. 7 (June 15, 1926), pp. 31-32.

148. The first quotation is from Soupault, "Que reste-t-il de nos amours?" *Réalités*, no. 166 (Nov. 1959), p. 121. The second is from his "Whither French Literature?" *Transition*, June 1929, p. 285.

149. From Mar. 1923 to July 1931, Soupault was the *gérant* and one of the four editors (along with the nonsurrealists Edmond Jaloux, Valery Larbaud, and André Germain) of *La Revue européenne*, published by Kra of Les Editions du Sagittaire. Grasset was the publisher of *Les Frères Durandeau*. Soupault speaks of "l'insolite" and its importance in the preface to his *Chansons* (Rolle: Eynard, 1949), p. 18. Its resemblance to

the Apollinaire-surrealist concept of surprise and to the surrealist *hasard objectif* is too obvious to need developing.

150. As Mallarmé wrote in "L'Art pour tous" (1863): "Toute chose sacrée et qui veut demeurer sacrée s'enveloppe de mystère." Reproduced in the appendix to E. Noulet's *Dix poèmes de Stéphane Mallarmé* (Genève: Droz, 1948), p. 148.

151. Soupault, *Essai sur la poésie* (Eynard, 1950), pp. 20-21.

152. *Ibid.*, p. 21.

153. See Pierre Naville's *La Révolution et les intellectuels* (Gallimard, 1927), parts of which appeared in *La Révolution surréaliste*, no. 9-10 (Oct. 1927), pp. 54-61. Curiously enough, some two years earlier Pierre Drieu La Rochelle had abandoned the group because it was moving too far to the left. See P. Drieu La Rochelle, "La Véritable erreur des surréalistes," *NRF*, no. 143 (Aug. 1, 1925), pp. 166-71, and Aragon's reply "Lettre à Drieu La Rochelle," *NRF*, no. 144 (Sept. 1925), pp. 381-84.

154. Artaud's last major contribution to the cause was his flamboyant issue of *La Révolution surréaliste*, no. 3 (Apr. 15, 1925), sufficiently extravagant to alienate the more cautious Breton and to lead to Artaud's elimination from the editorial board. His exacerbated mysticism was not to Breton's taste. Play, yes; belief, no. Roger Vitrac's departure, for reasons similar to those of Soupault, is discussed in the notes to Antonin Artaud's *Oeuvres complètes*, vol. 2 (Gallimard, 1961). From 1926 on, Desnos was contributing articles to *Paris-Soir, Ce Soir*, etc. Max Ernst joined Joan Miró in preparing the sets for Diaghilev's *Roméo et Juliette*, May 18, 1926. See "Protestation," signed by Aragon and Breton, in *La Révolution surréaliste*, no. 7 (June 15, 1926), p. 31, reprinted in Nadeau, *Histoire du surréalisme*, p. 227.

155. Fragments of *L'Homme approximatif* first appeared in *La Révolution surréaliste*, no. 12 (Dec. 15, 1929), pp. 18-20, in second place immediately following Breton's *Second manifeste du surréalisme*.

156. *La Première aventure céleste de Monsieur Antipyrine* was first published in Zurich in 1916. The quotation is taken from Tristan Tzara, *Morceaux choisis*, Jean Cassou, ed. (Bordas, 1947), p. 19. The few lines from *L'Homme approximatif* first appeared in *La Révolution surréaliste*, no. 12 (Dec. 15, 1929), p. 18.

157. See Colin Wilson, *The Outsider* (Boston: Houghton Mifflin Co., 1956).

CHAPTER IV

1. Breton, "La Confession dédaigneuse" (1924), *Les pas perdus*, p. 9.

2. Our information on Vaché comes almost exclusively from his *Lettres de guerre*, a slim volume of some fifteen short letters edited by Breton. The most recent edition (K éditeur, 1949) also contains Vaché's prose poem, "Blanche acétyline" (2 pp.), a short story, "Le Sanglant symbole" (2 pp.), and the reproduction of two newspaper clippings announcing his suicide (on Jan. 6, 1919). The whole is preceded by four prefaces written by Breton: "Introduction, 1919," which served to introduce the first edition; the last half of "La Confession dédaigneuse" (1924), first printed in *Les Pas perdus*, 1924; the extract relating to Vaché in the 1940 edition of Breton's *Anthologie de l'humour noir*, "Jacques Vaché. 1896-1919"; and "Trente ans après" (1948). The quotations are from the first of the prefaces (s.p. [pp. 2-3]).

3. The first quotation is from Breton's "Introduction, 1919," *Lettres de guerre*, s.p. (p. 5); the second is from his "La Confession dédaigneuse," *Pas perdus*, p. 17.

4. "La Confession dédaigneuse," *Les Pas perdus*, p. 18.

5. Breton: "Sans lui [Vaché] j'aurais peut-être été un poète; il a déjoué en moi ce complot de forces obscures qui mène à se croire quelque chose d'aussi absurde qu'une vocation" (*ibid.*, p. 9). (The fragment of this article reprinted in *Lettres de guerre* begins at the bottom of p. 16 of the version in *Les Pas perdus*.) Shortly thereafter, with a note of scorn in the voice, "Il n'est pas de semaine où l'on n'apprenne qu'un esprit estimable vient de 'se ranger'" (*ibid.*, p. 13). In spite of this, "je tiens encore la poésie pour le terrain où ont le plus de chances de se résoudre les terribles difficultés de la conscience avec la confiance, chez un même individu" (*ibid.*, p. 15). But here poetry becomes a tool of *self knowledge*, of insight, rather than a literary exercise.

6. *Ibid.*, pp. 19-20. Another escapade indicating a similar confusion of respect and meaningless insolence is recounted on pp. 21-22 of the same article. An attitude of this type, where the gesture masks a fundamental disgust or indifference, recalls Stavrogin and his "unaccountable" marriage in Dostoevski's *The Possessed*.

7. "La Confession dédaigneuse," *Pas perdus*, pp. 23-24. Vaché was found in a Nantes hotel room, next to an American soldier, both of whom had taken an overdose of opium. According to Breton, Vaché had some experience with the drug, and the double death may not have been as accidental as it seemed. A final, irrevocable joke indeed, but scarcely representative of *l'humour noir*, for it no more permits man to rise above his fate than does Roquentin's projected suicide in Sartre's *La Nausée*.

8. At one point Breton speaks of the attitude revealed in Tzara's *Manifeste Dada 1918*, "ce qui va m'amener à reporter sur lui [Tzara] une

bonne part de la confiance et des espoirs que j'avais pu mettre en celui-ci [Vaché]" (*Entretiens*, 1952, p. 53).

9. In his *Anthologie de l'humour noir* (1940), Breton speaks of Vaché in the following terms: "A la désertion à l'extérieur en temps de guerre, qui gardera toujours pour lui quelque côté *palotin*, Vaché oppose une autre forme d'insoumission qu'on pourrait appeler la désertion à l'intérieur de soi-même. Ce n'est même plus le défaitisme rimbaldien de 1870-1871, c'est un parti-pris d'indifférence totale, au souci près de ne servir à rien ou plus exactement de *desservir* avec application" (*Lettres de guerre*, s.p., p. 14).

10. Breton, in the last preface to *Lettres de guerre*, "Trente ans après," s.p. (p. 17).

11. "L'ART EST UNE SOTTISE" is from Vaché's letter to Breton of May 9, 1918. In *Lettres de guerre*, s.p. (p. 2 of that letter). The previous letter, also to Breton (Aug. 18, 1917), contains the longer quotation.

12. Paul Eluard, *Les Dessous d'une vie, ou La Pyramide humaine* (1919-26), in *Donner à voir* (Gallimard, 1939), p. 24.

13. Breton to his fellow "surrealist" Roger Vitrac, in an interview published in *Le Journal du peuple*, Apr. 7, 1923, p. 1; in Sanouillet, *Dada à Paris*, p. 377. Sanouillet makes the point that Breton's radical despair may have been occasioned not only by the Dada fiasco and his inability to come up with a viable program to replace Dada, but also by his recent discovery of Marcel Duchamp. See *Littérature*, no. 5 (Oct. 1, 1922), pp. 7-10. In Feb. 1923, on the occasion of his third return to Paris from the U.S.A., Duchamp definitively renounced all artistic activity; as Sanouillet suggests, this could not fail to have an effect on his admirers. "J'ai l'intention de ne plus écrire d'ici peu de temps," said Breton in the interview cited above. "Par exemple d'ici deux mois et demi. . . . Nous [Breton, Eluard, Desnos] publierons un dernier manifeste signé de nos trois noms, si nous nous mettons d'accord sur un texte." Needless to say, this literary suicide never took place.

14. T. S. Eliot, "The Waste Land" (1922), in *Collected Poems, 1909-1935* (London: Faber & Faber, 1949), pp. 62, 74; *Collected Poems 1909-1962* (Harcourt, Brace and World, 1963), pp. 54, 66.

15. The first quotation is from "The Hollow Men" (1925), *ibid.* (N.Y. edition), p. 80; the second is from the conclusion to "Ash Wednesday" (1930), *ibid.*, p. 95.

16. The most authoritative description of the *soirée du Coeur à barbe* is found in M. Sanouillet, *Dada à Paris*, pp. 380-87. The title *Coeur à barbe* is derived from a Mar. 1922 pamphlet (*Le Coeur à barbe*) pub-

lished by Tzara. This attack on Breton and his defunct Congrès de Paris included contributions by Duchamp, Eluard, Soupault, Satie, Théodore Fraenkel, and M. Josephson. The Apr. 1922 issue of *Littérature,* with Breton's anti-Dada call to arms "Lâchez tout," brought at least two of the recalcitrants (Eluard and Soupault) to heel. Victor Crastre, in Le *Drame du surréalisme* (Les Editions du Temps, 1963), in spite of a number of documentary gaps and typographical errors in dating, is the best single source for information concerning the brief marriage between the politically oriented group around *Clarté* and the surrealists. Unless otherwise indicated, our commentary will follow Sanouillet and Crastre quite closely.

17. Sanouillet devotes a detailed chapter to the Congrés de Paris in his *Dada à Paris,* pp. 319-47, and concludes that (a) the idea of such a Congress was "reactionary" with regard to Dada and (b) Breton's ambition was more in evidence than was his tact. Breton had hoped to bring together representatives of various "modern" tendencies in order to determine what the "esprit moderne" was and where it was going. The furor lasted from Jan. to Apr. 1922, at which time Breton's initiative was so discredited that the proposal collapsed.

18. One of the side effects of the riot was that Tzara filed a damage suit against Eluard for 8000 francs, followed by a countersuit by Eluard. The whole affair apparently lapsed when Eluard left France the following year (Mar. 15, 1924) and gave no indication he intended to return. See Sanouillet, *Dadu à Parts,* p. 386. There is reason to believe that this "romantic" departure was at least in part due to Tzara's suit. Of such stuff are legends made.

19. From Mar. 1922 to May of that year, and from Sept. 1922 to Feb.-Mar. 1923, the magazine had appeared monthly—which suggests a certain vitality; number 10 appeared two months later in May 1923.

20. See note 13 of this chapter for Breton's decision to leave literature.

21. In *NRF,* no. 125 (Feb. 1924), pp. 219-22: "Il [Breton] se refuse, chaque année plus habilement, à représenter, à participer. Il cesse d' écrire des poèmes charmants, qui eussent suffi peut-être à la gloire d'un autre. Il abandonne pour l'inhumain les singulières découvertes humaines qu'il commençait de faire. Il choisit d'être personnage plutôt qu'auteur, et mystère plutôt que dissertation. [ . . . ] Non que je veuille définir Breton: il échappe à tout portrait. Quant au reste, au mystère lui-même, il déplaît d'en parler. Nous en sommes encore à admettre qu'André Breton existe" (pp. 221-22). One must assume that Paulhan, an early contributor to *Littérature* and friend of Breton, knows whereof he speaks. Parts of his *Jacob Cow, le pirate; ou, Si les mots sont des signes* (Au Sans Pareil, 1921), first appeared in that periodical. See also his Les *Fleurs de Tarbes*

*ou La Terreur dans les lettres* (Gallimard, 1941) for a more elaborate development of Paulhan's views on literature and the avant-garde.

22. According to Arland, Aragon is "un écrivain véritable. . . . Il écrit avec ses nerfs; sa phrase est incisive et tendue." In "Le Libertinage," *NRF,* no. 131 (Aug. 1924), p. 235. Several months earlier he had condemned the unproductive (literarily unproductive) extravagances of the period in "Sur un nouveau mal du siècle," *NRF,* no. 125 (Feb. 1924), pp. 149-58.

23. 44 numbers, 1923-25. According to Sanouillet (*Dada à Paris,* p. 380), Aragon was for a time its editor and wrote several unsigned editorials. He left Apr. 20, 1923, to be replaced by Max Morise. (Aragon continued to publish in the review until Mar. 1924. See André Gavillet, *Aragon surréaliste: La Littérature au défi* [Neuchâtel: La Baconnière, 1957], p. 320.) Given the numerous political difficulties of the surrealist group, it is worth pointing out that all of its new members had begun as writers in non-Dada, nonsurrealist and nonpolitically oriented journals. They had started out as writers, not as doctrinaires. Crevel, Desnos, Jacques Baron, Georges Limbour, Max Morise, and Roger Vitrac came to "surrealism" after their periodical *Aventure* folded (no. 1, Nov. 1921; no. 2, Dec. 1921; no. 3, Jan. 1922; edited by Vitrac, with Crevel as *gérant*: among its contributors were Valéry, Max Jacob, Cendrars, Paul Dermée, Jean Paulhan, Tzara, and Aragon). Another avant-garde literary review of the type Breton would presumably have vomited was *Action, cahiers de philosophie et d'art,* whose 12 numbers run from Feb. 1920 to Mar.-Apr. 1922. In addition to Aragon and Eluard, it published Apollinaire, Cocteau, Malraux ("La Genèse des Chants de Maldoror," no. 3, Apr. 1920), Cendrars, Jacob, Pascal Pia—and Artaud, Rigaut and Péret (no. 4, July 1920). While it would be presumptuous to attribute the transfer of the last three to Breton's group because *Action* ceased publication, there can be little doubt that all three began as *gens de lettres.* Much the same can be said about those around *L'Oeuf dur* (16 numbers, Mar. 1921-Summer 1924), whose contributors included Aragon, Jacob, Cocteau, Reverdy, Cendrars, Soupault, Drieu La Rochelle and Pierre Naville. One of the editors of *L'Oeuf dur,* Gérard Rosenthal (pseud. Francis Gérard) was the first director of the Bureau de Recherches Surréalistes (Breton, *Entretiens,* p. 108; *La Révolution surréaliste,* no. 2, Jan. 15, 1925, p. 31); Drieu La Rochelle and Pierre Naville were for a brief period very active surrealists, until the first moved right and the second left on the political spectrum.

24. *Les Plaisirs de la capitale, ses Bas-Fonds, ses Jardins secrets* bears on its authorless title page, "Par l'auteur du Libertinage, de la Bible dépouillée, etc." (Berlin, s.d. [1923]). See also Matthew Josephson, *Life Among the Surrealists* (Holt, Rinehart, and Winston, 1962), pp. 196-98.

Aragon's decision to seek a career in literature was confirmed and made almost irrevocable in Jan. 1922 when he resolved, just prior to his final examinations for the M.D. degree, not to take them. (Josephson, *ibid.*, p. 126.) The Josephsons, it would appear, were on very close terms not only with Aragon (who dedicated to Matthew Josephson a "Préface à la Maldoror," in *Ecrits nouveaux*, Aug.-Sept. 1922, pp. 27-28), but also with Breton (with whom they had dined both at his apartment and at theirs), Tzara, and the others of the early Dada-surrealists.

25. See René Lacôte, "La Vie et l'oeuvre," *Europe*, no. 91-92 (July-August 1953), p. 19. Another motive for Eluard's trip to Rome in late 1923 may have been his desire to put an end to the legal proceedings resulting from the *soirée du Coeur à barbe* of July of that year.

26. The financial backing for *La Revue européenne* came from André Germain, whose secretary was Jacques Rigaut. See Matthew Josephson, *Life Among the Surrealists*, p. 201.

27. The *procès Barrès* took place on May 13, 1921 and was reported (in part) in *Littérature*, no. 20 (Aug. 1921). See also Sanouillet, *Dada à Paris*, pp. 254-66. This "trial," in which Barrès was accused of moral treason, was the occasion for the first overt confrontation of Breton and Tzara—Breton, the self-appointed presiding judge, striving for a "serious" parody of a court trial; Tzara preferring to view the legal circus as a variation on a Dada theme. The text of Breton's address in Barcelona, "Caractères de l'évolution moderne. . . ," can be found in his *Pas perdus*, pp. 181-212.

28. The surrealist *enquête* "Le Suicide est-il une solution?" appeared in *La Révolution surréaliste*, no. 2 (Jan. 15, 1925), pp. 8-15. *Clarté*, though clearly Marxist oriented, was not an official organ of the French Communist Party. It was founded by Henri Barbusse in 1922 and continued, in various forms, until 1928.

29. In V. Crastre, *Le Drame du surréalisme*, pp. 38-39. Crastre implies that the article in question was published in May 1924 (p. 38), for which read 1925. The error was probably occasioned by his recollection that at this time Aragon's *Le Paysan de Paris* was appearing in serial form in *La Revue européenne* (see Crastre, pp. 40-41), but *Le Paysan* appeared in eight different numbers, from June 1924 through June 1925.

30. Crastre, *Le Drame du surréalisme*, p. 41.

31. Aragon refers to Hegel's "idéalisme absolu" in a letter to his employer, the couturier Jacques Doucet, dated "février 1922." See R. Garaudy, *L'Itinéraire d'Aragon* (Gallimard, 1961), p. 131. Hegel, if we follow Aragon, was the philosophic keystone of any modern library. At that time Aragon was in the employ of Doucet, to whom he wrote some two letters

a week on literary subjects for which he received 500-800 francs per month. (Breton, also in the employ of Doucet, received 1000 francs for his advice on artistic matters. See Breton, *Entretiens*, p. 98.) These manuscript items are in the collection of the Fonds Doucet at the Bibliothèque Sainte-Geneviève, Paris. Both men were fired by Doucet after the publication of the collective pamphlet against Anatole France, *Un Cadavre* (Oct. 1924). In his first Manifesto, Breton inveighs against "L'intraitable manie qui consiste à ramener l'inconnu au connu," to which he prefers "L'esprit qui plonge dans le surréalisme et revit avec exaltation la meilleure part de son enfance" (*Manifestes*, pp. 21, 55).

32. Reproduced in M. Nadeau, *Histoire du surréalisme* (1964), pp. 197-200. It includes "L'Erreur" by Ph. Soupault, "Un Vieillard comme les autres" by Paul Eluard, "Refus d'inhumer" by André Breton, and "Avez-vous déjà giflé un mort?" by Aragon. It is interesting to note that, according to Aragon, *Un Cadavre* was published on the initiative of Drieu La Rochelle, whose political views came more and more to resemble those of *l'Action française*. See Aragon, "Lettre à Drieu La Rochelle," *NRF*, no. 144 (Sept. 1925), p. 382. This was in answer to Drieu's "La Véritable erreur des surréalistes," which had appeared in the previous issue Aug. 1925, pp. 166-71. Drieu's reply to Aragon, "Deuxième lettre aux surréalistes," came one and one-half years later in a magazine he and his conservative colleague Emmanuel Berl were editing: *Les Derniers jours, cahier politique et littéraire*, no. 2 (Feb. 15, 1927), pp. 3-5. A "Troisième lettre aux surréalistes sur l'amitié et la solitude" appeared in the same journal, no. 8 (July 8, 1927), pp. 1-17.

33. *Un Cadavre*, in Nadeau, *Histoire du surréalisme*, pp. 197-200.

34. Aragon, in an open letter to Bernier, dated "le 25 november 1924," and printed in both *Clarté*, Dec. 1, 1924, and in *La Révolution surréaliste*, no. 2 (Jan. 15, 1925), p. 32.

35. Both comments appeared originally in *Clarté*, Dec. 1, 1924, and are reproduced in *La Révolution surréaliste*, no. 2 (Jan. 15, 1925), p. 32.

36. The difficulties with Le Bureau de Recherches Surréalistes are alluded to in an unsigned statement of *La Révolution surréaliste*, no. 2 (Jan. 15, 1925), p. 31. See also, no. 3 (Apr. 15, 1925), p. 31, "L'Activité du Bureau de Recherches surréalistes," signed by Artaud. In that later issue, Naville notes "Plus personne n'ignore qu'il n'y a pas de *peinture surréaliste*" (no. 3, p. 27)—just prior to the beginning of Breton's serial publication of "Le Surréalisme et la peinture," in no. 4 (July 15, 1925), the first issue edited by Breton alone.

37. Breton, "Leon Trotsky: Lénine," *La Révolution surréaliste*, no. 5 (Oct. 15, 1925), p. 29.

38. Aragon, "Note sur la liberté," *La Révolution surréaliste,* no. 4 (July 15, 1925), p. 30. In this brief article Aragon had stressed an almost Dadaist conception of total liberty: "J'affirme qu'il n'y a d'autre système philosophique que l'idéalisme. . . . Il s'ensuit que je commettrai à toute occasion n'importe quel attentat contre la liberté d'autrui, en [eu?] égard à la liberté. L'homme libre est celui qui n'a de volonté que ce qui concourt à l'idée. L'homme parfaitement libre est parfaitement déterminé dans le devenir. Mort aux mécaniques qui remontent le courant!" One can only assume that Breton at the time agreed with this sentiment, as he alone was editor. If this is so, the crucial shift in attitude took place some time between July and October 1925.

39. Breton, "Léon Trotsky: Lénine," *La Révolution surréaliste,* no. 5 (Oct. 15, 1925), p. 29. See note 32 of this chapter for the reference to the Aragon-Drieu La Rochelle correspondance. It should be mentioned that Drieu and Aragon were sufficiently friendly for Aragon to spend the summer of 1924 with him at Drieu's place in Guéthary. See R. Garaudy, *L'Itinéraire d'Aragon,* p. 130.

40. Breton, "Léon Trotsky: Lénine," *La Révolution surréaliste,* no. 5 (Oct. 15, 1925), p. 29. It is ironic to note that by the time Breton became aware of Trotsky's existence Trotsky had lost his position as War Minister (Apr. 1925) and, with Zinoviev and Kamenev, was in the process of establishing his shortlived Opposition to Stalin. In November 1927 he and Zinoviev were expelled from the Party—at about the same time as the surrealists left. By January 1928 Trotsky was exiled to Siberia. Having entered the Party under the aegis of Trotsky, the surrealists could not fail to be suspect!

41. Victor Crastre, *Le Drame du surréalisme,* p. 74.

42. The surrealist *Declaration du 27 janvier 1925* was signed by twenty-six members of the inner circle. In Nadeau, *Histoire du surréalisme,* p. 219. This same *Déclaration* says elsewhere "Nous n'avons rien à voir avec la littérature" (p. 218) and concludes with a redefinition of surrealism: "Il est un cri de l'esprit qui retourne vers lui-même et est bien décidé à broyer désespérément ses entraves, et au besoin par des marteaux matériels!" (p. 219). The tone recalls far more the anarchists of a previous day than their highly disciplined communist contemporaries, with whom the surrealists obviously had little contact at that time. A document dated two months later (Apr. 2, 1925) speaks of "un certain état de fureur" as being crucial to surrealism, for it is this surrealist fury which will bring about "l'illumination surréaliste." A second document from the same period gives the primary goal of the surrealist revolution as "un mysticisme d'un nouveau genre." Both in Nadeau, *Histoire du surréalisme,* p. 220. It is quite clear that statements of that type reflect a disposition anti-

thetical to that of any modern political party, the Communist Party included.

43. The above-cited document of Apr. 2, 1925, begins: "Les membres soussignés de la *Révolution surréaliste* réunis, le 2 avril 1925, dans le but de déterminer lequel des deux principes surréaliste ou révolutionnaire était le plus susceptible de diriger leur action, sans arriver à une entente sur le sujet, se sont mis d'accord sur les points suivants. . . ." In *La Révolution d'abord et toujours!*—which Crastre tells us he and Aragon put together, and which was signed by some fifty-two persons associated with the periodicals *Clarté, Correspondance, Philosophies, La Révolution surréaliste*, and a number of independents—five points are made: (1) a call for disarmament, (2) a rejection of nationalism, and implicitly a refusal to serve in the armed forces, (3) a condemnation of the Moroccan war, (4) a denunciation of those who signed the manifesto "Les Intellectuels aux côtés de la Patrie," which supported French intervention in Morocco, and (5) an affirmation of their belief in a social revolution. First printed in *La Révolution surréaliste*, no. 5 (Oct. 15, 1925), pp. 31-32, reprinted in Nadeau, *Histoire du surréalisme*, pp. 215-18. Breton dates this declaration "septembre 1925" in "A suivre. . . ," *Variétés. Le Surréalisme en 1929* (Bruxelles, June 1929), p. ii.

44. The lecturer was Robert Aron; the subject, the "Français moyen." See V. Crastre, *Le Drame du surréalisme*, p. 72, for a brief account of this affair. Also Nadeau, *Histoire du surréalisme*, p. 81, who quotes the report published by the *Journal littéraire* of June 13, 1925. Oddly enough, the title of the play to be performed is never mentioned, nor is there any indication that Aragon was present at the disturbance which followed. According to Yvette Gindine (*Aragon, prosateur surréaliste*, 1966, p. 53), the play was *Au pied du mur* and the date of performance June 13, 1925. It was first published in Aragon's *Le Libertinage*, 1924.

45. See Nadeau, *Histoire du surréalisme*, pp. 81-85, and Breton, *Entretiens*, pp. 111-14, for two complementary accounts.

46. In an interview given to the Italian periodical *Il Secolo*, reprinted by *Comoedia*, June 17, 1925, Claudel is quoted as saying: "Quant aux mouvements actuels, pas un seul ne peut conduire à une véritable rénovation ou création. Ni le dadaisme, ni le surréalisme qui ont un seul sens: pédérastique." Nadeau reproduces the "Lettre ouverte à M. Paul Claudel," including the relevant section of the Claudel interview, in his *Histoire du surréalisme*, pp. 214-15.

47. "Il ne saurait y avoir pour nous ni équilibre ni grand art. Voici déjà longtemps que l'idée de beauté s'est rassise. [Rimbaud, at the beginning of his *Saison en Enfer,* had written: "Un soir, j'ai assis la Beauté sur mes genoux.—Et je l'ai trouvée amère.—Et je l'ai injuriée." In "Après le déluge,"

the first section of *Illuminations,* we find "Aussitôt que l'idée du Déluge se fut rassise. . . ."] Il ne reste debout qu'une idée morale, à savoir par exemple qu'on ne peut être à la fois ambassadeur de France et poète. Nous saisissons cette occasion pour nous désolidariser publiquement de tout ce qui est français, en paroles et en actions. . . . C'est une singulière méconnaissance des facultés propres et des possibilités de l'esprit qui fait périodiquement rechercher leur salut à des goujats de votre espèce dans une tradition catholique ou gréco-romaine. Le salut pour nous n'est nulle part. . . Catholicisme, classicisme gréco-romain, nous vous abandonnons à vos bondieuseries infames. . . . nous réclamons le déshonneur de vous avoir traité une fois pour toutes de cuistre et de canaille." From the "Lettre ouverte à M. Paul Claudel," in Nadeau, *ibid.*

48. In Nadeau, *Histoire du surréalisme,* pp. 82-83. As Nadeau points out, no two witnesses agree completely as to what happened. The version given here is probably accurate, as far as it goes.

49. *Ibid.,* p. 83.

50. Quoted by Nadeau, *Histoire du surréalisme,* p. 84. It is not clear from the context whether this comes from *L'Action française* or from *Le Journal littéraire* of July 4, 1925.

51. Victor Crastre notes that several months after the *union sacrée* confirmed by *La Révolution d'abord et toujours!,* "Les surréalistes. . . commencent à se rendre compte que *Clarté n'est pas* le Parti communiste et que leur alliance avec nous n'a pas résolu toutes les difficultés puisqu'elle ne leur ouvre pas les portes du Parti. *Clarté* fait de plus en plus figure de groupe d'opposition. . . l'orthodoxie de la revue est de plus en plus sujette à caution" (*Le Drame du surréalisme,* p. 89).

52. Marcel Fourrier in *Clarté,* Nov. 1925; quoted by Crastre, *Le Drame du surréalisme,* p. 74.

53. Nadeau, *Histoire du surréalisme,* p. 86. Pierre Naville's disaffection with surrealism is spelled out in his *La Révolution et les intellectuels: Mieux et moins bien, 1927. Que peuvent faire les surréalistes? 1926* (Gallimard, 1927). *Mieux et moins bien* originally appeared in *La Révolution surréaliste,* no. 9-10 (Oct. 1, 1927), pp. 54-61, in reply to Breton's *Légitime défense* (Editions Surréalistes, Sept. 30, 1926), subsequently published in *La Révolution surréaliste,* no. 8 (Dec. 1, 1926), pp. 30-36. (Curiously enough, in the reprinting of this item in Breton's *Point du jour,* it carries the date "Décembre 1926." Can he have forgotten the autographed copy he sent "A mon Ami Louis de Gonzague Frick / André Breton / Café Cyrano / 8 octobre 1926?" See the 1960 Catalogue of the Librairie Nicaise, 145, boulevard Saint-Germain, entry no. 289.) *Légitime défense,* in its turn, was Breton's uncertain answer to Naville's *La Révolu-*

*tion et les intellectuels* (1926): See the note to "Mieux et moins bien," *La Révolution surréaliste* (Oct. 1, 1927), p. 54. Though the dating is not always clear, the problem is. Naville was moving faster than Breton, and the latter feared a political heresy which might destroy the movement quite as much as he did a literary one.

54. See Breton, "Légitime défense," *Point du jour* (1934), p. 62.

55. *"L'Humanité,* puérile, déclamatoire, inutilement *crétinisante,* est un journal illisible. . . ." (*ibid.,* p. 41).

56. *Ibid.,* p. 58. On p. 66 he adds: ". . . j'ai jugé inutile de me faire *inscrire* au Parti communiste. Je ne veux pas être rejeté arbitrairement dans *l'opposition* d'un parti auquel j'adhère sans cela de toutes mes forces. . . ." Benjamin Péret, however, if we may believe his answer on the questionnaire completed in Brazil many years after the fact, did join the Party in 1925. See the photo of this questionnaire in Claude Courtot, *Introduction à la lecture de Benjamin Péret* (1965), p. 21.

57. Breton, "Légitime défense," *Point du jour,* pp. 58-59.

58. At the end of Naville's "Avertissement" to *La Révolution et les intellectuels. . .* (Gallimard, 1927), p. 8. This is aimed directly at Breton, who at the time was playing a waiting game: *"dans la période d'attente que nous vivons,"* as he wrote in "Légitime défense," and given "l'impossibilité de ne vouloir 'connaître que la consigne' au moins déroutante donnée par le Parti française," he could only wait and hope (*Point du jour,* pp. 44, 65).

59. Naville, *La Révolution et les intellectuels. . . ,* p. 128.

60. "Abstraitement, le surréalisme part de l'anarchie. . ."(*ibid.,* p. 82). "Un mouvement comme le surréalisme, aussi purement cérébral et dont l'expérience des choses est nettement romantique. . ."(*ibid.,* p. 125). "Si le surréalisme nie l'individualité, il ne nie pas l'individu" (*ibid.,* p. 134). Naville eventually became one of the leaders of the French section of the IVth (Trotskyite) International, which led to a *rapprochement* between him and Breton. See Breton, *Entretiens,* p. 133.

61. Crastre notes that "Antonin Artaud. . . disparut presque complètement lorsque les surréalistes se rapprochèrent du groupe *Clarté"* (*Le Drame du surréalisme,* p. 69). The expulsion of Soupault and Artaud took place at the end of Nov. 1926, at the café Le Prophète. (See the article by Aragon and Breton, "A suivre. Petite contribution au dossier de certains intellectuels à tendances révolutionnaires," *Variétés. Le Surréalisme en 1929* [June 1929], p. i.)

62. Included in Nadeau, *Histoire du surréalisme,* pp. 260-74. The brochure is composed of five letters and a brief introductory statement, each

of the six sections signed by Aragon, Breton, Eluard, Péret, and the young
Pierre Unik. The letters are addressed to (1) Paul Nougé and Camille
Goemans, the leaders of the Belgian branch of surrealism and editors of
*Correspondance*, Bruxelles, nos. 1-12/13, Aug. 1923-Dec. 1939 (Nadeau,
pp. 262-64), (2) Marcel Fourrier, sole editor of the new series of *Clarté*,
16 nos. from June 15, 1926-Dec. 1927/Jan. 1928 (Nadeau, pp. 264-65),
(3) "Aux surréalistes non communistes" (Nadeau, pp. 265-67), (4)
Pierre Naville: "Cher ami, Ce n'est pas sans penser à vous que nous
écrivons ces lettres. . ." (Nadeau, pp. 265-71), (5) "Aux communistes"
(Nadeau, pp. 271-74). In the introduction, the authors speak of "la
grande concordance d'aspirations qui existent entre les communistes et
lui [le surréaliste qui n'a pas encore adhéré au Parti]" (Nadeau, p. 262).

63. At one point they even parrot a list of party slogans—"Defense des
salaires. Respect intégral des huit heures. Lutte contre le chômage,
contre la rationalisation capitaliste et la vie chère. Amnistie générale et
totale! A bas la loi Paul Boncour! A bas la militarisation des syndicats!
Debout contre la guerre impérialiste! A bas l'intervention en Chine!"—and
affirm "Pas un seul de ces mots d'ordre à l'application duquel nous ne
demandions à nouveau qu'on nous fasse servir" (Nadeau, pp. 272-73).

64. Breton, *Entretiens*, p. 127. According to Garaudy, Aragon was the
first to join the Party, on Jan. 6, 1927, followed shortly thereafter by
Breton, "peu soucieux de se laisser déborder à gauche," and several
others (*L'Itinéraire d'Aragon*, p. 189). Their departure was probably
not unconnected with the expulsion of Trotsky and Zinoviev from the
Russian Communist Party on Nov. 12 of that year.

65. Breton, *Entretiens*, pp. 120-21.

66. After the controversy due to Naville's *La Révolution et les intellectuels* (1926), Breton's *Légitime défense* (Sept. 1926) and the collective
obeisance of *Au grand jour* (May 1927), Breton welcomed Naville's
"Mieux et moins bien" in *La Révolution surréaliste*, no. 9-10 (Oct. 1,
1927), pp. 54-61. The quotation is from this last article by Naville, p. 55.

67. Artaud, *A la grande nuit, ou le Bluff surréaliste* (June 1927), in Antonin Artaud, *Oeuvres complètes* (Gallimard, 1956), t. I, pp. 287, 290. *A
la grande nuit* is also to be found in Nadeau, *Histoire du surréalisme*, pp.
274-80.

68. Péret had married a Brazilian citizen, a certain Elsie Houston, in
1927. From 1929 to 1931 he was in Brazil, where his political activities
finally led the authorities to arrest him and ultimately to expel him. While
there he was a member of the Left (Trotskyite) Opposition. See Claude
Courtot, *Introduction à la lecture de Benjamin Péret* (Le Terrain Vague,
1965), p. 22.

69. Ernest Gengenbach, who on occasion used the pseudonym Jean Genbach, first made his appearance in surrealism with a letter dated July 10, 1925, to *La Révolution surréaliste*, no. 5 (Oct. 15, 1925), pp. 1-2. For Breton, he was the major find of the season: a young abbé who had had an unhappy love affair with an actress (she would have become his mistress if only his bishop had permitted him to continue wearing the cassock). Defrocked and depressed, he concludes his confession with: "je veux que l'on sache ce que les gens d'Eglise ont fait de moi: un désespéré, un révolté et un nihiliste." On Apr. 3, 1927, he was presented to the Paris public, at the Salle Adyar, by André Breton. The subsequent political commitment of the surrealists led to his virtual disappearance from the group: satanism and politics do not mix very well. There is at least one other attempted suicide and several returns to the Church which mark his career. See his *Satan à Paris* (H. Meslin, 1927), signed "Jean Genbach"; *Surréalisme et christianisme* (chez l'auteur, 1938), in which he prepares for his readmittance to the Church by rejecting surrealism, a move required by the ecclesiastical authorities, says Gengenbach in "Un Surréaliste à la Santé," *Les Temps modernes*, no. 17, (Feb. 1947), pp. 907-8; *l'Expérience démoniaque* (Editions de Minuit, 1949), *Judas ou le vampire surréaliste* (Les Editions Premières, 1949), *Adieu à Satan* (Bruxelles: L'Ecran du Monde, 1952). For Gengenbach, the surrealists (even when he admired them) were "nouveaux Lucifériens" and surrealism "une mystique sans théologie" (*L'Expérience démoniaque*, p. 99; *Adieu à Satan*, p. 41). He was quite close to Artaud, whom he knew and so resembled spiritually, when he wrote: "il faut bien avouer que dans une société que refuse le salut par le Christ, la Poésie représente la seule cause défendable, et que les seuls titres de noblesse de l'espèce humaine sont encore les rêves, les contes de fées. . . bref tout ce qui fait vibrer la lyre des âmes assoiffées d'amour et de connaissance. . ." (*Adieu à Satan*, p. 86). A similar *rapprochement* between surrealism and Christianity was attempted by Michel Carrouges between 1945-51. See my article on "L'Affaire Pastoureau," *Yale French Studies*, Spring 1964.

70. This tale has been told by several of the participants. The most thorough account can be found in "A suivre: Petite contribution au dossier de certains intellectuels. . ." (by Breton and Aragon), in *Variétés. Le Surréalisme en 1929* (June 1929), pp. i-xxxii. See also Georges Ribemont-Dessaignes, *Déjà jadis* (Julliard, 1958), pp. 139-43; and Nadeau, *Histoire du surréalisme*, pp. 122-31 and 287-96, where parts of "A suivre. . ." are reproduced.

71. From "A suivre. . .," *Variétés* (June 1929), p. vii.

72. One of the more revealing bits of information to come from this meeting was that Breton had recently sent copies of two of his books (probably *Le Surréalisme et la peinture* and *Nadja*) to the conservative

Ecole Normale with the dedication "hommage à la bibliothèque de l'E.N.S." See "A suivre. . .," *Variétés* (June 1929), p. xxv. This was the same meeting in which some were denounced for writing for the bourgeois press (Your livelihood or your principles!) and others, such as certain members of *Le Grand jeu,* were condemned for lacking the courage to risk almost certain expulsion from the Ecole Normale Supérieure in defense of their revolutionary convictions. That Breton saw no reason to let his public convictions stand in the way of his reputation is amply attested to by the dedications in the copies of his works sent to Edmond Jaloux, Henri Massis, Eugène Monfort. See Catalogue no. 10 (1960) of the Librairie Nicaise, Paris, pp. 72, 74-75, 78, 81-82, 86.

73. Breton, for example, did not hesitate to defend *l'Humanité* when it was attacked by the former Communist leader Boris Souvarine. See "Hola!" *Le Surréalisme au service de la révolution,* no. 1 (July 1930), pp. 45-48. He had earlier, however, quoted with cautious approval a remark attributed to the Romanian novelist and short story writer Panaït Istrati: "Trotsky, ou l'opposition, c'est la réserve d'or de la révolution russe. Sans cette réserve, vraiment, je ne sais pas comment il y aurait un progrès révolutionnaire en Russie et dans le monde. Ce serait déjà le piétinement, l'enlisement." After which Breton adds: "Il ne saurait s'agir, d'ailleurs, d'adopter d'enthousiasme cette conception." In "A suivre. . . ," *Variétés* (June 1929), p. xxiii.

74. The *Second Manifeste* gave rise to a second *Un Cadavre,* this one directed at Breton, in which Desnos, Jacques Prévert, Georges Ribemont-Dessaignes, Jacques Baron, Georges Limbour, and Roger Vitrac all attacked "le contrôleur du Palais des Mirages" (Prévert's phrase). Sections from this 1930 *Un Cadavre* are reproduced in Nadeau, *Histoire du surréalisme,* pp. 300-303, as is Breton's answer "Avant-après" (pp. 304-5), which originally appeared as an addendum to the Manifesto when it was published in book form (Kra, 1930).

75. See the first page of the first issue of *Le Surréalisme au service de la révolution* (hereinafter abbreviated SASDLR), July 30.

76. The most thorough single account of the *affaire Aragon* can be found in Breton's *Misère de la poésie* (Editions Surréalistes, 1932). See also Breton, *Entretiens,* pp. 163-66, R. Garaudy, *L'Itinéraire d'Aragon,* pp. 203-236, and the Mar. 1932 brochure published by the surrealists, *Paillaise! Fin de l'affaire Aragon.'* (Reproduced in Nadeau, *Histoire du surréalisme,* pp. 353-63.) Breton refers to Elsa Triolet's ambiguous role in this trip in his *Entretiens,* p. 163; Garaudy remarks that he went "pour des raisons privées: voir la soeur d'Elsa, Lili Brik, veuve de Maiakovsky" (*L'Itinéraire d'Aragon,* p. 212). For *veuve* read *bien-aimée.*

The sad tale of Sadoul can be found in the first issue of *SASDLR*

(July 1930), pp. 34-40—letters, deposition, and the rest. Sadoul and a friend, Jean Caupenne, had written an insulting letter to a certain Keller, who had placed first in the entrance examination for admission to Saint-Cyr. This letter, dated Sept. 16, 1929, eventually found its way into the hands of the commanding general of the famed military academy. Charges were filed, and Sadoul (Caupenne had apologized and was not further involved), defended by Marcel Fourrier, was found guilty of threatening to assault the cadet. As it is manifestly clear that the letter was the result of a drunken lark, and that Sadoul had no intention of putting his verbal violence to the test, we can only conclude that his conviction was prompted by his unflattering allusions to patriotism, the flag, and the officer corps. Shades of Meursault, who was condemned for not having wept at his mother's funeral! (Camus, *L'Etranger*, 1942).

77. Mayakovsky had invited Aragon, to whom he had been introduced at a banquet given the year before by *Clarté*, to join him at his table in La Coupole (Montparnasse), on Nov. 5, 1928. The following day, "dans le même lieu de confusion et de courants d'air," he was introduced to Elsa Triolet. Garaudy, *L'Itinéraire d'Aragon*, p. 204.

78. Aragon's attempted suicide occurred in Venice, Sept. 1928. The only extracts of *La Défense de l'infini* published were the fragments entitled "Le Cahier noir," in *La Revue européenne*, no. 36 (Feb. 1, 1926), pp. 1-17; no. 37 (Mar. 1, 1926), pp. 28-38. A note at the bottom of the first page (Feb. 1926) indicates that the completed work was to be published by Gallimard.

79. *Entretiens*, p. 163.

80. Garaudy assures us, following Aragon, that the invitation to Aragon and Sadoul was tendered "de façon tout à fait fortuite" (*L'Itinéraire d' Aragon*, p. 214). Here is what Aragon had written shortly before his expulsion from the surrealist group: "D'une façon fortuite, mis en rapport avec les organisateurs du congrès de Kharkov, nous avons été invités à ce congrès. Nous n'étions mandatés par personne et nous n'avons pas été considérés comme tels. Nous avons été invites *à titre purement consultatif*, nous n'avions pas part aux votes" ("Le Surréalisme et le devenir révolutionnaire," *SASDLR*, no. 3, Dec. 1931, p. 4.) Far more likely the invitation was carefully arranged by Elsa, an author in her own right and not unknown to her Russian colleagues, with the tacit approval of the surrealists, who in this way hoped to circumvent their Paris opponents. Breton implies as much when he refers to this invitation to sit in on the meetings as "un incontestable succès," especially as it led to a resolution condemning Henri Barbusse's publication *Monde* (*Entretiens*, p. 164). It is worth noting that Aragon, probably encouraged by Elsa, had requested readmission to the French Communist Party shortly before his

projected trip. While in Kharhov, he had written Breton: "Nous sommes délégués officiellement pour la France au plénum du bureau international de littérature révolutionnaire"—a misunderstanding of short duration. See *Paillasse!* in Nadeau, *Histoire du surréalisme*, pp. 354-55.

81. Breton, *Entretiens*, p. 165. This is a brief résumé of the letter Aragon and Sadoul signed Dec. 1, 1930. The complete letter is reprinted in *Paillasse!* in Nadeau, *Histoire du surréalisme*, pp. 357-58.

82. Aragon's *Front rouge* was first published in Russian, in a 16-page edition (translated by Elsa?), in Moscow, 1931. It subsequently appeared in French in the second number of *Littérature de la révolution mondiale*, where it was pulled from the stands and the author charged (Jan. 16, 1932) with inciting to riot—a charge which could have led to a five-year prison sentence. (See Garaudy, *L'Itinéraire d'Aragon*, p. 233.) As it was the charge was ultimately dropped, even though the poem was reprinted in Aragon's collection *Persécuté persécuteur* (Editions Surréalistes, achevé d'imprimer 25 octobre 1931). *Front rouge* is included in Nadeau, *Histoire du surréalisme*, pp. 333-42.

83. Breton, *Misère de la poésie* (Editions Surréalistes, 1932), p. 10.

84. Romain Rolland's letter to the surrealists, dated Feb. 4, 1932, is perhaps the best illustration of this inability to distinguish poetry from prose, the imaginative flight from the political tract. "Nous sommes des combattants. Nos écrits sont nos armes. Nous sommes responsables de nos armes comme nos compagnons ouvriers ou soldats. Au lieu de les renier, nous sommes tenus de les revendiquer" (*Misère de la poésie*, p. 30).

85. On Feb. 9, 1932, *Humanité* published an announcement rejecting the surrealist defense of Aragon as inadmissible. (Included in *Misère de la poésie*, pp. 16-17.) This was followed by Breton's *Misère de la poésie* (Mar.). The circle was completed when *Humanité* announced, on Mar. 10, 1932, that Aragon formally disassociated himself from Breton's defense as elaborated in *Misère de la poésie*. (See the first paragraph of *Paillasse!* in Nadeau, *Histoire du surréalisme*, p. 353.) *Le Monde réel* is the general title for a series of novels Aragon began in 1934.

86. This copy of *Paillasse!* can be found in the Bibliothèque Littéraire Jacques Doucet (Fonds Doucet), in the collection Eluard, call number AI4.1. Our page references will be to the more accessible version in Nadeau, *Histoire du surréalisme*, pp. 353-63. Eluard's *Certificat*, dated Mar. 23, 1932, is included in Nadeau, *ibid.*, pp. 363-64. In a personal communication Mme Cécile Dreyfus-Valette, the poet's daughter, suggests that the annotations are René Char's, not her father's. There is at present no simple way of resolving this question, short of graphological

analysis of the handwriting of both men in early 1932. But, for the purpose of our argument, the annotator could as easily be René Char: a surrealist "insider," one who knew Aragon well, had substantive doubts concerning sections of *Paillasse!* The Eluard copy of this pamphlet has recently been published by Robert D. Valette in his *Eluard, livre d'identité* (Tchou, 1967), p. 111.

87. The letter from Ferdinand Alquié, who has since written an excellent *Philosophie du surréalisme* (Flammarion, 1955, tr. *The Philosophy of Surrealism*, Univ. of Michigan Press, 1965), appeared in *SASDLR*, no. 5 (May 15, 1933), p. 43. See also Breton, *Entretiens*, p. 169. The letter, dated Mar. 7, 1933, is essentially a note thanking Breton for having sent *Les Vases communicants*.

88. For example, it caused not the least stir in the movement when Tristan Tzara and René Crevel joined Aragon's "Maison de la Culture" in early 1934. See Tzara, *Le Surréalisme et l'après-guerre* (Nagel, 1948), p. 31. This is the text of a lecture first delivered at the Sorbonne, Apr. 11, 1947. Much the same could be said for Dali's estrangement, caused by his careless flirtation with Naziism and a sudden desire for wealth. See Marcel Jean, *Histoire de la peinture surréaliste* (Editions du Seuil, 1959), pp. 220-23, 261. But, as Marcel Jean points out (*ibid.*, p. 223), Dali's expulsion in Jan. 1933 did not preclude his taking part in certain surrealist-sponsored activities. For much of the literate public it was he, not Breton, who was the typical surrealist.

89. On Feb. 10, 1934, the "Maison des Syndicats" brought out a one-page *Appel à la lutte* signed by Communists and surrealists alike (also Fernand Léger, André Malraux, and others), calling for a general strike, if necessary, to defend the Republic. In March, Jean Cassou presided over a "grande réunion" to protest the Fascist uprisings in Paris. (Jean-Pierre Maxence, *Histoire de dix ans: 1927-1937*, Gallimard, 1939, p. 336.) This was followed by a surrealist sponsored *Enquête sur l'unité d'action*, dated Apr. 18. Then on Apr. 24 appeared the collective statement *La Planète sans visa* in defense of Trotsky, and another brief honeymoon was over. The three tracts are all found in Nadeau, *Histoire du surréalisme*, pp.381-88.

90. *L'Homme révolté* (Gallimard, 1951), p. 123.

91. H. Pastoureau, "A suivre: Petite contribution au dossier d'un écrivain à prétentions révolutionnaires (Paris 5 mai 1932-12 février 1951)," *En Marge*, no. 1 (Jan.-Feb. 1955), p. 37. The dates in the title of the article refer to Pastoureau's sojourn among the surrealists. The article describes how and why he made the trek from communism to surrealism at about the time Aragon was moving in the opposite direction. His departure is briefly summarized in H. Gershman, "L'Affaire Pastoureau," *Yale French*

*Studies,* no. 31 (Spring 1964), pp. 154-58. Pastoureau is the only surrealist of any note who has left a record of why he joined the *bretonistes* and why he left. "Sur le plan révolutionnaire," wrote Breton with reference to Pastoureau, "l'activité poétique et l'activité politique doivent rester libres, indépendantes l'une de l'autre, sous peine de se limiter." A. Breton, preface to H. Pastoureau, *Le Corps trop grand pour un cercueil* (Editions Surréalistes, 1936), s.p.

92. In the Breton anthology *Poésie et autre,* Gérard Legrand, ed. (Le Club du Meilleur Livre, 1960), the date given for his marriage is 1935 (p. 116). The correct date is given by Breton in his *L'Amour fou* (Gallimard, 1937), p. 97; see also *L'Amour fou,* pp. 63-83, and 94, where the year 1934 is mentioned in each case. The *Times* of London briefly described the Pan-Soviet Literary Congress on Sept. 1, 1934, p. 9.

93. Breton, "Du temps que les surréalistes avaient raison" (Aug. 1935), in *Manifestes du surréalisme* (Pauvert, 1962), pp. 289-90. Interestingly enough, this collective statement, which first appeared in book form along with several other articles of a similar nature (*Position politique du surréalisme,* Editions du Sagittaire, 1935), bore the signature of Dali, among others. It would seem clear, given Dali's fascist sympathies (see note 88 of this chap.), that Breton's principles were highly disciplined: an exclusion that is not an exclusion is a true surrealist paradox. Of course a number of the surrealists owned paintings by Dali. Except where otherwise indicated our account of the *Congrès international pour la défense de la culture* is based on the information contained in *Position politique du surréalisme,* as reprinted in *Manifestes* (1962).

94. Pierre Laval, who was to become better known during World War II as Pétain's right-hand man, signed for France. Breton quotes the reaction of the Communist *L'Humanité* as "c'est dur"—but *L'Humanité* had no choice about accepting the new line, Breton did. See Breton's "Discours au Congrès des écrivains" (June 1935), in *Manifestes,* p. 277.

95. Crevel committed suicide on June 22, 1935; Breton's "Discours au Congrès des écrivains" was read on June 25 and first published in the *Bulletin international du surréalisme* (Bruxelles), no. 3 (Aug. 20, 1935), pp. 4-8. Part of the Ehrenburg book in question, *Vus par un écrivain de l'U.R.S.S.,* specifically the section Breton objected to, was early translated into English as "The Surrealists," *Partisan Review,* no. 9 (Oct.-Nov. 1935), pp. 11-16. Two revealing statements on Crevel's suicide appeared in *NRF,* one by Marcel Jouhandeau, in the July 1935 issue (no. 262, pp. 121-22), the other by Breton the following month (no. 263, pp. 291-93), in which the surrealist leader denies that loss of faith in surrealism led to Crevel's taking of his life. Carlos Lynes, incidentally, in his "Solitude de René Crevel," *French Studies,* XII, 2 (Apr. 1958), pp. 125-42, has writ-

ten an excellent study of Crevel's six "novels." Of all the surrealists of the second generation, he was probably their most talented polemicist.

96. Both quotations are from the "Préface" to *Position politique du surréalisme* (achevé d'imprimer, novembre 1935), in *Manifestes du surréalisme* (1962), pp. 242-43.

97. Breton and Eluard spent the latter part of Mar. and the beginning of Apr. in Prague, helping inaugurate an international surrealist exhibition sponsored by a number of left-wing groups. The occasion was commemorated by a *Bulletin international du surréalisme*, in Czech with French translations, on Apr. 9, 1935. (It was in Prague, incidentally, on Mar. 17, that the Breton-Aragon play, *Le Trésor des Jésuites*, one of the earlier examples of the theater of the absurd, was first performed. The text can be found in the periodical *Variétés. Le Surréalisme en 1929*, June 1929.) In mid-May, Breton, accompanied by his wife, Péret, and others, was in Tenerife, in the Canary Islands, where friends of Oscar Dominguez (a recent convert to the movement) had succeeded in putting together another surrealist exhibition (May 11-21). The second *Bulletin international du surréalisme* (publ. Oct. 1935), in Spanish and French this time, brought to the fore the same themes as the earlier Czech number, specifically "the relationship of art and revolution" (Marcel Jean, *Histoire de la peinture surréaliste*, p. 264).

98. In "Du temps que les surréalistes avaient raison" (Aug. 1935), *Manifestes du surréalisme*, p. 297. The source for the *Comité de Vigilance* statement is Breton's "Discours au Congrès des écrivains" (June 1935), in *Manifestes*, p. 282. For a brief chronology of the German rearmament and the French reaction, see J.-B. Duroselle, *Histoire diplomatique de 1919 à nos jours* (Librairie Dalloz, 1962), pp. 191-94.

99. *Minotaure*, founded in June 1933, was rapidly "infiltrated" by the surrealists. By the winter of 1937, with no. 10 of that periodical, Tériade was replaced by a *comité de rédaction* composed of Breton, Duchamp, Eluard, Maurice Heine, and Pierre Mabille. Its final issue appeared in May 1939 (no. 12/13). The *Cahiers d'art*, directed for a period by the early Dadaist and friend of Picabia, Christian Zervos, while never "taken over" by the surrealists, was regularly receptive to their contributions. See, for example, no. 6-7 (1936), devoted to the *Exposition surréaliste d'objets*, held at the Charles Ratton Gallery, 14 rue Marignan, from May 22-31, 1936.

100. The London exhibition, including lectures, poetry readings, and the like, was commemorated in an *International Surrealist Bulletin*, no. 4 (Sept. 1936) and in a surrealist issue of *Contemporary Poetry and Prose* (June 1936), with contributions by Breton, Eluard, Péret, Dali (!), Georges Hugnet, René Char, Jarry, and a number of Englishmen. It is

undoubtedly this exhibition, and the English-language publications it gave rise to, that served to bring the movement to the serious attention of many who had previously dismissed it as a Daliesque aberration. Not the least of these publications, incidentally, is that edited by one of the exhibition's sponsors, Herbert Read: *Surrealism* (London: Faber and Faber, 1936), which includes Breton's "Limits not Frontiers of Surrealism," Eluard's "Poetic Evidence," and Hugnet's "1870 to 1936."

101. His financial situation was such that, in the period before the Mexican opportunity presented itself, he had been reduced to accepting the offer of a friend (name never mentioned) to direct an art gallery, *Gradiva*, rue de Seine (See Breton, *Entretiens*, p. 182). Breton stayed in Mexico from Apr. to mid-Aug. 1938, a house guest of the painter Diego Rivera, who arranged the numerous meetings between Breton and Trotsky. The latter had arrived in Mexico the year before and occupied a separate house (also owned by Rivera). Breton's few comments on this period can be found in *Entretiens*, pp. 187-91; in three of the articles collected in *La Clé des champs* (Editions du Sagittaire, 1953), pp. 29-54: "Souvenir du Mexique," the Breton-Trotsky manifesto "Pour un art révolutionnaire indépendant," and "Visite à Léon Trotsky," extracts of a speech delivered before the Parti Ouvrier International, in Paris, Nov. 11, 1938. It is in this last item, p. 42, that he alludes to his return: "Près de trois mois se sont écoulés depuis mon retour du Mexique. . ."; and the brief article on "Frida Kahlo de Rivera," Diego's wife and a painter in her own right, in *Le Surréalisme et la peinture* (Brentano's, 1945), where, among other things, we learn that Breton was in Mexico as of Apr. 20, 1938 (p. 140).

102. In *La Clé des champs*, pp. 36-41. The manifesto, signed July 25, 1938, originally bore the signatures of Breton and Diego Rivera. But as Breton later revealed, Trotsky was his coauthor: "Pour des raisons tactiques, Trotsky demanda que la signature de Diego Rivera fût substituée à la sienne" (*ibid.*, p. 41 note). The manifesto is reproduced in Nadeau, *Histoire du surréalisme*, pp. 471-76.

103. *La Clé des champs*, p. 41.

104. Breton in "Visite à Léon Trotsky," in *La Clé des champs*, p. 52. As finally published, the phrase reads: *"toute licence en art"* (*La Clé des champs*, p. 39).

105. "Pour un art révolutionnaire indépendant," *La Clé des champs*, p. 37.

106. *Ibid.*, p. 39.

107. *Ibid.*, p. 39.

108. After condemning "l'indifférentisme politique" and the "soi-disant art 'pur' " (*ibid.*, pp. 39-40), they pinpoint the problem—without, however, so labeling it! (*ibid.*, p. 40).

109. Breton, "Visite à Léon Trotsky," *La Clé des champs*, p. 51.

110. *Entretiens*, p. 191. According to Breton, he first became aware of Eluard's leanings while he was in Mexico, when some of Eluard's poems appeared in the Communist periodical *Commune* (*ibid.*,). See also Francis J. Carmody, "Eluard's Rupture with Surrealism," *Publications of the Modern Language Society*, LXXVI, no. 4, Part 1 (Sept. 1961), pp. 436-46. Carmody fixes "the final decision to leave Breton, as early as April" (*ibid.*, p. 446). This would imply that whatever his reasons for leaving, he felt sufficiently unsure of them to prefer to wait until Breton had left the country before having his defection known. A *fait accompli* is easier to defend than a poor argument. Perhaps not completely unrelated to Eluard's departure is an anecdote recounted by the Cuban novelist Alejo Carpentier, who revealed that on one occasion he told Breton that surrealism in South America was known through the poems of Eluard. Breton is said to have replied that if that were so surrealism was "foutu," for Eluard's poems were "à l'opposé de la poésie" and Eluard himself "n'y comprenait rien" (A. Carpentier, "Témoignage," *Un Cadavre*, 1930, p. 4). *Un Cadavre*, being the tract of the post-*Second Manifeste* dissidents (Ribemont-Dessaignes, Prévert, Vitrac, Georges Limbour, Queneau, Max Morise, Jacques Baron, Michel Leiris, J.-A. Boiffard, Georges Bataille, Carpentier, and Desnos), its testimony is subject to some caution.

111. In *Ni de votre guerre ni de votre paix!* dated "le 27 septembre 1938" (in Nadeau, *Histoire du surréalisme*, pp. 476-77.) Exceptionally, the statement is signed "Le groupe surréaliste." Was this due to a passing fear of political reprisal (quite real), or was Breton hesitant to publicize Eluard's recent defection by printing a list of names that did not include his?

112. This evaluation of Western policies comes from *Ni de votre guerre ni de votre paix!* (in Nadeau, *Histoire du surréalisme*, p. 477).

113. This is the final hopeful (if empty) phrase of *Ni de votre guerre ni de votre paix!* (ibid.).

114. See Breton, *Entretiens*, p. 192, and the brief extracts from *Clé*, no. 1 (Jan. 1939), no. 2 (Feb. 1939)—the only issues to appear—in Nadeau, *Histoire du surréalisme*, pp. 479-82; also an undated tract by the F.I.A.-R.I. against police terror in France, *A bas les lettres de cachet! A bas la terreur grise!*, in Nadeau, pp. 482-84. The Fonds Doucet has a copy of both issues of *Clé, Bulletin mensuel de la F.I.A.R.I.* The editorial administrator ("Rédaction-Administration") was Maurice Nadeau. Its

"comité national" included Yves Allégret, Breton, Michel Collinet (the second husband of Breton's first wife?), Jean Giono, Maurice Heine, Pierre Mabille, Marcel Martinet, André Masson, Henry Pouaille, Gérard Rosenthal, and Maurice Wullens.

115. By Simone de Beauvoir. See her *La Force de l'âge* (Gallimard, 1960), p. 395.

116. Patrick Waldberg, *Max Ernst* (Pauvert, 1958), pp. 329-42. In Dec. 1940 Ernst was permitted to go to Marseilles, but visa difficulties prevented his departure (to Madrid and Lisbon) until May of the following year. He arrived in New York on July 14, 1941.

117. See B. Péret, *La Parole est à Péret* ([New York], Editions Surréalistes, 1943), reprinted as the first part of the Introduction to his *Anthologie des mythes, légendes et contes populaires d'Amérique* (Albin Michel, 1960), pp. 16-18. As he notes (*Anthologie*, p. 18), "je suis sorti de la prison de Rennes le 22 juillet en payant une rançon de mille francs aux nazis."

118. See Marcel Jean, *Histoire de la peinture surréaliste*, p. 300. The first "official" recognition of their presence in New York was the special issue of *View*, no. 7-8 (Oct.-Nov. 1941), edited by Charles Henri Ford and devoted to surrealism.

119. Marcel Jean, *Histoire de la peinture surréaliste*, p. 301.

120. *VVV*, published in New York, and edited by David Hare, had four numbers: no. 1 (June 1942), no. 2-3 (Mar. 1943), no. 4 (Feb. 1944). The *VVV* statement of principles is included in Breton's *La Clé des champs*, pp. 74-75, suggesting that he was its author. The first issue of *VVV*, incidentally, included Breton's "Prolégomènes à un troisième manifeste du surréalisme ou non," and the Mar. 1943 issue contained the first printing of his lecture at Yale University of Dec. 10, 1942: "Situation du surréalisme entre les deux guerres." Perhaps the best indication of Breton's prudence at this time can be found in such a statement as: "La seule tradition dont *VVV* se réclame est celle des revues de combat qui se sont appelés *les Soirées de Paris, Maintenant, Nord-Sud, la Révolution surréaliste* à Paris, *Lacerba* à Rome, *291* à New-York, *Cabaret Voltaire* à Zurich" (*La Clé des champs*, p. 75). Neither the recent *Clé* nor even *Le Surréalisme au service de la révolution* merits listing, but dadaist and pre-dadaist periodicals do.

121. "Situation du surréalisme entre les deux guerres" (Dec. 10, 1942), *La Clé des champs*, p. 60.

122. *Ibid.*, p. 73.

123. From "Prolégomènes à un troisième manifeste du surréalisme ou non," first published in *VVV*, no. 1 (June 1942), pp. 18-26—French and English in juxtaposed columns. Here quoted in my translation from *Manifestes du surréalisme* (1962), p. 341.

124. From "Prolégomènes. . . ," *Manifestes*, p. 345.

125. The catalogue for this Exhibition, organized by Breton and Marcel Duchamp for the Coordinating Council of French Relief Societies, bore the title *First Papers of Surrealism* (New York, 1942), 48 pp., unnumbered. Germany occupied the Zone libre on Nov. 11, 1942.

126. Tzara, *Le Surréalisme et l'après-guerre* (Nagel, 1948), p. 74.

127. Breton had arrived in Haiti in early Dec., with the intention of giving several lectures. On Jan. 1, 1946, *La Ruche*, a Haitian periodical, printed one of his typical statements in praise of liberty—which led to the banning of the magazine by the government (Jan. 4). Then, in rapid sequence there followed a street demonstration (Jan. 7), the cancellation of Breton's lecture on Victor Hugo (Jan. 8), and the fall of Elie Lescot's dictatorship (Jan. 10).

128. *Les Quatre vents; Cahiers de littérature* brought out nine numbers between 1945-47. It published Breton, Péret, Artaud, Gracq, René Char, Jean Paulhan, Henri Michaux, Clément Pansaers, Prévert, Queneau, and others. Henri Parisot, for example, gathered together an anthology which he published in no. 4 (Feb. 1946) under the title, *L'Evidence poétique;* no. 8 (1947) was devoted to *Le Langage surréaliste.* The specific manifestation I have in mind is the one announced in *Les Lettres françaises* of May 24, 1946 (p. 4), in honor of Antonin Artaud, recently released from the asylum at Rodez. Present and participating were Maria Casarès, Jean-Louis Barrault, Madeleine Renaud, Adamov, Dullin, Jouvet, Vialar, and Breton. (Gide and Paulhan were on the organizing committee.) On the following Jan. 13 Breton and Gide were both present at a lecture given by Artaud at the Théâtre du Vieux-Colombier.

129. The collective tract, *Liberté est un mot vietnamien*, s.l.n.d., is included in Jean-Louis Bédouin's *Storia del surrealismo dal 1945 ai nostri giorni* (Milan: Schwarz, 1960), tr. by Livio Maitan and Tristan Sauvage. The French edition, *Vingt ans de surréalisme: 1939-1959* (Denoël, 1961), does not contain this item. Ho Chi Minh proclaimed the independence of Viet-Nam on October 15, 1945; armed hostilities broke out in December. Bédouin refers to the similarity of surrealist reaction to both the Riff and Vietnamese conflicts in his *Vingt Ans de surréalisme*, p. 98.

130. This was a theme Breton repeatedly came back to in the thirties. In his Apr. 1935 lecture in Prague he remarked, "la civilisation bourgeoise se trouve plus inexorablement condamnée du fait de son manque absolu

de justification poétique." From "Position politique de l'art d'aujourd'hui," *Manifestes*, p. 264. Later in the same lecture he noted, " 'Plus de conscience', tel est, en effet, le mot d'ordre que nous aimons par excellence retenir de Marx" (p. 268). In his "Discours au congrès des écrivains" of June of that year, quoting Romain Rolland: " 'Il faut rêver', a dit Lénine; 'il faut agir', a dit Goethe. Le surréalisme n'a jamais prétendu autre chose, à ceci près que tout son effort a tendu à la résolution dialectique de cette opposition" (*Manifestes*, p. 279). And he concludes this "Discours" with: " 'Transformer le monde', a dit Marx; 'changer la vie', a dit Rimbaud: ces deux mots d'ordre pour nous n'en font qu'un" (p. 285).

131. See the collective declaration drafted by Henri Pastoureau: *Rupture inaugurale; Déclaration adoptée le 21 juin 1947 par le Groupe en France pour définir son attitude préjudicielle à l'égard de toute politique partisane*, 14 pp. (In J.-L. Bédouin, *Storia del surrealismo*, pp. 255-63; not included in his *Vingt ans de surréalisme*, though a key extract is quoted there on p. 100.)

132. *Vingt ans*, pp. 152-57. The collective letter to Garry Davis, dated "Février 1949" and signed by thirty-five surrealists proclaiming their adhesion to his movement, can be found in the above work, pp. 309-10.

133. See the letter cited in note 132, in which Breton mentions "nous étions à votre côté, le 19 novembre dernier. . ." (*ibid.*, p. 310). Among those who signed this letter were Bédouin, Breton, Jean-Pierre Duprey, Maurice Henry, Pierre Mabille, Jehan Mayoux, Henri Pastoureau, Péret, and Jean Schuster. Breton had taken his first steps in the direction of world government (as distinguished from Garry Davis's more "populist" movement) when he addressed the first public meeting of Front Humain, Apr. 30, 1948. The address is reproduced in Breton, *La Lampe dans l'horloge* (Editions Robert Marin, 1948), pp. 63-82. Front Humain appears to have been the French version of the World Federalist movement.

134. This figure is given by Bédouin, *Vingt ans de surréalisme*, p. 152, whose account we follow for the remainder of this exposé.

135. "Nous laissons à André Breton toute la responsabilité de son discours" (*ibid.*, p. 154). The speech was delivered at the Palais de la Mutualité on Oct. 21, 1949, which can be taken as the terminal date of surrealist involvement with the Citizens of the World. Some ten months before (Dec. 1948), at a public meeting at the Salle Pleyel, Breton had shared the platform with Sartre, Camus, Carlo Levi, and others in defending this same partisan of world government. But in Apr. 1949 the N.A.T.O. treaty had been signed and left-wing sentiment with regard to things American was becoming noticeably cooler.

136. In 1948, for example, the surrealists published a 16-page pamphlet, *A la niche, les glapisseurs de dieu!* (In Bédouin, *Vingt ans de surréalisme,* pp. 305-8.) It seems quite clear on reading this manifesto (written by Pastoureau) that the surrealists had no intention of having their views assimilated to those of any organized religion.

137. The *lettristes,* who saw salvation in the careful arrangement of letters (leading to sound poems recalling those of Hugo Ball at the Cabaret Voltaire), appeared on the scene as early as 1945. Their consecration came when Gallimard published their leader's rambling 400-page manifesto: Isidore Isou, *Introduction à une nouvelle poésie et à une nouvelle musique* (Gallimard, 1947). See also, I. Isou, "Qu'est-ce que le lettrisme?" *Fontaine,* XI, no 62 (Oct. 1947), pp. 529-50. One has the impression that Isou was insufficiently familiar with the early Dada-surrealist current.

138. That their elders were indeed established is suggested by (1) the fact that Breton was being considered for the Prix de la Ville de Paris in 1950, which award he publicly announced he would refuse (see Bédouin, *Vingt ans de surréalisme,* p. 165); (2) Aragon's elevation to deputy member of the Central Committee of the French Communist Party (1950)— in July 1956, he became a permanent member of that committee; and (3) Eluard's consecration as one of *the* great French poets—the first volume of the Poètes d'aujourd'hui series (Pierre Seghers, ed.) was devoted to him, the second to Aragon. Dali, Picasso, and other *surréalisants* were, of course, world renowned. As far as the *lettristes* were concerned, the time was ripe for younger blood.

139. Camus, *L'Homme révolté* (Gallimard, 1951), pp. 118-19.

140. "La révolution pour les surréalistes n'était pas une fin qu'on réalise au jour le jour, dans l'action, mais un mythe absolu et consolateur" (*ibid.,* p. 123). Breton's reply appeared in an interview with Aimé Patri, in *Arts,* Nov. 16, 1951, where he defends himself (inadequately) against Camus' description: calling his antagonist humorless and unpoetic, for example, is quite irrelevant. See also Breton, "Sucre jaune," *Arts,* Oct. 12, 1951, included in *La Clé des champs,* pp. 250-53, a defense of Lautréamont, one of the surrealist idols, against Camus' "incomprehension."

141. I have been unable to examine all the relevant numbers of this periodical. Bédouin discusses this collaboration in *Vingt ans de surréalisme,* pp. 203-7; this summary is based essentially on his account.

142. This short-lived periodical ceased publication in June 1953, after eight numbers. It was replaced by the more elegant *Médium, communication surréaliste,* also edited by Schuster, whose four numbers appeared Nov. 1953, Feb. 1954, May 1954, and Jan. 1955.

143. See H. Gershman, "L'Affaire Pastoureau," *Yale French Studies*, no. 31 (Spring 1964), pp. 154-58. Among those who left at this point, in addition to the protagonists Michel Carrouges and Henri Pastoureau, were the biographer and art critic Patrick Waldberg, the cartoonist Maurice Henry, and the painter-historian Marcel Jean.

144. From "Comme toujours et comme jamais," *Médium, communication surréaliste*, no. 1 (Nov. 1953), p. 16.

145. First sentence of "Du surréalisme dans ses oeuvres vives," *Médium, communication surréaliste*, no. 4 (Jan. 1955), p. 2. This article is the final item in Breton's *Manifestes du surréalisme* (Pauvert, 1962), pp. 355-63, and we can assume it represents his most recent thinking on the subject, as of 1962.

146. See Gérard Legrand, "P.M.F. = 1788?" *Médium, communication surréaliste*, no. 4 (Jan. 1955), pp. 15-16. Mendès-France was at the time a member of the center, so-called "Radical" party.

147. Shortly after the Hungarian revolt, the surrealists brought out the tract entitled *Hongrie, soleil levant*, s.l.n.d. [1956]. Included in Bédouin, *Vingt ans de surréalisme*, pp. 323-24.

148. See *Au tour des livrées sanglantes!* dated Apr. 12, 1956, and containing fifteen names. (Included in Bédouin, *Vingt ans du surréalisme*, pp. 319-22.) Its principal theme, however, was not Algeria but the reconstruction of the Communist Party, which was presumably inevitable following the denunciation of Stalin's excesses at the XXth Party Congress. It was for a time felt that Trotsky might be rehabilitated, the old-line Stalinists brought to heel, and so on.

149. The title of this manifesto, published Sept. 1960, was *Déclaration sur le droit à l'insoumission dans la guerre d'Algérie*. See *Le Monde*, Sept. 30, 1960, p. 6. The government immediately banned the declaration and took steps to sanction the signers. As José Pierre points out, "Parmi les 121 signataires, figurent tous les membres du Mouvement Surréaliste de nationalité française." In "La Déclaration des 121. . . ," *La Brèche*, no. 2 (May 1962), p. 61. The above article by José Pierre (pp. 61-70) presents both a summary of the text and an indication of what several different groups understood it to say.

150. *Le Surréalisme, même*, 5 numbers between Oct. 1956 and the spring of 1959. *Bief, jonction surréaliste*, 12 thin numbers (4-10 pp. each) from Nov. 15, 1958, through Apr. 15, 1960. *La Brèche, action surréaliste*, 8 numbers from Oct. 1961 to Nov. 1965. The first was edited by Jean Schuster (rédacteur en chef; André Breton, directeur) and published by Jean-Jacques Pauvert; the second was edited by Gérard Legrand, an-

other of Breton's new stalwarts and one of his closest collaborators. Its publisher was Eric Losfeld of Le Terrain Vague. *La Brèche,* also published by Le Terrain Vague, was edited by Breton, with an advisory committee composed of Robert Benayoun, Gérard Legrand, José Pierre, Jean Schuster, and Vincent Bounoure (the last as of no. 4, Feb. 1963). The most recent periodical, *Archibras,* edited by Jean Schuster, has had four numbers from April 1967 to June 1968.

CHAPTER V

1. Claude Cahun, quoting the views of friends in the Communist Party on his report to the Association des Ecrivains et Artistes Révolutionnaires, later published as *Les Paris sont ouverts* (Corti, achevé d'imprimer le 25 mai 1934), pp. 30-31. Extracts from this report, but not the above passage, can be found in Nadeau, *Histoire du surréalisme* (1964), pp. 388-95. The copy I examined at the Fonds Doucet has the following dedication: "A Paul Eluard / ce pamphlet où la véritable poésie tient trop peu de place."

2. Robert Benayoun speaks of "la véritable extériorisation de libido que suppose l'automatisme," in his article criticizing a recent flurry of "Happenings": "Où rien n'arrive," *La Brèche,* no. 6 (June 1964), p. 18. José Pierre, in the same issue of *La Brèche,* refers to "la peinture rendue à sa mission essentielle qui est, selon Hegel, d'exprimer 'l'intériorité spirituelle.' " In "Peinture et autre," *La Brèche,* no. 6 (June 1964), p. 2. P. A. (Philippe Audoin?) suggests that a truly impressive work is one in which "l'Imaginaire. . . tend à devenir réel." In "A d'autres!" *La Brèche,* no. 7 (Dec. 1964), p. 105.

3. Mircea Eliade, *Le Sacré et le profane* (Gallimard, [1957] 1965), p. 18.

4. On several occasions Breton has referred to the long list of obtuse reviews and obituary notices the movement and its work have elicited. See, for example, his introduction to the 1947 International Exhibition of Surrealism, "Devant le rideau," *Le Surréalisme en 1947* (Maeght Editeur, 1947), pp. 13-19; included in Breton, *La Clé des champs* (Editions du Sagittaire, 1953), pp. 87-95.

5. "Qu'est-ce que la littérature," *Situations II,* (Gallimard, 1948), p. 174.

6. *Ibid.,* p. 175, where Sartre condemns the irresponsibility of the surrealists; p. 176, where he contrasts the amateur *révolté* with the more efficient revolutionary; p. 326 note 9, where he remarks on the frivolousness of surrealist literature in a time of war. It might be mentioned in this context that Camus, writing somewhat earlier, is far more sympathetic to the *révolté,* the moral man who reluctantly takes up arms for his cause, and rejects the assumption that morality can be divorced from revolution-

ary activity without the latter losing much of its significance. See A. Camus, "Remarque sur la révolte," *L'Existence*, ed. Jean Grenier (Gallimard, 1945), pp. 9-23. In that respect Camus is quite close to the surrealists.

7. Sartre, *L'Existentialisme est un humanisme* (Nagel, 1946), pp. 36-37. This idea recurs constantly in his work. See, for example, *Les Mouches*, II, 5; III, 2 and elsewhere.

8. See the first part of Sartre's "Qu'est-ce que la littérature," "Qu'est-ce qu'écrire," esp. pp. 63, 69-71, and 87 note 5 (*Situations II*). But here, too, there is a contradiction, for he had earlier written approvingly of Francis Ponge's hermetic poetry. See Sartre, "L'Homme et les choses" (Dec. 1944), *Situations I* (Gallimard, 1947), pp. 245-93. See also Alain Robbe-Grillet's recent evaluation of the problem: "Nature, humanisme et tragédie" (1958), *Pour un nouveau roman* (Gallimard, Coll. Idées, 1963) esp. pp. 76-80.

9. "On sait maintenant que la poésie doit mener quelque part." Breton, in his review of Lautréamont's *Les Chants de Maldoror*, in *NRF*, no. 81 (June 1920), p. 918; later misquoted as "Nous savons à présent que la poésie doit mener quelque part," in A. Breton and Gérard Legrand, *L'art magique* (Club Française du Livre, 1957), p. 231. See also Breton, *La Position politique du surréalisme* (Editions du Sagittaire, 1935), which is his most detailed attempt to show what role surrealism could play in society. As he summed up in the speech presented to the Congrès des Ecrivains pour la Défense de la Culture (June 1935), " 'Transformer le monde,' a dit Marx; 'changer la vie,' a dit Rimbaud: ces deux mots d'ordre pour nous n'en font qu'un." *Position politique du surréalisme* in *Manifestes du surréalisme* (J.-J. Pauvert, 1962), p. 285.

10. Sartre, "Qu'est-ce que la littérature," *Situations II*, p. 64.

11. The passing difficulties that a number of *normaliens*, specifically a certain Bénichou, had with the surrealists are detailed in Breton and Aragon, "A suivre: Petite contribution au dossier de certains intellectuels à tendances révolutionnaires (Paris 1929)," *Variétés. Le Surréalisme en 1929* (Brussels, June 1929), pp. xxiii-xxv. Sartre was at the Ecole Normale Supérieure from 1924-28, and passed the *agrégation* in 1929.

12. "Je disais que le monde est absurde et j'allais trop vite. Ce monde en lui-même n'est pas raisonnable, c'est tout ce qu'on peut dire. Mais ce qui est absurde, c'est la confrontation de cet irrationnel et de ce désir éperdu de clarté dont l'appel résonne au plus profond de l'homme" (Camus, *Le Mythe de Sisyphe*, Gallimard, 1942, p. 37).

13. *Ibid.*, pp. 37, 48. Camus had earlier noted that recognition of the absurd could only be a beginning, never an end: "Constater l'absurdité de la vie ne peut être une fin, mais seulement un commencement." In his review of "*La Nausée* de J.-P. Sartre" (Oct. 20, 1938), in Camus, *Essais* (Bibl. de la Pléiade, 1965), p. 1419. Carrouges, therefore, is clearly in error when he attributes to Camus a belief in the absurd as a terminal principle, while the surrealists, according to Carrouges, consider the absurd a transition. See Michel Carrouges, "Le Surréalisme, doctrine et méthode de l'humanisme dialectique," in Marc Eigeldinger, ed., *André Breton, essais et témoignages* (Neuchâtel: A la Baconnière, 1950), p. 76.

14. Camus, *Le Mythe de Sisyphe*, pp. 88-89.

15. Claude Roy, "Sur divers points de littérature," in his *Le Commerce des classiques* (Gallimard, 1953), p. 10.

16. *Ibid.*, p. 15.

17. *Ibid.*, p. 13, where Claude Roy rejects the use of literature as an opiate. Jean Larnac had previously condemned the surrealists for preaching "la démission de l'homme." In *La Littérature d'aujourd'hui* (Editions Sociales, 1948), p. 70. According to Roger Garaudy, one of the major younger theoreticians of the French Communist Party, Aragon, even while a surrealist, had fought "cette prétention d'effacer le monde, par un acte de l'esprit devant la réalité 'supérieure' de cet automatisme mental." In *L'Itinéraire d'Aragon* (Gallimard, 1961), p. 252.

18. Aragon, *Pour un réalisme socialiste* (Denoël et Steele, 1935), pp. 81-82.

19. *Commerce*, no. 2 (Autumn 1924), pp. 89-122.

20. A. Robbe-Grillet, "Une Voie pour le roman futur" (1956), one of a series of his essays collected under the title *Pour un nouveau roman* (Gallimard, Coll. Idées, 1963), p. 26.

21. See Breton, *Manifestes du surréalisme* (Pauvert, 1962), p. 22.

22. *Ibid.*, p. 23.

23. Aragon, "Une Vague de rêves," *Commerce*, no. 2 (Autumn 1924), p. 102.

24. Aragon had noted that "*le nominalisme absolu* trouvait dans le surréalisme une preuve éclatante" (*ibid.*, p. 102).

25. Robbe-Grillet, "Sur quelques notions périmées" (1957), *Pour un nouveau roman*, p. 38.

26. "Le récit moderne a ceci de remarquable: il affirme de propos délibéré ce caractère [d'inventer en toute liberté, sans modèle], à tel

point même que l'invention, l'imagination, deviennent à la limite le sujet du livre" (*ibid.,* p. 36).

27. *Ibid.,* p. 48.

28. "Il [l'écrivain] a, en tête, des mouvements de phrases, des architectures, un vocabulaire, des constructions grammaticales, exactement comme un peintre a en tête des lignes et des couleurs" (*ibid.,* p. 49). This recalls Valéry's statement on the origin of *Le Cimetière marin*: "Il [*Le Cimetière marin*] est né, comme la plupart de mes poèmes, de la présence inattendue en mon esprit d'un certain rythme." In Frédéric Lefèvre, *Entretiens avec Paul Valéry* (1926), reprinted in Valéry, *Oeuvres* (Gallimard, Bibliothèque de la Pléiade, 1957), vol. I, p. 1674. In his lecture, "Situation du surréalisme entre les deux guerres" (Dec. 10, 1942), Breton noted that "J'ai dit qu'il [le hasard] pourrait être la forme de manifestation de la nécessité extérieure qui se fraie un chemin dans l'inconscient humain" (*La Clé des champs,* Editions du Sagittaire, 1953, p. 72). Earlier he had approvingly quoted Engels' definition of objective chance as the "forme de manifestation de la nécessité." See Breton, "Limites non frontières du surréalisme" (1937), *ibid.,* p. 18.

29. And he then adds: "Il doit créer un monde, mais c'est à partir de rien, de la poussière. . ." Robbe-Grillet, "Sur quelques notions perimées" (1957), *Pour un nouveau roman,* p. 51.

30. In the concluding paragraph of "Sur quelques notions perimées," Robbe-Grillet defends his new formalism with still another insight the surrealists could endorse: "Le public. . . associe volontiers le souci de la forme à la froideur. Mais cela n'est plus vrai du moment que la forme est invention, et non recette" (*ibid.,* p. 53).

31. Breton (quoting an article by Reverdy in *Nord-Sud,* Mar. 1918) *Manifeste du surréalisme* (1924) in *Manifestes* (1962), p. 34.

32. Breton, "Le Maître de l'image" (1925), in Eigeldinger, ed., *André Breton, essais et témoignages,* p. 27. Lest there be any doubt about the romantic tenor of this definition, Breton approvingly cites Saint-Pol Roux's sometime motto, "L'émotion, ce sillon du vrai" (*ibid.,* p. 27).

33. F. T. Marinetti, *Zang Tumb Tuuum,* sometimes referred to as *Zang-Tuum-Tumb* (Milano: Edizioni Futuriste di "Poesia," 1914), p. 194. It is not generally known that *Les Mots en liberté futuristes* (1919) is scarcely more than a revised (and translated) version of *Zang Tumb Tuuum.* Given Marinetti's friendship with Apollinaire, and the latter's influence on the surrealists, both directly and through Reverdy, there can be little doubt as to one of the sources of the surrealist definition of the image.

34. *Zang Tumb Tuuum,* p. 4. This theme is expanded in Apollinaire's essay on "L'Esprit nouveau et les poètes," *Mercure de France,* CXXX, no. 491 (Dec. 1, 1918), pp. 384-86. It should be mentioned, however, that in a letter to Raoul Dufy, dated Aug. 29, 1910, Apollinaire remarked to his correspondant that he took as his own the motto "J'émerveille."

35. In his "Notice" (1868)) to Baudelaire's *Fleurs du mal,* (Calmann Lévy, 1894), p. 21, Théophile Gautier had noted that in order to heighten the sensation of beauty Baudelaire added "un certain effet de surprise, d'étonnement et de rareté." In this same "Notice" he points out that the poet "sait découvrir par une intuition secrète des rapports invisibles à d'autres et rapprocher ainsi par des analogies inattendues que seul le *voyant* peut saisir les objets les plus éloignés et les plus opposés en apparence" (p. 31). Who first recognized the importance of surprise and spelled out the technique of unlikely analogies: Breton? Reverdy? Marinetti? Apollinaire? Baudelaire? . . . or Gautier? Whatever the answer, it is clear that the Futurists were the first to use these *trouvailles* systematically.

36. Michel Beaujour, "André Breton ou la transparence," in Breton, *Arcane 17. . .* (1944) (Pauvert, Coll. "Le Monde en 10/18," 1965), p. 183.

37. Robbe-Grillet, "Nature, humanisme, tragédie" (1958), *Pour un nouveau roman,* p. 60. And shortly thereafter: "Il faut même ajouter que le surcroît de valeur descriptive n'est ici qu'un alibi: les vrais amateurs de métaphore ne visent qu'à imposer l'idée d'une communication"(*ibid.,* p. 61).

38. *Ibid.,* p. 63.

39. See the section "Surréalisme et révolution," in Camus, *L'Homme révolté* (Gallimard, 1951), pp. 115-27.

40. The image is borrowed from Frederick Brown, "The Inhuman Condition: An Essay Around Surrealism," *Texas Quarterly,* V, no. 3 (Autumn 1962), p. 162.

41. Robbe-Grillet, "Nature, humanisme, tragédie" (1958), *Pour un nouveau roman,* p. 64.

42. See Breton, *Arcane 17. . .* (1944) (Pauvert, Coll. "Le Monde en 10/18," 1965), pp. 59-71; pp. 83-102 in the earlier edition of *Arcane 17 enté d'ajours* (Sagittaire, 1947). Breton returns to "la nécessité de reconstitution de l'*Androgyne primordial*" in "Du surréalisme en ses oeuvres vives" (1953), *Manifestes du surréalisme* (Pauvert, 1962), p. 360.

43. See Robbe-Grillet, "Nature, humanisme, tragédie" (1958), *Pour un nouveau roman,* pp. 66-68.

44. *Ibid.*, pp. 70-78.

45. Robbe-Grillet, "Enigme et transparence chez Raymond Roussel" (1963), *Pour un nouveau roman*, p. 88.

46. "Roussel est surréaliste dans l'anecdote." Breton, *Manifeste du surréalisme* (1924), in *Manifestes.* . . (1962), p. 41. Breton rarely misses an opportunity to extol Roussel. See, for example, his preface "Fronton virage" to Jean Ferry, *Une Etude sur Raymond Roussel* (Arcanes, 1953).

47. Robbe-Grillet, *Pour un nouveau roman*, p. 88.

48. *Ibid.*, p. 89.

49. *Ibid.*, p. 90.

50. See Raymond Roussel, *Comment j'ai écrit certains de mes livres* (Lemerre, 1935), pp. 4 sq. Another of his techniques was to connect two words, not normally juxtaposed, by the preposition *à* (*ibid.*, p. 7). Needless to say, this would give him a new "creation."

51. Robbe-Grillet, "Enigme et transparence. . .," *Pour un nouveau roman*, pp. 92-95.

52. Such is Rimbaud's description of the academician in his *lettre du voyant* (to Paul Demeny) of May 15, 1871.

53. Caillois joined the group with a brief note, "Spécification de la poésie," *Le Surréalisme au service de la révolution*, no. 5 (May 1933) and "resigned" with a letter to Breton dated Dec. 27, 1934. See his *Procès intellectuel de l'art*, 2e éd. (Marseille: Cahiers du Sud, 1936). It should be mentioned that Caillois' ideals—liberty, love and poetry—were and are still those held by the surrealist group.

54. See R. Caillois, *Les Impostures de la poésie* (Gallimard, 1945), p. 25, in which he speaks of the "confessions naïves. . . images forcées. . . [and] expression prétentieuse" of a certain type of poetry—which in context is clearly either surrealist or surrealist-inspired.

55. Caillois condemns "la sincérité [qui] tient lieu de tout effort et de tout mérite" (*ibid.*, p. 26). He subsequently indicates his impatience with those who call themselves "mage ou prophète, *voyant*, ou métaphysicien" (*ibid.*, p. 26). The Breton quotation is from his *Second Manifeste* (1930), in *Manifestes*. . . (1962), p. 154.

56. Caillois, *Les Impostures de la poésie*, pp. 33 and 71.

57. *Ibid.*, p. 38.

58. See Melville's essay on "Hawthorne and His Mosses" (1850), in R. W. B. Lewis, ed., *Herman Melville* (Dell, 1962), p. 48.

59. Sir Lewis Namier, *Personalities and Powers* (Harper & Row, [1955] 1965), pp. 4-5.

60. Colin Wilson, *Religion and the Rebel* (Boston: Houghton Mifflin Co., 1957), p. 300.

61. *Poèsies* (1870), in *Oeuvres complètes* (Corti, 1946), pp. 243 and 255. Surrealist interest in Lautréamont, as I have indicated, goes back to the early years of the movement and has in no way diminished. See, for example, Lautréamont's *Poésies*, with commentary by Georges Gold-fayn—a fleeting member of the group—and Gérard Legrand (Le Terrain Vague, [1960] 1962), and Radovan Ivsic's meticulous study of misreadings (printer's errors?) in the principal editions of Lautréamont's *Chants de Maldoror*: "Le Plagiat de coquilles n'est pas nécessaire," *La Brèche*, no. 6 (June 1964), pp. 59-66, followed by his note in no. 7 (Dec. 1964), pp. 106-7.

62. Henry Miller, "Of Art and the Future," in *Sunday after the War* (New Directions, 1944), pp. 155-56.

63. Henry Miller, "Original Preface to [Parker Tyler's] *Hollywood's Hallucination*," in *Sunday after the War*, p. 47. Miller, in context, is referring to Hollywood's Production Code and its stress on conformity.

64. Henry Miller, "The Gigantic Sunrise," *Sunday after the War*, p. 59.

65. Henry Miller, "An Open Letter to Surrealists Everywhere," *The Cosmological Eye* (Norfolk, Conn.: New Directions, 1939), p. 181.

66. "A few of them [the surrealists] have committed suicide, but not one of them has as yet assassinated a tyrant. They believe in revolution but there is no revolt in them" (*ibid.*, p. 182). He had earlier rejected metaphysics, "from which there is no escape, except into life" (*ibid.*, pp. 165-66.

67. "The brotherhood of man is a permanent delusion common to idealists everywhere in all epochs" (*ibid.*, p. 152). He subsequently lumps together the Fascist, Communist, and capitalist societies as being all equally uninteresting: "It is the individual who interests me—not the society" (*ibid.*, p. 162). "It seems to me that it is a very simple error which the Surrealists are guilty of; they are trying to establish an Absolute. They are trying with all the powers of consciousness to usher in the glory of the Unconscious" (*ibid.*, p. 181).

68. The opening sentence of "An Open Letter to Surrealists Everywhere" (*ibid.*, p. 151).

69. See his article, "Dernier Etat de la poésie surréaliste," *NRF*, no. 221 (Feb. 1, 1932), pp. 284-93. In this review of some seven surrealist works,

he points to *L'Immaculée conception* of Breton and Eluard as an example
of questionable automatism. Breton's reply, "Lettre à Rolland de Renéville," can be found in his *Point du jour* (Gallimard, 1934), pp. 122-32.
See also Breton and Eluard, "Note à propos d'une collaboration," *Cahiers
d'art*, X, no. 5-6 (1935), p. 137, in which they claim that *L'Immaculée
conception* "fut écrit en quinze jours." Roland de Renéville wrote with
some regularity on modern poetry in the pages of the *NRF*. See his
*L'Expérience poétique* (Gallimard, 1938) and *L'Univers de la parole*
(Gallimard, 1944).

70. See Julien Benda, *La France Byzantine* (Gallimard, 1945), p. 16.

71. From the *NRF* of Feb. 1, 1930, quoted by Marcel Raymond, *De
Baudelaire au surréalisme* (Corti, 1940), p. 344.

72. From Rimbaud's letter of May 15, 1871, to Paul Demeny.

73. Breton, who claimed to dislike such terms as "school" and "movement," refers to "notre organisation" in his statement, "Pourquoi je prends
la direction de *La Révolution surréaliste*," *La Révolution surréaliste*, no. 4
(July 15, 1925), p. 3.

74. P. Geyl, *Debates with Historians* (Philosophical Library, 1956), p. 18.

75. Baudelaire, *Mon coeur mis à nu* (1862-64), in *Oeuvres complètes*
(Gallimard, Bibliothèque de la Pléiade, 1954), p. 1222. Camus has Tarrou, one of the essential characters of *La Peste* (Gallimard, 1947), give
flesh to this ideal. "En somme, dit Tarrou avec simplicité, ce qui m'intéresse, c'est de savoir comment on devient un saint. . . Peut-on être un
saint sans Dieu, c'est le seul problème concret que je connaisse aujourd'-
hui." *La Peste*, in *Théâtre, récits, nouvelles* (Gallimard, Bibliothèque de
la Pléiade, 1962), p. 1425. But Camus, of course, has Dr. Rieux, the
main character, answer: "Ce qui m'intéresse, c'est d'être un homme." And
Tarrou replies: "Oui, nous cherchons la même chose, mais je suis moins
ambitieux" (*ibid.*). Has the saint been out-sainted?

76. Baudelaire jotted down this ambiguous phrase in *Mon coeur mis à
nu*. See his *Oeuvres complètes*, p. 1211.

77. This is one of the more common errors concerning the movement,
implied in both hastily written reviews as well as in some serious studies.
Even Marcel Raymond remarks, in an otherwise superb work, "chaque
texte surréaliste présuppose un retour au chaos." In *De Baudelaire au
surréalisme* (Corti, 1940), p. 286. Breton, it may be added, was quite
aware that he was open to "accusations de mysticisme." See his *Prolégomènes à un troisième manifeste du surréalisme ou non*, in *Manifestes du
surréalisme* (J.-J. Pauvert, 1962), p. 348. My own reference to "mystic
flight" (chap. I) is to be understood, as I hope the context makes clear,

in a metaphorical sense. Having rejected traditional rationalism, the surrealists proceed by a series of almost existential leaps to conclusions un-
supported by conventional logic.

78. Breton first referred to "la *création d'un mythe collectif*" in a lecture
delivered April 1, 1935, in Prague, "Position politique de l'art d'aujourd'
hui," first published in *Position politique du surréalisme* (1935) and included in his *Manifestes du surréalisme* (Pauvert, 1962), p. 272. The
second quotation appears earlier in the same lecture (*ibid.*, p. 264). The
third quotation is from the *Second manifeste du surréalisme* (*ibid.*, pp.
167-68). It may be mentioned in this context that the search for a new
myth was the subject of the 1947 International Exhibition of Surrealism.
See Breton and Duchamp, eds., *Le Surréalisme en 1947* (Maeght, 1947),
esp. Breton's letter of invitation, "Projet initial," pp. 135-38, and his opening statement, "Devant le rideau," pp. 13-19.

79. This he makes very clear in his *Prolégomènes à un troisième manifeste ou non*: "Il faut que l'homme passe, avec armes et bagages, du côté
de l'homme" (*Manifestes*, p. 341).

80. Rimbaud was one of the earliest French poets to describe a universe
that would later be called surrealistic. As we know, he ultimately abandoned his attempt to live "surrealistically"—hence his comment "La vraie
vie est absente," from "Délires I," *Une Saison en Enfer* (1873).

81. Colin Wilson, *Religion and the Rebel* (Boston: Houghton Mifflin
Co., 1957), p. 16.

82. See, for example, Antonin Artaud, *Le Théâtre et son double* (1938),
which contains his various comments on "Le Théâtre de la Cruauté." In
Artaud, *Oeuvres complètes* (Gallimard, 1964), esp. pp. 101-53 and related notes. The first manifesto of "Le Théâtre de la Cruauté" appeared
in *NRF,* no. 229 (Oct. 1, 1932), but the fundamental themes clearly go
back to an earlier period. Roger Vitrac's *Théâtre* has been published by
Gallimard, in 4 volumes, 1946, 1948, and the last two in 1964. His first
play, *Les Mystères de l'amour*, subtitled "drame surréaliste," had its première on June 2, 1927, at the Théâtre de Grenelle, and was performed by
the group of the Théâtre Alfred Jarry, which Artaud and Vitrac were
instrumental in forming.

83. Ado Kyrou probably exaggerates this influence in his enthusiastic
study *Le Surréalisme au cinéma* (Le Terrain Vague, 1963), first published
by Arcanes in 1953. See also the two issues of *Etudes cinématographiques*, nos. 38-39 (1st trimestre 1965) and nos. 40-42 (2nd trimestre
1965), both devoted to *Surréalisme et cinéma*.

84. Philippe Audoin, "L'Air de fête," *L'Oeil*, no. 131 (Nov. 1965), p. 51.
Audoin was one of the three organizers of the so-called 11th International

Surrealist Exhibition, held at the Galerie de l'Oeil, 3 rue Séguier, Paris VIᵉ. The other two were Breton and J.-F. Revel. The theme of this exhibition, *L'Ecart absolu,* recalls the clown's *grand écart* (split) and the anchorite's withdrawal from the world of appearances, though the surrealists seek neither to amuse nor to leave the world.

85. T. S. Eliot, Part III of "East Coker," *Four Quartets,* in *Collected Poems 1909-1962* (New York: Harcourt, Brace & World, 1963), pp. 185-86; *Four Quartets* (London: Faber and Faber, 1950), pp. 18-19.

86. *Ibid.,* p. 187 (Faber and Faber, p. 20).

87. Title and refrain of a poem by Dylan Thomas, *Collected Poems* (New Directions, 1953), p. 77.

# Index